BIOMECHANICS & KINESIOLOGY OF HUMAN MOTION

SINKU KUMAR SINGH

KHEL SAHITYA KENDRA
7/26, Ansari Road, Darya Ganj,
New Delhi-110 002 (India)

Published by:

KHEL SAHITYA KENDRA

(The Largest Stockist of Physical Education Books in India)

Office Address: 7/26, Ansari Road, Darya Ganj, New Delhi-110 002 (India)
Phone : (O) 011-42564726, 47090343, 43551324 (M) 9811088729,
E-mail: khelsahitya1@rediffmail.com, vivekthani@gmail.com,
khelsahitya.sales@gmail.com
Website:

ISBN: 978-81-7524-566-2

PRINTED IN INDIA 2008

RE-PRINTED IN INDIA 2026

Typeset by:
K.S.K. DTP UNIT, DELHI

Printed at:
ASIAN OFFSET, DELHI

Contents

1

BIOMECHANICS — AN INTRODUCTION

Biomechanics in the field of sports, is a quantitative based study and analysis of professional athletes and sports' activities in general. It can simply be described as the Physics of Sports. In this subfield of biomechanics the laws of mechanics are applied in order to gain a greater understanding of athletic performance through mathematical modeling, computer simulation and measurement.

Biomechanics is the application of mechanical principles to living organisms. This includes bioengineering, the research and analysis of the mechanics of living organisms and the application of engineering principles to and from biological systems. This research and analysis can be carried forth on multiple levels, from the molecular, wherein biomaterials such as collagen and elastin are considered, all the way up to the tissue and organ level. Some simple applications of Newtonian mechanics can supply correct approximations on each level, but precise details demand the use of continuum mechanics.

The application of biomechanical principles to plants and plant organs has developed into the sister field of Plant biomechanics. The many strands of plant biomechanics are described in a text book on the subject by Karl Niklas Plant Biomechanics: An Engineering Approach to Plant Form and Function.

Applied mechanics, most notably thermodynamics and continuum mechanics, and mechanical engineering disciplines such as fluid mechanics and solid mechanics, play prominent roles in the study of biomechanics. By applying the laws and concepts of physics, biomechanical mechanisms and structures can be simulated and studied. Such concepts are found in the field of Sports Biomechanics where we apply the laws of mechanics and physics to human performance in order to gain a greater understanding of performance in athletic events through modeling, computer simulation and measurement. Elements of Mechanical Engineering (e.g., strain gauges), Electrical Engineering (e.g., digital filtering), Physics/Dynamics (e.g., moments of inertia), Computer Science (e.g., numerical methods) and Clinical Neurophysiology (e.g., surface EMG) are common methods used for the analysis.

Relevant mathematical tools include linear algebra, differential equations, vector and tensor calculus, numerics and computational techniques such as the finite element method.

The study of biomaterials is of crucial importance to biomechanics. For example, the various tissues within the body's organs, such as skin, bone, and arteries each possess unique material properties. The passive mechanical response of a particular tissue can be attributed to characteristics of the various proteins, such as elastin and collagen, living cells, ground substances such as proteoglycans, and the orientations of fibers within the tissue. For example, if human skin were largely composed of a protein other than collagen, many of its mechanical properties, such as its elastic modulus, would be different.

It has been shown that applied loads and deformations can affect the properties of living tissue. There is much research in the field of growth and remodeling as a response to applied loads. For example, the effects of elevated blood pressure on the mechanics of the arterial wall, the behaviour of cardiomyocytes within a heart with a cardiac infarct, and bone growth in response to exercise, and the acclimative growth of plants in response to wind movement, have been widely regarded as instances in which living tissue is remodelled as a direct consequence of applied loads.

Chemistry, molecular biology, and cell biology have much to offer in the way of explaining the active and passive properties of living tissues. For example, in muscle contractions, the binding of myosin to actin is based on a biochemical reaction involving calcium ions and ATP.

History

Aristotle wrote the first book on biomechanics, De Motu Animalium, or On the Movement of Animals. He not only saw animals' bodies as mechanical systems, but pursued questions such as the physiological difference between imagining performing an action and actually doing it. Some simple examples of biomechanics research include the investigation of the forces that act on limbs, the aerodynamics of bird and insect flight, the hydrodynamics of swimming in fish, and locomotion in general across all forms of life, from individual cells to whole organisms. The biomechanics of human beings is a core part of kinesiology.

Applications

The study of biomechanics ranges from the inner workings of a cell to the movement and development of limbs, to the mechanical properties of soft tissue, and bones. As we develop a greater understanding of the physiological behavior of living tissues, researchers are able to advance the field of tissue engineering, as well as develop improved treatments for a wide array of pathologies.

Biomechanics is also applied in studying human muscleskeletion systems. In recent years, research applied force platform to study human joint reaction forces, 3D human movement. Human motion is also captured through the human Motion capture systems (e.g. Vicon systems) to study human 3D motion. With the help of force platform and vicon systems. It is possible to study the human muscleskeletion behavior, including joint reaction forces, human postural control etc. Research also applies Electromyography system to study the muscle activation. By this, it is feasible to investigate the muscle responses to the external forces as well as perturbations.

Biomechanics is the study of the structure and function of biological systems by means of the methods of "mechanics." – which is the branch of physics involving analysis of the actions of forces. Within "mechanics" there are two sub-fields of study: (1) statics, which is the study of systems that are in a state of constant motion either at rest (with no motion) or moving with a constant velocity; and (2) dynamics, which is the study of systems in motion in which acceleration is present, which may involve kinematics (i.e., the study of the motion of bodies with respect to time, displacement, velocity, and speed of movement either in a straight line or in a rotary direction) and kinetics (the study of the forces associated with motion, including forces causing motion and forces resulting from motion).

Biomechanics is therefore not kinesiology (which is often another name for physical education). There are numerous titles of books that are confusing, especially since the titles suggest more than the definition of biomechanics that was stated earlier. Examples include, but are limited to, Fundamentals of Sports Biomechanics, The Mechanics of Athletics, Scientific Principles of Coaching, Biomechanic Analysis of Sport, Biomechanics of Sports Techniques, Biomechanics of Human Motion, and Mechanical Kinesiology.

BIOMECHANICAL ANALYSES

In general, there are two approaches used to study mechanical aspects of human movement. There is the quantitative approach that involves the use of numbers. This approach helps to eliminate subjective description and relies on data from the use of different instruments. It is a more scientific, publishable, and predictable analysis than the qualitative approach that implies that the movement is described without the use of numbers. This approach is used a lot in coaching and during the teaching of sports skills. Both quantitative and qualitative descriptions play important roles in the biomechanical analysis of human movement.

Biomechanical analyses can be divided into four areas. (1) noncinematographic analysis; (2) basic cinematographic analysis; (3) intermediate cinematographic analysis; and (4) Biomechanics research.

- Noncinematographic analysis is the most common analytical technique used in sports by coaches, athletes, and others. No film or videotape is used in capturing the performance and/or component parts of the execution of the motor skill. It requires a disciplined approach to observing and, then, analyzing skills, but does not require intricate mathematical calculations. It does require a full understanding of biomechanical principles. Obviously, a qualitative analysis is subject to some error in interpretation.
- Basic cinematographic analysis involves the use of film or videotape for improving performance. It does not involve any mathematical calculations. One advantage of noncinematographic analysis is that you can see the movements in slow motion (frame by frame). The analysis allows for seeing what actually occurred versus what you may think took place. It is helpful in reducing the amount of guess work and, thus error in correcting motor skills since it is a qualitative analysis.
- Intermediate cinematographic analysis requires some mathematical computations to enhance the analysis. The use of film is necessary to capture the motor skill and subsequent analysis. It is a quantitative analysis, where velocity and force (along with other data) are calculated, thus

allowing for a significant reduction in guess work in analysis of component parts of a given skill. As a result, the analysis increases the chances of teaching the skill correctly.

- Biomechanics research involves highly sophisticated biomechanical equipment, such as high speed cameras, EMG for muscle involvement, force plates, transducers, computers, and much more. The equipment allows for very accurate determination of factors that influence human performance. It is the method for publishing in scientific journals, and usually a doctorate in biomechanics is needed. As you might imagine, it takes a lot of time to reduce the data before treated with statistical procedures.

NEWTONIAN LAWS

Law of Inertia

Newton's 1st Law states that an object continues in a state of rest or of uniform motion in a straight line unless acted upon by an external force. Inertia is Latin for idleness or laziness. The Law of Inertia can be interpreted as everything in the universe is lazy, thus requiring a force to get it on the move (which then occurs in a straight line). Once moving, more force is needed to slow it, stop it, or to speed it up or to change direction.

Inertia is the body's resistance to change in movement. It is proportional to mass, thus the mass of an object is the measure of its inertia. Therefore, mass is the quantity of resistance to change. It should not be confused with weight. The weight of a person (or an object) is the measure of force with which the earth pulls on the body's mass. This downward gravitational force is the body's weight directed towards the earth's center. Understandably so, a body's mass and weight are directly proportional. The more mass a body has, the greater the earth's attraction on it, the more it will weigh. Weight is a force; whereas, mass is not. It has no direction. Mass is the resistance to change (i.e., inertia).

Newton's 2nd Law (the Law of Acceleration)

When a body is acted upon by a force, its resulting acceleration is proportional to the force and inversely proportional to the mass. Hence, with a constant mass, the greater the force, the greater the acceleration. And, with a constant force applied, the greater the mass, the less the acceleration. Another way of saying the same thing is: "The velocity of a moving object will remain constant unless a force acts on it."

Newton's 3rd Law (the Law of Action and Reaction)

The third principle of motion can be stated as follows: If one body exerts a force on another body, the second body will exert an equal and opposite force on the first body. Hence, it is sometimes referred to as the principle of action and reaction, which can be stated: "For every force, there is an equal and opposite reaction force. Essentially, Newton's 3rd Law is a statement that forces always exist in pairs. For example, when we take a step forward, we press our foot against the floor. Because of the friction between the foot and the floor, we exert a backward force on the floor. The reaction force is the equal and opposite force exerted by the floor on our foot. It is this force, which acts in the forward direction, that moves us in the forward direction.

PRINCIPLES RELATED TO THE LAW OF INERTIA

Combining translatory and rotary motions

The combined motions, if performed correctly with proper timing and sequence, will produce maximum final velocity of 'an object' in the desired direction of release (e.g., discus toss, bike riding, car, wheelchair).

Continuity of Motion

The accomplishment of the first motion represents the overcoming of a certain amount of inertia and, therefore, any hesitation prior to the next motion will result in loss of some or all of the advantage gained by the previous motion" (e.g., backward roll, pole vaulting). Interruption of motion costs energy.

Effects of Momentum

More momentum can be produced with a longer implement in that the end will move faster than a shorter implement" (e.g., don't choke up on a tennis racket or baseball bat).

Transfer of Momentum

Momentum develop in a body segment may be transferred to the total body, but only while the body is in contact with the supporting surface (e.g., earth, diving board).

PRINCIPLES RELATED TO THE LAW OF ACCLERATION

Acceleration is proportional to the force causing it

A sprinter can increase acceleration by increasing the force that he/she applies backward and downward against the surface on which he/she is running" and, if he/she should double the force, then acceleration would double and, similarly, if he/she should keep the force constant and reduce mass, he/she would increase acceleration.

Maximum acceleration and efficiency of motion

To achieve maximum acceleration, all available forces should be applied sequentially with proper timing and as directly as possible in the intended line of motion.

Effects of body's radius on angular velocity

The rate of rotation is increased as the radius of rotation is decreased (e.g., tuck head and bend knees; a shorter person will have a higher rate of rotation).

Conservation of momentum in swinging movements

To build or to conserve momentum in any swinging movement, the radius of rotation should be shortened on the upswing and lengthened on the downswing.

Movements while unsupported

When the body is unsupported, movements may occur to aid in controlling balance, but the flight path (trajectory angle) will be unaffected by the movements.

Twisting movements

Are based on the transfer of momentum from part to whole, when in contact with a surface (have to initiate the twist in some way at take off).

PRINCIPLES RELATED TO THE LAW OF COUNTER FORCE

Surface variation and the amount of counterforce

The counterforce is equal to the applied force when a stable surface is used. The less stable the surface, the less will be the counterforce. Examples include: (a) decreased friction on ice (fast skating); (b) increased friction running in the sand; and (c) quality of a trampoline bed (i.e., new vs. old, as in sagging).

Direction of the counterforce

The direction of the counterforce is directly opposite that of the applied force. The counterforce is most effective when it is perpendicular to the supporting surface. If not perpendicular, the force is separated into two components, vertical and horizontal. Hence, it is important to consider the trajectory angle.

Counterforce in striking activities

The amount of force a striking implement imparts to an object depends upon the combined momentum of the implement and the object at the moment of impact (i.e., how is the force dissipated). Also, it depends on the mass of the object and the implement. Examples include baseball bat hitting a baseball or a tennis racket hitting a tennis ball.

Temporarily stored counterforce

If a surface or implement used in a performance has elasticity, then an applied force produces bend or compression that represents stored force, and the stored force increases the propulsive force over what it would be if elasticity were not present. Examples include pole vaulting (e.g., fiberglass poles bend more and store more energy than aluminum poles) and diving boards (the aluminum board vs. the wooden board).

Surface contact while applying forces to external objects

In throwing, pushing, pulling, and striking activities, one or both feet should be keep in firm contact with the supporting surface until the force providing motion is complete, otherwise the maximum force is decreased.

PRINCIPLES RELATED TO FORCE

General Principles of Force

Total Force

A total force is the sum of the forces of each body segment contributing to the act, if the forces are applied in a single direction and in proper sequence with timing.

Constant Application of Force

A force should be constant in which a minimum amount of energy is used to overcome inertia. To do otherwise is to waste the effort (energy) put into the activity (e.g., pushing a car or some other object).

Direction of Force Application

All forces should be applied as directly as possible in the direction of the intended motion (e.g., running with feet pointed straight forward).

Distance of Force Application

A body develops greater velocity as the distance over which the force is applied increases (e.g., for martial arts performer rotates first to increase the force of the kick, as does the athlete who throws the shot).

SELF-PRODUCED AND OTHER FORCES

Correct Muscle Selection

The performer must select the muscles that are most effective for the task at hand.

Stability and the Loss of Effective Force

A spotter must be stable before he/she can prevent a loss of force to the performer.

Effect of the Angle of Application on the Force Produced

In angular movements of body segments, the maximum effective force and velocity occur when the limb is at right angles to the direction in which the object is moved" (e.g., karate punches in which the arm straight forward, not up or down, so the arm is perpendicular to the body).

Initial Muscular Tension

Placing muscles on stretch before contraction increases in the force of muscular contraction.

APPLICATION OF THE PRINCIPLES TO THE TENNIS SERVE

Of all the skills involved in tennis, the serve is the most individual. Beginning players simply attempt to tap the ball into the appropriate court. The more advanced players learn to place various slices and spins on the ball as it is struck. Although an effective serve is possible, the beginning player rarely serves with much powcr. This important factor in the tennis game is most often the most difficult to learn as well as to teach or coach.

The power serve, as it is often called, is a skill that

requires understanding of mechanical power gained through the laws of motion and force. The technique is essentially the same throughout all individual variations and styles. Through careful analysis of the applicable principles of motion and force, the performer of this serve should produce the desirable results.

Principles of Motion

Principle – Combining translatory (linear) and rotary motion. Effective execution of a successful performance combines translatory and rotary motions.

Application. Since the serve involves synchronized motion of body levers, rotary motion is the most essential of the two motions. The shift of weight from the back foot to the front foot as the movement begins requires rotary motion with only limited linear motion. As the feet shift, the racket arm is extended at the side and slightly behind the hip. The elbow then bends and the arm abducts. As the elbow reaches the height of the shoulder, the wrist is abducted allowing the racket head to drop to a position behind the scapula. The elbow is held high, allowing it to lead the motion of the forward swing which follows.

This back swing motion must be executed in a fluent manner with the toss of the ball from the opposite arm (ball arm). The ball arm begins its rotary motion to propel the ball upward into the air for striking. This arm is fully extended in front of the server as the levers of the arm act to push and lift the ball. This action gives the ball motion of its own, curvilinear motion and momentum. Timing and the speed of the toss must be equal to that of the back swing for proper execution of the move.

No pause is experienced prior to the beginning of the forward swing. The forward swing is begun by the racket elbow leading the upward motion, and flexion and lateral rotation of the glenoid cavity (shoulder) complete the upward move. When the arm approaches a position above and forward of the shoulder, the forearm starts its rapid extension. At a point where the racket arm is fully extended and the wrist is adducted, the ball is struck with the upper center strings of the racket.

Principle – Continuity of motion. When performing activities in which two or more consecutive motions contribute toward movement in the same direction, the performer should not pause between motions.

Application. Each motion of the back swing and ball toss should be done by successively moving complete body parts. This same successive motion of body parts should be executed from the termination of the back swing to the forward swing carrying through the follow-through. Unless one wishes to overcome inertia twice, there should be no sustained pauses or jerking in the motion. Energy is conserved in the fluent motion of performing the serve.

Principle – Effects of momentum. When a moving object strikes another object, the greater its momentum at impact, the greater the force will be.

Application. Since momentum is the product of velocity and mass, increasing either factor will increase momentum. In a serve it is possible to increase velocity only. The racket may in fact be larger but is rarely significantly heavier, so mass is constant. To increase velocity, the server can produce a harder swing by increasing muscular strength of the involved muscles and can more effectively hyperextend the back to generate more stretch of the involved muscles. These work together to product greater velocity and a more forceful movement.

Principle – Transfer of momentum. Momentum developed in a body segment is transferred to the rest of the body only while the body is still in contact with the supporting surface.

Application. The momentum generated as the forward swing begins will pull the whole body off balance. The racket pulled, as is the arm, into a position out of the center of gravity.

Principle – Maximum acceleration and efficiency of motion. All available forces should be applied sequentially with proper timing, and as directly in the intended line of motion as possible. Body motions extraneous to the desired motion should be minimal.

Application. The major forces in the serve follow this essential sequence:

1. Passive extension of the racket elbow.

2. Arm abduction along with outward rotation of the arm.

3. Scapular adduction and upward rotation of the glenoid cavity.

4. Rotation of the thoracic spine.

5. Elbow flexion of the ball arm.

6. Elbow extension of the ball arm along with relaxation of the finger flexors.

7. Elbow extension of the racket arm with hyperextension of the back.

8. Adduction of the arm, inward rotation of shoulder and hyperextension of the racket elbow.

9. Trunk flexion with hip flexion.

The follow-through is a continuation of all of these. Because of the strength and speed necessary for the serve, it must be executed in this sequence vigorously. The ball arm is usually carried behind the server to maintain balance.

Principle – Counterforces in striking activities. The amount of force a striking implement imparts to an object depends upon the combined momentum of the implement and the object at the moment of impact. Give in the implement reduces propulsive force.

Application. Strong muscular contractions of the involved muscles are essential for reducing the loss of force due to the give in both the racket and ball. Grip on the racket should be firm, and the back foot must push strongly. Tension increases on the strings of the racket may reduce loss of force as well.

Principle – Direction of the counterforce. The counterforce is directly opposite and equal to the applied force.

Application. The push of the back foot along with the strong adduction of the arm overhead produce the applied force of the swing. The first force requires a strong push to propel the server upward and slightly outward leaving the ground. The tendency to push too far forward reduces the advantage of the downward swing of the racket. Full power is attained when hitting the ball at the top of the forward swing. A broader starting stance insures more weight transfer is placed on the back foot.

Principle – Temporarily stored counterforce. If a surface, implement, or object used in a performance has elasticity, then an applied force produces bend or compression, which represents stored energy.

Application. Rackets may be strung at various tensions. Some players prefer more tension on the strings to product more power to the serve. A reduced tension adds energy to the striking force, but at the same time may reduce momentum of ball placement.

Principle – Leverage. By changing the amount and type of leverage, either speed (and distance) or force can be gained at the sacrifice of the other.

Application. The serve uses third class body levers. These levers produce speed and range of motion (distance) at the expense of force. Third class levers are especially effective in producing a fast striking force with a relatively light object. By applying a total range of motion to each lever and utilizing great muscular force, the optimum effect can be obtained.

Principles of Force

Since there is a direct relationship between force and motion, many principles of force have already been discussed. The principles not yet identified are:

Principle - Total force. The total force is the sum of the velocities of all contributing movements, if the movements are applied in a single direction, in the proper sequence, with proper timing.

Application. At the moment of contact, the racket head has a velocity approximately equal to the sum of the velocities of the contributing levers from the forward swing. In order to maximize velocity, the forward swing should be performed in the proper sequence already discussed. If the proper sequence is applied but timing is off, the performer will not produce the most effective serve. Timing takes considerable practice, since the toss of the ball and the height at which the forward swing is applied requires precise motions.

Principle – Duration of force application. If a constant force is applied to a body, the body develops greater acceleration as the distance over which the force is applied increases.

Application. For maximum duration (distance) of force application, the back swing should be executed with hyperextension of the back and the racket head at the scapular level. The hyperextension of the back allows the performer more distance for stretch of muscles necessary to perform the forward swing. An optimum back swing and total body shift will produce the optimum duration of force.

Principle – Follow-through. Emphasis on a correct follow-through eliminates a tendency to decelerate the striking action prior to contact.

Application. During the follow-through, the racket arm descends toward the ground under the influence of gravity. The weight then shifts from the back foot, the front foot as the back foot is thrust forward. The ball arm is carried back to act as a counter-balance to maintain balance. Adequate follow-through is vital to a forceful and complete serve. Lack of follow-through increases the force applied by antagonistic muscles and reduces the force applied at the moment of ball contact. Concentrating on the follow-through may help control the consistency of agonist muscular contractions during the forward swing.

Principle – Effects of spin on the ball. The flight of an object is influenced by the direction and amount of spin on it.

Application. We know that a spinning ball curves from an accumulation of air resistance on the forward spinning side of the ball. The amount and direction of wind must be considered when application of the height of the toss is made. The toss must be executed at a height approximately equal to the reach of the racket head at the peak of the forward swing.

Principle – Force causing the projection. The force causing the projection produces varying effects depending upon its point of application.

Application. The position of the racket head as it contacts the ball will produce the desired slice. Off-center contact produces rotation. To produce the desired spin, the ball will have to be hit slightly over the top and mostly on the right (right-handed player) side. Hitting the ball on the upper right quarter segment will maximize the desired slice. The imparted slice will cause the ball to curve in flight from the server's right to left and away from the receiver.

Final Thoughts

The analysis of the mechanics of the tennis serve is rather detailed; however much detail has been omitted due to length and space to do so. The essence of the mechanics have been covered in an attempt to aid the performer eliminate common errors. Major forces have been identified and the proper sequence and timing were emphasized.

For the serve to be executed with the maximum success, a full baseball-throw arm motion is necessary. It may be helpful for the beginner to pretend the racket handle is a baseball and attempt to "throw" the head of the racket at the ball. It may be questionable as to whether or not a pause or hesitation is experienced between the forward swing and the back swing. In order to avoid overcoming inertia twice, the serve should be executed without hesitation.

For the teacher/coach wishing to improve the performance of a player, encouragement should be given to provide adequate and essential practice time on the serving skill. Strengthening exercises for the arm and shoulder, which can also improve the speed and flexibility of these areas, should be encouraged. To attain the maximum degree of power and skill, both beginning adults and children should engage in such exercises.

FORCE ABSORPTION

An athlete prepares for impact (as when falling) by placing the shock absorbing joints in extension, but not locked. The same is true when catching a baseball. The position of the limbs provides more distance to absorb the force compared to a flexed position (shorter distance).

As contact is made, the extended joints flex due to the impact and immediately absorb the force of impact. The force is gradually reduced by eccentric (i.e., lengthening) contraction of the (e.g., elbow) extensors (and shoulder flexors). The force of impact is distributed over either a greater time (distance) or area of the body or both.

TYPES OF MOTION

When static balance has been upset, the body has been put into MOTION. Thus, what is implied is a change of place or position involving direction and speed. There are three major classifications of motion:

- Linear motion
- Curvilinear motion
- Rotary motion

Linear motion (also known as translation or translatory motion). Meaning, a person is said to move as a whole with all parts moving in the same direction. If the path is straight, it is linear. Linear motion is also referred to as rectilinear motion, although it has become customary to use only the word linear. The distance moved (i.e., the linear displacement) is measured in linear measurement units, such as feet, meters, inches, centimeters, miles, etc. Curvilinear motion (also known as translatory non-rectilinear motion) is defined as an object that moves in a curved path. The motion has a horizontal (straight) component plus a force that pulls it inward. Rotary (or angular) motion occurs when some point within a system is secured or restricted so that the system will rotate around this point when it receives force. The point serves as its axis.

Linear Motion

When we see something or someone move we know a force is responsible for the motion. We know this because Newton's first law of motion says that a body at rest will remain at rest unless acted upon by a force. This is called the Law of Inertia. The inertia of a person or thing is essentially its mass. Inertia is resistance to movement. The more mass (weight) a person has the less easy it is to move that person. Another way of saying the same thing is -- the more inertia a person has the more force which will be necessary to move that person.

A force may be generally defined as a push, pull or tendency to distort. In other words, if we see movement (push or pull) we know a force is present. The reverse is not necessarily so, however. It is possible to have a force (tendency to distort) without any movement. This would happen if the force were not of a magnitude sufficient to overcome the inertia of the body. The formula for calculating force is mass times acceleration.

Acceleration is defined as a change in velocity. Velocity is the rate (speed) at which a body might move per a specific unit of time (such as feet per second or miles per hour). Therefore, when we see a body change its velocity, we know a force has acted on it. In the simplest sense, this could mean that a body was standing still and then moved. It could also mean that a body was moving and then changed its velocity (as in speeding up or slowing down). If this were the case, again, we would know by Newton's first law that a force is present. We know this because Newton's first law states that a body in motion will continue in motion in the same direction at the same velocity unless acted upon by some force. This introduces another possibility, that is, a body could move in one direction and then change direction. When this happens, we know that a force caused the change in direction.

Once a body has been put in motion, it has momentum. How much momentum it has is determined by how fast it is moving and how much mass it has (by formula, Momentum = Mass x Velocity). This would imply that while a force acted on the body to move it (a force sufficient to overcome its inertia), the force is no longer acting on it. Since Newton's Law of Inertia says that the body will continue to move unless acted on by another force we would expect to observe the momentum of that body continue unless resistance forces (such as gravity, friction, or air resistance) slow it to a stop.

It should be obvious that it is going to take more force to move a large mass. Ten pounds is twice as much as five pounds. It will take twice as much force to move 10 pounds as it will to move five pounds. When enough force is applied to move either 10 pounds or five pounds and they were both given the same speed of movement (velocity), the 10-pound weight would have twice as much momentum. Remember that momentum is not just velocity. While momentum is movement, it is made up of both velocity and mass. For example, it would take more effort (force) on your part to catch the 10-pound weight (twice as much effort) as it would for the five-pound weight if both traveling at the same speed (velocity).

The Effect of Gravity on the Body

Gravity is a force because it tends to accelerate a

body. Gravity is a phenomenon that exists on earth. It is a force that attracts everything in the earth's atmosphere to the center of the earth. It is as if the center of the earth is a magnet that draws everything with mass towards it. The attraction is greatest the closer a body is to the center of the earth. For example, the gravitational attraction is greater for someone in Wisconsin than it would be for the same person in the mountains of Colorado.

Gravity is what causes our weight. How much mass we have and what that mass is made of will determine the attraction of our bodies towards the center of the earth. When we place a scale between the center of the earth and us, the scale will measure that attraction. A person with more mass will be heavier.

It is important to understand that the effect of gravity is very close to being a constant. That is, the force of gravity will accelerate any body at the same rate (e.g., 32 feet per second per second). That means that as long as a body is free to fall it will accelerate at a rate of 32 feet per second every second. A body dropped from a plane will have a velocity of 32 feet per second at the end of one second, 64 feet per second at the end of the second second, 96 feet per second at the end of the third second and so on.

Although, in most sports situations, we will not reach these velocities, the principle remains the same – as a body is allowed to fall, it will accelerate at a rate of 32 feet per second every second regardless of its weight. Air resistance becomes a retardant force when the shape of the body is such that it will present more surface area to the air below it. A skydiver will slow down in the air as he/she becomes spread eagle, and will speed up if he/she drops feet or head first. The effect of air resistance is very dependent also on the speed of the object. It becomes more of a factor when a body is going a great speed. For all practical purposes it does not affect athletes in sports such as various gymnastics activities.

While it is important to understand that a light body will fall at the same rate as a heavy body, the momentum of each will be different. Taking the two weights we used before (five and ten pounds) and dropping them from the same height will give us the example that we need. Both weights will fall at the same rate. They would both hit the ground at the same time. However, the ten-pound weight will have twice as much momentum or twice as much impact as it hits the ground. It would take twice as much resistive force to stop the ten-pound weight at any time in the air.

Application of these Linear Forces to the Body

All of this knowledge is necessary to understand how to get force, how to direct it, and some of the problems of moving and/or stopping bodies that have more mass. Muscles are responsible for generating much of the force to move the body and to redirect it once it is moving. How well it moves depends on how much force can be generated (strength and/or power) and how much inertia (body weight) there is to overcome.

Athletes need to know what the objective of each skill is and how to position the body to direct the necessary forces appropriately. When gravity is used as the prime mover of the body, athletes must come to an understanding of its positive and negative effects. In so doing, they are able to adjust body parts and/or position to, for example, spot gymnast during the learning phase of the gymnastic skills. Similarly, mats should be arranged in anticipation of landing areas based the coach's ability to control the momentum of the gymnast.

Angular Movement

Angular movement is rotational movement. When something rotates, it always turns about an axis. The axis may be real as in the hinge of a door, the center of a turnstile, the axle of a wheel, or a horizontal bar. It may be imaginary, as a body rotates in the air, free of support. In this case, the axis of rotation is the exact center of gravity of the body. This is the point at which all of the weight of the individual is centered (i.e., the exact middle of the body). That middle or center changes every time the body changes shape. If the arms are raised overhead, weight is moved away from the original center of the body and now the center has moved in that direction. When a body is in the air rotating, it always rotates around its exact center no matter where that center is located. Angular motion is described by degrees through which something moves.

The concepts of angular motion are similar to linear motion, but the terms change in order to specifically identify an association with rotation. It still takes a force to overcome inertia in order to produce momentum. The force of rotation is called torque. Torque is required in order to rotate a body. Instead of having to overcome simple inertia (weight or mass), we must now overcome angular inertia. Not only does mass resist movement but also, when you are trying to turn a body, the length of the body has an effect on how easy it is to turn. The longer a body is, the more difficult it becomes to turn the body. So now there are two factors that constitute the angular inertia of a body–the mass and the length of the body. There will be more angular inertia (more resistance to torque or angular force) the more mass the body contains and the longer it is when the force is applied.

Once a force (torque) of sufficient magnitude (enough to overcome the angular inertia) is applied to a body, angular momentum will be produced. The total amount of angular momentum will depend on the angular inertia (i.e., how much mass and how long the body is) and the speed (angular velocity) the body is turning. It is important to know how torque is created. Generally it is a combination of two forces (in physics terms – a force couple). For example, it is possible to cause rotation of a body by what we might call a "tripping effect." Much the same as one might trip over something when walking (the effect of which would be to rotate forward and possibly fall on the face) and thereby fall into or "trip" into a forward roll. A gymnast does this by first running forward (creating horizontal momentum). By bringing the feet together (hurdling) and planting the feet on a vaulting board or mat the feet stop by virtue of a restraining force (friction). With the combination of horizontal momentum and stopping of the feet, the gymnast creates a force couple. During the time the feet are in contact with the board or mat, the body is free only to rotate. The axis of rotation becomes the point at which the feet are in contact with the board or mat. If the feet remain in contact, the body would literally fall flat on its face. What usually happens is that the person pushes with the legs downward on the takeoff surface with enough force to raise the body go into the air. When it goes in the air it will (depending on the magnitude of all these forces) continue to move forward as a result of the run, move upward as a result of the push down, and rotate as a result of the "tripping effect" created by stopping the feet and having the body move forward.

It is also possible to rotate the body by applying what is called an eccentric force (i.e., a force that is not directed through the center of gravity of a body). For example, when we walk through a revolving door, we direct our push close to a right angle (90°) to the door. We do not push on the end of the door in the direction of the axis of rotation that would also be the center of weight. If we think of a circle with the axis of rotation of the door in the center, then the door would become the radius of the circle. Rather than apply a force in the direction of the radius, it applied at a right angle to the radius (tangent to the circle). Another example might be to balance a stick (not on end) in the middle of your finger. If you now push up and send the stick into the air it should not rotate (not if your finger was directly below its center of weight – the condition necessary to balance). However, if you place your finger away from the center of gravity and conduct the same experiment you will find that the stick will not only go up but will also rotate. The further away from the center that you place your finger the more rotational and less vertical effect you will have on the stick. We use this method of producing rotation by having the body lean in one direction or another while a force is not directed through the exact center of gravity of the body. As a result, the force, in the case of a gymnast or a diver leaving the springboard, will initiate a flipping or turning effect. The more lean there is the more flipping and the less vertical effect there will be.

It is important to realize that all the angular momentum one creates is created while the body is still in contact with the ground or the apparatus, in other words, at the time of the take off. This angular momentum is a product of the angular inertia (mass and the length of the body) and the angular velocity created. Once in the air, it is impossible to create any more angular momentum.

However, when a person is in the air, free of support and rotating, it is possible to change the variables that make up angular momentum. Remember that Angular Momentum = Angular Inertia x Angular Velocity. What we can easily see while a person is multiple somersaulting from a great height is a change in angular velocity. What we sometimes do not perceive is a concurrent (at the same time) change in angular inertia. While it is impossible to change the mass of the body while it is in the air, we can change the shape of the body at will. When we extend the body (stretched body position) it is the longest it can possibly be relative to forward, backward or sideward rotation. If the body were rotating forward then we would have the most angular inertia in a stretched body position and the least in a tucked position. While in the air rotating around a horizontal axis (somersaulting), we could increase our angular inertia (lengthen our body) in order to slow the angular velocity, or we could decrease our angular inertia (shorten our body) in order to speed up our angular velocity. One factor will decrease by the same amount that the other will increase so that the total angular momentum will never change.

Pendulum Swing

When on the apparatus we can develop angular momentum in a fashion similar to the "tripping effect." The major difference is that instead of a horizontal force initiating movement, a vertical force is responsible. That vertical force is gravity. It acts the same on all bodies regardless of size or weight. By virtue of a downward force (gravity) and fixing the hands or some other part of the body on the apparatus, we can create a force couple. Because the hands or other part of the body become fixed that becomes an axis about which the rest of the body (which is free to move) will rotate.

We create what we call a pendulum swing. It is possible to swing back and forth continuing to build a bigger swing or it is possible to rotate completely around a piece of apparatus. In either case, we are rotating during this time. We have angular momentum. In order to take the greatest advantage of gravity we lengthen our bodies on the down swing. This allows the center of gravity to fall a greater distance which will give it a greater velocity at the bottom. We must decide whether the individual has the strength to maintain the fixed contact with the apparatus. In other words, because of an increase in angular momentum as a result of an increase in angular inertia (either because of large mass or increased length of body), the body will need an increased ability to control the increase in angular momentum. In order to reduce the inertia at any time, but in particular, on the up swing, we shorten the body the same as we would in the air. This will increase our angular velocity and help us achieve a complete revolution if desired. By utilizing the same principles which governed learning to swing on the playground swings when we were youngsters, we can learn to "swing" our bodies on gymnastics apparatus.

Theoretically, a person could continue a pedulum swing indefinitely without any more effort at the level they started out. However, friction would continuously reduce the height of the swing until the person came to a stop. Air resistance might also be a negative factor. What is it then which causes the person to be able to swing higher? Since the only force that is available is the effect of gravity, the objective is try to put the body at a higher level in order that gravity has a longer time to act. In this way the body will have a greater velocity at the bottom of the swing (which is, theoretically, the greatest velocity point during the entire arc) and will rise to a higher point on the up swing. The only way this can be done is to reduce the angular inertia so that the angular velocity is increased. The increase in angular velocity will result in a higher peak of up swing each consecutive time until it is possible that a body will attempt to make a complete revolution (something virtually impossible on a playground swing because the chains are not rigid and would collapse after rising beyond a horizontal position). Since the angular inertia of the pendulum consists of its mass (weight) and its length and, since we can do nothing practical to reduce the body weight itself we have to work with the length of the pendulum. We reduce the angular inertia by shortening the radius of rotation (bring the body closer to the axis of rotation) on the up swing. By the same principle then, in order to maximize the effect of gravity on the down swing, we should do just the opposite, i.e., lengthen the radius of rotation by moving the body weight further away from the axis of rotation.

When learning any skill involving swing we should first be concerned with developing the skill pattern with the least amount of swing possible. The appropriate changes of shape of the body and the correct timing of those changes of shape should be learned first. As the essential characteristics of the skill are learned, more force can be added to the skill by moving the center of weight further away from the axis of rotation on the down swing. Since this will produce more angular momentum, there should be a concern for the safety of the individual and a preliminary judgment of whether the individual is capable of maintaining their contact with the apparatus at the bottom of the swing. Every skill involving swings becomes a process of learning the basic movements with a minimum of swing and then adding swing in order to increase the amplitude of the skill keeping in mind that the more the body is lengthened on the down swing the greater will be the total momentum of the body at the bottom of the swing.

Continuum Mechanics

Human muscleskeletton system.It is often appropriate to model living tissues as continuous media. For example, at the tissue level, the arterial wall can be modeled as a continuum. This assumption breaks down when the length scales of interest approach the order of the micro structural details of the material. The basic postulates of continuum mechanics are conservation of linear and angular momentum, conservation of mass, conservation of energy, and the entropy inequality. Solids are usually modeled using "reference" or "Lagrangian" coordinates, whereas fluids are often modeled using "spatial" or "Eulerian" coordinates. Using these postulates and some assumptions regarding the particular problem at hand, a set of equilibrium equations can be established. The kinematics and constitutive relations are also needed to model a continuum.

Second and fourth order tensors are crucial in representing many quantities in electromechanical. In practice, however, the full tensor form of a fourth-order constitutive matrix is rarely used. Instead, simplifications such as isotropy, transverse isotropy, and incompressibility reduce the number of independent components. Commonly-used second-order tensors include the Cauchy stress tensor, the second Piola-Kirchhoff stress tensor, the deformation gradient tensor, and the Green strain tensor. A reader of the mechanic's literature would be well-advised to note precisely the definitions of the various tensors which are being used in a particular work.

Circulation

Red blood cells Under most circumstances, blood flow can be modeled by the Navier-Stokes equations. Whole blood can often be assumed to be an incompressible Newtonian fluid. However, this assumption fails when considering flows within arterioles. At this scale, the effects of individual red blood cells becomes significant, and whole blood can no longer be modeled as a continuum. When the diameter of the blood vessel is slightly larger than the diameter of the red blood cell the Fahraeus–Lindquist effect occurs and there is a decrease in wall shear stress. However, as the diameter of the blood vessel decreases further, the red blood cells have to squeeze through the vessel and often can only pass in single file. In this case, the inverse Fahraeus–Lindquist effect occurs and the wall shear stress increases.

Bones

Bones are anisotropic but are approximately transversely isotropic. In other words, bones are stronger along one axis than they are along a pivotal (i.e., normal or orthogonal) axis, and are approximately the same strength no matter how they are rotated around the one axis.

The stress-strain relations of bones can be modeled using Hooke's law, in which they are related by elastic moduli, e.g., Young's modulus, Poisson's ratio or the Lamé parameters. The constitutive matrix, a fourth-order tensor, depends on the isotropy of the bone.

$$\sigma_{ij} = C_{ijkl}\varepsilon_{kl}$$

Muscles

There are three main types of muscles:

Skeletal muscle (striated): Unlike cardiac muscle, skeletal muscle can develop a sustained condition known as tetany through high frequency stimulation, resulting in overlapping twitches and a phenomenon known as wave summation. At a sufficiently high frequency, tetany occurs, and the contracticle force appears constant through time. This allows skeletal muscle to develop a wide variety of forces. This muscle type can be voluntary controlled. Hill's Model is the most popular model used to study muscle.

Cardiac muscle (striated): Cardiomyocytes are a highly specialized cell type. These involuntarily contracted cells are located in the heart wall and operate in concert to develop synchronized beats. This is attributable to a refractory period between twitches.

Smooth muscle (smooth - lacking striations): The stomach, vasculature, and most of the digestive tract are largely composed of smooth muscle. This muscle type is involuntary and is controlled by the enteric nervous system.

Soft Tissues

Soft tissues such as tendon, ligament and cartilage are combinations of matrix proteins and fluid. In each of these tissues the main strength bearing element is collagen, although the amount and type of collagen varies according to the function each tissue must perform. Elastin is also a major load-bearing constituent within skin, the vasculature, and connective tissues. The function of tendons is to connect muscle with bone and is subjected to tensile loads. Tendons must be strong to facilitate movement of the body while at the same time remaining compliant to prevent damage to the muscle tissues. Ligaments connect bone to bone and therefore are stiffer than tendons but are relatively close in their tensile strength. Cartilage, on the other hand, is primarily loaded in compression and acts as a cushion in the joints to distribute loads between bones. The compressive strength of cartilage is derived mainly from collagen as in tendons and ligaments, however because collagen is comparable to a "wet noodle" it must be supported by cross-links of glycosaminoglycans that also attract water and create a nearly incompressible tissue capable of supporting compressive loads.

Recently, research is growing on the biomechanics of other types of soft tissues such as skin and internal organs. This interest is spurred by the need for realism in the development of medical simulation.

Viscoelasticity

Viscoelasticity is readily evident in many soft tissues, where there is energy dissipation, or hysteresis, between the loading and unloading of the tissue during mechanical tests. Some soft tissues can be preconditioned by repetitive cyclic loading to the extent where the stress-strain curves for the loading and unloading portions of the tests nearly overlap. The most commonly used model for viscoelasticity is the Quasilinear Viscoelasticity theory (QLV). In addition, soft tissues exhibit other viscoelastic properties, including creep, stress relaxation, and preconditioning.

Nonlinear Theories

Hooke's law is linear, but many, if not most problems in biomechanics, involve highly nonlinear behavior, particularly for soft tissues. Proteins such as collagen and elastin, for example, exhibit such a behavior. Some common material models include the Neo-Hookean behavior, often used for modeling elastin, and the famous Fung-elastic exponential model. Non linear phenomena in the biomechanics of soft tissue arise not only from the material properties but also from the very large strains (100% and more) that are characteristic of many problems in soft tissues.

Measurement, Description, and Monitoring

It is difficult to separate the two functions of measurement and description. However, for clarity the student should be aware that a given measurement device can have its data presented in a number of different ways. Conversely, a given description could have come from several different measurement devices.

Earlier biomechanical studies had the sole purpose of describing a given movement, and any assessments that were made resulted from visual inspection of the data. The description of the data can take many forms: pen recorder curves, plots of body coordinates, stick diagrams, or simple outcome measures such as gait velocity, load lifted, or height of a jump. A movie camera, by itself, is a measurement device, and the resulting plots from the description of the event in time and space.

A system incorporating a cinema camera and two different descriptive plots. The coordinates of anatomical landmarks can be extracted and plotted at regular intervals in time. Time history plots of one or more coordinates are useful in describing detailed changes of a particular landmark. They also can reveal to the trained eye changes in velocity and acceleration. A total description in the plane of the movement is the stick diagram, in which each body segment is represented by a straight line or stick.

Joining the sticks together gives the spatial orientation of all segments at any point in time. Repetition of this plot at equal intervals of time gives a pictorial and anatomical description of the dynamics of the movement. Here trajectories, velocities, and accelerations can be visualized. To get some idea of the volume of the data present in a stick diagram, the student should note that one full page of coordinate data is required to make this complete plot for the description of the event. The coordinate data can be used directly for any desired analysis: reaction forces, muscle moments, energy changes, efficiency, and so on, Conversely, an assessment can occasionally be made directly from the description. A trained observer, can scan a stick diagram and extract useful information that will give some directions for training or therapy, or give the researcher some insight into basic mechanisms of movements.

The term monitor needs to be introduced in conjunction with the term describe. To monitor means top note changes over time. Thus a physically therapist will monitor the progress for each physically disabled person undergoing therapy. Only through accurate and reliable measurements will the therapist be able to monitor any improvement and thereby make inferences to the validity of the current therapy, What monitoring does not tell us is why an improvement is or is not taking place; it merely documents the change. All too many coaches or therapists document changes with the inferred assumption that their intervention has been the cause.

Biomechanics and Its Relationship with Physiology and Anatomy

Because biomechanics has been a recent entry on the research scene, it is important to identify its interaction with other movement sciences: ncural physiology and exercise physiology. The neuromuscular system acts as a control of the release of metabolic energy for the purpose of generating controlled patterns of muscle tension in the presence of passive structures. These muscles act at the joints to create moments of force which cause or resist movement, with a resultant generation or absorption of mechanical energy. It is at this biomechanical level that we see the net and final goal of the central nervous system. Neurologically in the motor unit we see a convergence of many excitatory and inhibitory signals, and this axon has been aptly called the final common pathway. However, at his micro level it is impossible to identify the total intent of the CNS. Within each muscle we see a second level of convergence in the summation of all motor unit forces in a process described as recruitment.

Then at the joint level we see a third level of convergence where the moment of force is an algebraic summation of all agonist/antagonist tension moment arm lengths. Thus the moment of force could be described as the final common mechanical pathway because it reflects the algebraic summation of all CNS controlled forces. Then, when we look at a total limb, or the total body, we see interactions between these moment patterns, and we can see an even higher level of integration of CNS control.

Thus from a performance of diagnostic approach the biomechanics is uniquely placed to analyze and assess the net output of both the neural and the metabolic systems and to identify and constraints of the anatomical system. If performance drops because of metabolic problems, it will be seen in the forces, moments, and mechanical powers.

2

MECHANICAL WORK, ENERGY AND POWER

If we were to choose which biomechanical variable contains the most information, we would be forced to look at a variable that relates to the energetics. Without that knowledge, we would to know nothing about the energy flows that cause the movement we are observing; and no movement would take place without those flows. Diagnostically, we have found joint mechanical powers to be the most discriminating in all our assessment of pathological gait. Without them, we could have made erroneous or incomplete assessments that would not have been detected by EMG or moment-or-force analyses alone. Also, valid mechanical work calculations are essential to any efficiency assessments that are made in sports and work-related tasks.

Internal Versus External Work

The only source of mechanical energy generation in the human body is muscles, and the major site of energy absorption is also muscles. A very small fraction of energy is dissipated into heat as a result of joint friction and viscosity in the connective tissues. Thus mechanical energy is continuously flowing into and out of muscles and from segment to segment. To reach an external load, there may be many energy changes in the intervening segments between the source and the external load. In a lifting task the work rate on the external load might be

200 W, but the work rate to increase the energy of the total body by the sources muscles of the lower limb might be 400 W. Thus the sum of the internal and external work rates would be 600 W, and this generation of energy might result from many source muscles, and shown, Or, during many movement tasks such as walking and running, there is no external load, and all the energy generation and absorption are required simply to move the body segment themselves.

A distinction is made between the work done on the body segments versus the work done on the load. Thus lifting weights, pushing a car, or bicycling an ergometer have well-defined external loads. One exception to external work definition includes lifting one's own body weight to a new height. Thus running up a hill involves both internal and external work. External work can be negative if an external force is exerted on the body and the body gives way. Thus in contact sports, external work is regularly done on players being pushed or tackled. A baseball does work on the catcher as his hand and arms give way.

In bicycle ergometry, the cyclist does internal work just to move his limbs through the cycle. This complex experiment has one bicycle ergometer connected via the chain to a second bicycle. Thus one cyclist can bicycle in the forward direction while the other cycles backwards. The assumption made by the researchers who introduced this novel idea was that each cyclist was doing equal amount of must do his her own internal work plus the internal work on the negative work cyclist plus any additional negative work of that cyclist. Thus if the internal work of each cyclist was 75W, the positive-work cyclist would have to do mechanical work at 150-

W rate just to freewheel both cyclists. Then as the negative-work cyclist contracted his or her muscles, an additional load would be added. Thus if the negative-work cyclist worked at 150W, the positive work cyclists would now be loaded to 300 W. It is no wonder that the negative work cyclists can cycle with ease while the positive-work cyclist rapidly fatigues. They are simply not working at the same mechanical work rate, plus the metabolic demands of positive work far exceeds that of negative that of negative work.

Law of Conservation of Energy

At all points in the body at all instants in time, the law of conservation of energy applies. Any body segment will change its energy only if there is a flow of energy into or out of any adjacent structure. A segment which is in contact at the proximal and distal ends and has four muscles attachments. In this situation, there are six possible routes for energy flow. The low of conservation of energy states that the algebraic sum of all the energy flows must equal the energy change of that segment. Thus if we are able to calculate each of the individual energy flows at the six attachment points, we should be able to confirm ΔE. The balance will not be perfect because of measurement errors and because our link-segment model does not perfectly satisfy the assumptions inherent in link-segment analysis. A second way to look at the energy balance is through a power balance.

Another aspects of energy conservation takes place within each segment. Energy storage within each segment takes the form the potential and kinetic energy. Thus the segment E_s at any given point in time could be made up of any combination of potential and kinetic energies, quite independent of the energy flows into or out of the segment. These components and the determination of the amount of conservation that occurs within a segment over any given period of time.

Mechanical Energy and Work

Mechanical energy and work have the same units but have different meanings. Mechanical energy is a measure of the state of a body at an instant in time as to its ability to do work. A body which has 200 J kinetic energy and 150 J potential energy is capable of doing 350 J of work. Work, on the other hand, is the measure of energy flow from one body to another, and time must elapse for that work to be done. It energy flows from body A to body B, we say that body A does work on body B; or muscle A can do work on segment B if energy flows form the muscle to the segment.

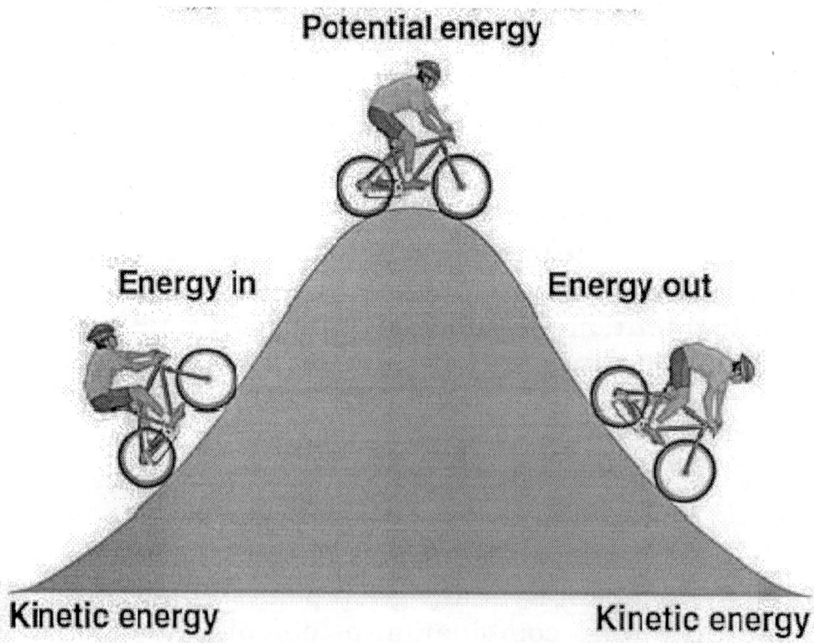

EFFICIENCY

The term efficiency is probably the most abused and misunderstood term in human movement energetics. Confusion and error result form an improper definition of both the numerator and the denominator of the efficiency equation. In the next section four causes of inefficiency are discussed in detail, and these next section four causes of inefficiency are discussed in detail, and these mechanisms must be recognized in whatever formula for inefficiency: inefficiency in the conversion of metabolic energy to mechanical energy, and neurological inefficiency in the control of that energy. Metabolic energy is converted to mechanical energy at the tendon, and the metabolic efficiency depends on the conditioning of each muscle, the metabolic state of muscle, the subject's diet, and any possible metabolic disorder.

Such an efficiency is impossible to calculate at this time because it is currently impossible to calculate the work of each muscle and to isolate the metabolic energy of these muscles. Thus we are forced to compromise and calculate an efficiency based on segmental work and to correct the metabolic cost by subtracting estimates of overhead cost not associated with the actual mechanical work involved.

In all of the efficiency calculations described there are varying amounts of positive and negative work. The metabolic cost of positive work exceeds that of equal levels of negative work. However, negative work is not negligible in most activities. Level gait has equal amounts of positive and negative work., Running uphill has more positive work than negative work and vice versa for downhill locomotion. Thus any of the efficiency calculations yield numbers that are strongly influenced by the relative percentages of positive and negative work.

The interpretation of efficiency is faulty if it is assumed to be simply a measure of how well the metabolic system converts biochemical energy into mechanical energy, rather than a measure of how well the neural system is performing to control the conversion of that energy. A normal healthy adult walks with 100 J mechanical work per stride. The metabolic cost is 300 J per stride, and this would yield an efficiency of 33%. A neurologically disabled adult would do considerable more mechanical work because of his or her jerky gait pattern, say 200 J per stride. Metabolically, the cost might be 500 J per stride, which would give an efficiency of 40%.

Obviously, the healthy adult is a more efficient walker, but our efficiency calculation does not reflect that fact. Neurologically, the disabled person is quite inefficient because he or she is not generating an effective and smooth neural pattern. However, the disabled is quite efficient in the actual conversion of metabolic energy to mechanical energy, and that is that is reflected in the higher efficiency score.

Mechanical Energy Transfer Between Segments

Each body segment exerts forces on tis neighboring segments, and if there is a translation movement of the joints, thee is a mechanical energy transfer between segments. In other words, one segment can do work on an adjacent segment by a force displacement through the joint center. In a joint system there will be n power flows but the algebraic sum of all those power flows will be zero, reinforcing the fact that these flows are passive and therefore do not add to or subtract from the total body energy.

This mechanism of energy transfer between adjacent segments is quite important in the conservation of energy of any movement because it is a passive process and does not require muscle activity. In walking, this has been analyzed in detail. At the end of swing. The swinging foot and leg lose much of their energy by transfer upward through the thigh to the trunk, where it is conserved and converted to kinetic energy to accelerate the upper body in the forward direction.

Mechanical Work Done on an External Load

When any part of the body exerts a force on a adjacent segment or on an external body, it can only do work if there is movement. In this case work is defined as the product of the force acting on a body and the displacement of the body in the direction of the applied force. The work dW a force.

Mechanical Work of Muscles

Until now we have used the terms power and work almost interchangeably. Power is the rate of doing work. Thus to calculate work done, we must integrate power over a period of time. The product of power and time is work, and it is measured in yules. If a muscles generates 100 W for 0.1 s, the mechanical work done is 10 J. This means that 10 J of mechanical energy has been transferred from the muscle to the limb segments. Power is continuously changing with time. Thus the mechanical work done must be calculated from the time integral of the power curve.

Muscle Mechanical Power

The rate of work done by most muscles is rarely

constant with time. Because of rapid time-course changes, it has been necessary to calculate muscle power as a function of time. At a given joint, muscle power is the product of the net muscle moment and angular velocity.

Negative Work of Muscles

Negative work is work done during an eccentric contraction when the muscle moment acts in the opposite direction to the movement of the joint. This usually happens when an external force F, acts on the segment and is such that it crates a joint moment greater than the muscle moment. The external force could include gravitational or ground reaction forces. Using the polarity convention that we have a flexor moment with an extensor angular velocity. The product yields a negative power, so that the work done during this angular change is negative.

Similarly, when there is an extensor moment during a flexor angular change the product is negative. Here the net work is being done by the external force on the muscles and represents a flow of energy from the limbs into the muscles.

Positive Work of Muscles

Positive work is work done during a concentric contraction, when the muscle moment acts in the same direction as the angular velocity of the joint. If a flexor muscle is causing a shortening, we can consider the flexor moment to be positive and the angular velocity to be positive. The product of muscle moment and angular velocity is positive; thus power is positive. Conversely, if an extensor muscle moment is negative and an extensor angular velocity is negative, the product is still positive.

The integral of the power over the time of the contraction is the net work done by the muscle and represents generated energy transferred from the muscles of the limbs.

FORMS OF ENERGY STORAGE

1. Total Energy and Exchange within a Segment. As mentioned previously, energy of a body exists in three forms.

2. Kinetic Energy - There are two forms of kinetic energy. Note that these two energies increase as the velocity squared. The polarity of direction of the velocity is unimportant because velocity squared is always positive. The lowest level of kinetic energy is therefor zero when a body is at rest.

3. Potential Energy - Potential energy is the energy due to gravity and, therefore, increases with the height of the body above ground or above some other suitable references datum, g = gyrational acceleration and h= height of center of mass, meter. With h= 0, the potential energy decreases to zero. However, the ground reference datum should be carefully chosen to fit the problem in question. Normally it is taken as the lowest point the body takes during the given movement. For a diver, it could be the water level; for a person walking, it would be the lowest point in the pathway.

Total Energy of Multi-segment System

As we proceed with the calculation of the total energy of the body, we merely sum the energies of each of the body segments at each point in time. The individual segment energies continuously change with time, so it is not surprising that the sum of these energies will also change with time. However, the interpretation of changes in E_b must be done with caution when one considers the potential for transfer of energy between segments and the number of possible generators and absorbers of energy at each joint. However, in other than the simplest movements there may be several simultaneous concentric and eccentric contractions. Thus over a period of time, two muscle groups may generate 30 J while one other muscle group may absorb 20 J. The net change in body energy over that time would be an increase of 10 J. Only through a detailed analysis of mechanical power at the joints are we able to assess the extent of such a cancellation. Such events are obviously inefficient, but are necessary to accomplish many desired movement patterns.

Consider now a simple muscular system which can be represented by a pendulum mass with a pair of antagonistic muscle groups m_1 and m_2, crossing a simple hinge joint. Such an arrangement is rotating counter clockwise at w1 to t2 the normal pendulum energy exchange takes place and the total energy remains constant. However, between t2 and t3 and t3 muscle m2 causes an increase in both kinetic and potential energies of the segment. The muscle moment has been in the same direction as the direction of rotation, so positive work has been done by the muscle on the limb segment, and the total energy of the limb has increased. Between t3 and t4 both muscles are inactive, and the total energy remains at the higher but constant level. At t4 muscle m1 contracts to slow down the segment. Energy is lost by the segment and is absorbed by m1. This is negative work being done by the muscle because it is lengthening during its contraction. Thus at t5 the segment has a lower total energy that at t4.

1. During cyclical activity, such as level running, the net energy change per stride equals zero. Thus the internal positive work done per stride equals the internal negative work done per stride.

2. When muscles do negative work, they decrease the total body energy.

3. When muscles do positive work, they increase the total body energy.

Energy of a Body Segment and Exchanges of Energy Within the Segment

Most body segments contain all three energies in various combination as at any point in time during a given movement. A diver at the top of a dive has considerable potential energy, and during the dive, converts it to kinetic energy. Similarly, a boomerang when released has rotational and translation kinetic energy, and at peak height of the translation kinetic energy has been converted to potential energy. At the end of its travel, the boomerang will have regained most of its translational kinetic energy.

In a multi-segment system, such as the human body, the exchange of energy can be considerably more complex. There can be exchanges within a segment or between adjacent segments. The upper part of the body has two peaks of potential energy each stride- during mid-stance of each leg. At this time HAT has slowed its forward velocity to a HAT picks up velocity at the expense of a loss in height. Evidence of energy exchange should be seen from a plot of the horizontal velocity and the vertical displacement of the center of gravity of HAT. The potential energy, which varies with height, changes roughly as a sinusoidal wave, with a minimum during double support and reaching a maximum during mid-stance. The forward velocity is almost completely out of phase, with peaks approximately during double support and minima during mid-stance.

Exchanges of energy within a segment are characterized by opposite changes of the potential and kinetic energy components. The total energy would remain constant over time in the presence of large changes of potential and kinetic energy. Consider the other extreme, in which no energy exchange takes place. Such a situation would be characterized by totally in-phase energy components, not necessarily of equal magnitude.

CAUSES OF INEFFICIENT MOVEMENT

It is often difficult for a therapist or coach to concentrate directly on efficiency. Rather, it is more reasonable to focus on the individual causes of inefficiency, and thereby automatically improve the efficiency of the movement. The four major causes of the mechanical inefficiency are now described.

Jerky Movements

Efficient energy exchanges are characterized by smooth-looking movements. A ballet dancer and a high jumper execute smooth movements for different reasons, one for artistic purposes, the other for efficient performance. Energy added to the body by positive work at one point in time is conserved, and very little of this energy is lost by muscles doing negative work. The jerky gait of a cerebral palsy child is quite the opposite. Energy added at one time is removed a fraction of a second later. The movement has a steady succession of stops and starts, and each of these bursts of positive and negative work has a metabolic cost. The energy cost due to jerky movement can be assessed in tow ways: by work analysis based on a segment-by-segment energy analysis or by a joint-by-joint power analysis. Both of these techniques are described later.

Generation of Energy at One Joint and Absorption at Another

The least known and understood cause of inefficiency occurs when one muscle group at one joint does positive work at the same time as negative work is being done at others. Such an occurrence is really an extension of what occurs during a contraction. It is quite difficult to visualize when this happens. During normal walking it occurs during double support when the energy increase of the push-off leg takes place at the same time as the weight-accepting leg absorb energy. There is no doubt that the instability of pathological gait is a major cause of this type of inefficient muscle activity. The only way to analyze such inefficiencies is to calculate the muscle power at each joint separately and to quantify the overlap of simultaneous phases of positive and negative work. In spite of the inefficiencies inferred by such events, it must be remembered that many complex movements such as walking or running require that several functional tasks be performed at the same time.

Isometric Contractions Against Gravity

In normal dynamic movement there is minimal muscle activity t hat can bc attributed to holding limb segments against the forces of gravity. This is because the momentum of the body and limb segments allows for a smooth interchange of energy. However, in many pathologies the movement is so slow that there are

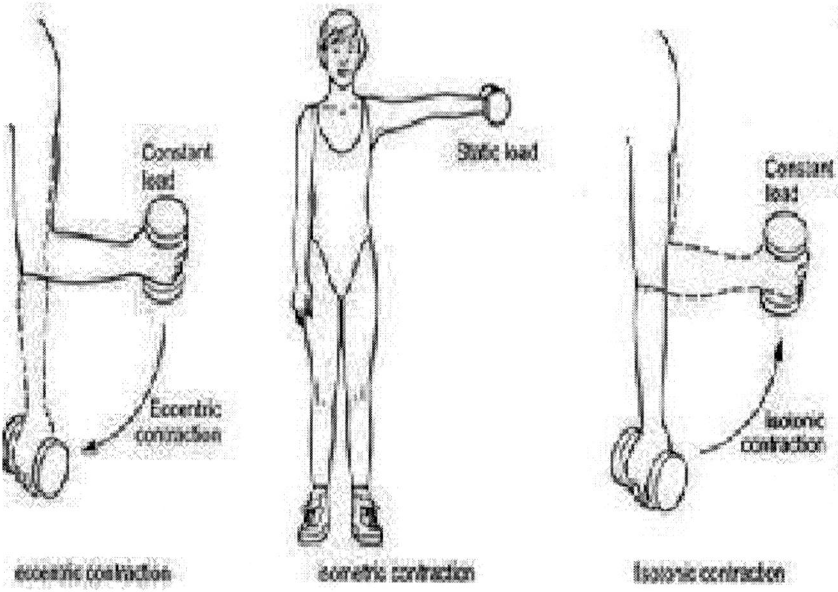

extended periods of time when limb segments or the trunk are being held in near-isometric contractions. Spastic cerebral palsy patients often crouch with their knee flexed, requiring excessive quadriceps activity to keep them from falling down. At the present time it is impossible to quantify work against gravity because there is no movement involved. The only possible technique that might be used in the EMG, and each muscle's EMG would have to be calibrated against the extra metabolism required to contract that muscle. At present no valid technique has been developed to separate the metabolic cost of this inefficiency.

Contractions

Obviously it is inefficient to have muscles contract because they fight against each other without producing a net movement. Suppose a certain movement can be accomplished with a flexor moment of 30 N m. The most efficient way to do this is with flexor activity only. However, the same movement can be achieved with 40 N. m. flexion and 10 N. m. extension, or with 50 n. m flexion and 20 n. m extension. In the latter case is an unnecessary 20 N. m moment in both the extensors and the flexors. Another way to look at this situation is that the flexors are doing unnecessary positive work to overcome the negative work of the extensors.

Contractions occur in many pathologies, notably hemiplegia and spastic cerebral palsy. They also occur to a limited extent during normal movement when it is necessary to stabilize a joint, especially if heavy weights are being lifted or at the ankle joint during walking or running. At present the measurement of unnecessary contractions is only possible by monitoring the EMG activity of the antagonistic muscles. Without an exact EMG calibration versus tension for each muscle it is impossible to arrive at the quantitative measure of contraction.

POWER BALANCES AT JOINTS AND WITHIN SEGMENTS

We can now look at one other aspect of muscle energetics that is necessary before we can effect a complete power balance segment by segment: the fact that active muscles can transfer energy from segment to segment in addition to their normal role of generation and absorption of energy.

Power Balance within Segments

Energy can enter or leave a segment at muscles and across joints at the proximal and distal ends. Passive transfer across the joint and active transfer plus absorption or generation must be calculated. The reaction forces and the velocities at the joint centers at the proximal and distal ends are shown plus the moments of force acting at the proximal and distal ends along with the segment angular velocity. The total energy of the segment E_s is the power balance for that segment, the arrows showing the directions where the powers are positive. If the force-velocity or moment- w product turns out to be negative, this means that energy flow is leaving the segment. According to the law of conservation of energy, the rate of change of energy of the segment should equal the four powers terms,

CALCULATION OF INTERNAL AND EXTERNAL WORK

Internal and external work has been calculated in a multitude of ways by different researchers. Some assume that the energy changes in the body center of mass yield the total internal work done by all the muscles. Others look only at the vertical work resulting from potential energy increases of the body center of gravity, while others even ignore internal work completely. It is therefore important to look at all possible sources of muscle activity that have a metabolic cost and keep those readily available on a checklist to see how complete any analysis really is. This some list serves a useful purpose in focusing our attention on possible causes of inefficient movement.

External Work Calculation

It was noted that the work calculation done automatically take into account all work done by the muscles independent of whether that work was internal or external. There is no way to partition the external work except by taking measurements at the interface between human and external load. A cyclist, would require a force transducer on both pedals plus a measure of the velocity of the pedal. Similarly, the analyze a person lifting or lowering a load would need a force transducer between the hands and the load, or an imaging record of the load and the body.

Isometric Work Against Gravity

Finally, there is one inefficiency that cannot be resolved at the muscle level: the work requirements to hold a body segment against gravity. Mechanically there is no movement, thus no mechanical work is being done; but metabolically there is cost. Such work is not unimportant in many pathologies and in work-related lifting or carrying tasks where loads are held momentarily against gravity or are carried with a forward body lean for extended periods.

Muscle Power and Work

We have underestimated the work done by co-contracting muscle. Joint power, as calculated is the product of the joint moment of force M_j and the angular velocity w_j. M_j is the net moment resulting from all agonist and antagonist activity and therefore cannot for simultaneous generation by one muscle group and absorption by the antagonist group, or vice versa. If M_j = 40N.m and w $_=$3 rad/s, the joint power would be calculated to be 120 W. However, if there was a contraction, the antagonists might be producing a resisting moment of 10n .m. Thus in this case, the agonists were generating energy at the rate of 50×3 = 150 W while the antagonists were absorbing energy at the rate of 10×3 = 30 W. Thus the net power and work calculations will underestimate both the positive and the negative work done by the muscle groups at each

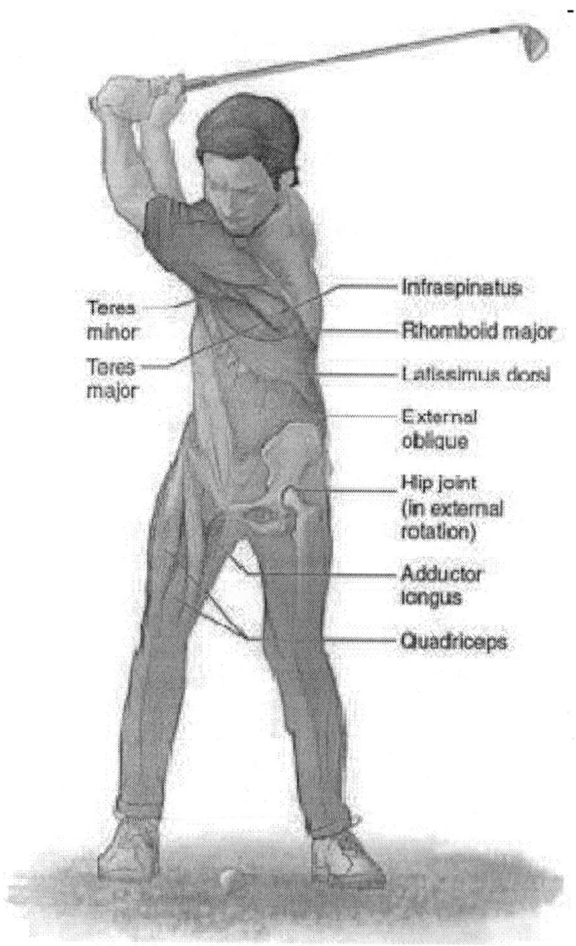

joint. To date three has been very limited progress to calculate the power and work associated with each muscle's action.

Joint Power and Work

Using the time integral of the power curve, we are able to get at the sources and sinks of all the mechanical energy. The power burst are labeled k_1..., k_5 , and the energy generation/ absorption resulting from the time integral of each phase. In this runner it is evident that the energies absorbed early in stance by the knee extensors and by the knee flexors in later swing dominate the profile; only J are generated by the knee extensors in middle and late stance.

It should be noted that this technique automatically calculates any external work that is done. The external power will be reflected in increased joint moments, which when multiplied by the joint angular velocity will show an increased power equal to that done externally.

Sum of Segment Energies

A major improvement on the previous techniques was made by Ralston and Lukin and Winter et al. Using displacement transducers and TV imaging techniques, the kinetic and potential energies of the major segment were calculated. A sum of the energy components within each segment recognized the conservation of energy within each segment and a second summation across all segments recognized energy transfers between adjacent segments.

Center of Mass Approach

Cavagna and Margria proposed in and in many subsequent papers a technique that is based on the potential and kinetic energies of the body's center of mass. Their data were based on force platform records during walking and running, from which the translational kinetic and potential energies were calculated. Such a model makes the erroneous assumption that the body's center of mass reflects the energy changes in all segments. The body center of mass is a vector sum of all segment mass-acceleration products, and, as such, opposite-polarity accelerations will cancel. But energies are scalars not vectors, and therefore the reciprocal movements that dominate walking and running will be largely canceled. Thus simultaneous increases and decreases in oppositely moving segments will go unnoticed. Also, Cavagna's technique is tied to force platform data, and nothing is known about the body center of gravity during non-data, and nothing is known about the body center of gravity during non-weight-bearing phases of running. Thus this technique has underestimation errors and limitations that have been documented. Also, the center of mass approach does not account for the energy losses due to the simultaneous generation and absorption of energy at different joints.

3

BIOMECHANICAL FOUNDATIONS OF STRENGTH AND POWER TRAINING

Introduction

The qualities of strength and power are most popularly associated with sports which require the obvious display of impressive muscular performance such as weightlifting, wrestling and track-and-field events. Consequently, whenever strength training was used as a method of supplementary sports preparation, it was applied most frequently in these types of 'strength' sports and minimally in those sports in which the role of the cardiovascular system was stressed at the expense of almost all other motor qualities.

However, all sports, and indeed all human movements, necessitate the generation of appropriate levels of strength and power in a variety of different applications and situations, as well be discussed later. Several factors have contributed to the prolonged reluctance to accept strength training as a relevant part of the repertoire for preparing all types of international athlete for the rigous of top level competition, in particular the pre-eminence bestowed by the medical profession on the role of cardiovascular fitness in cardiac

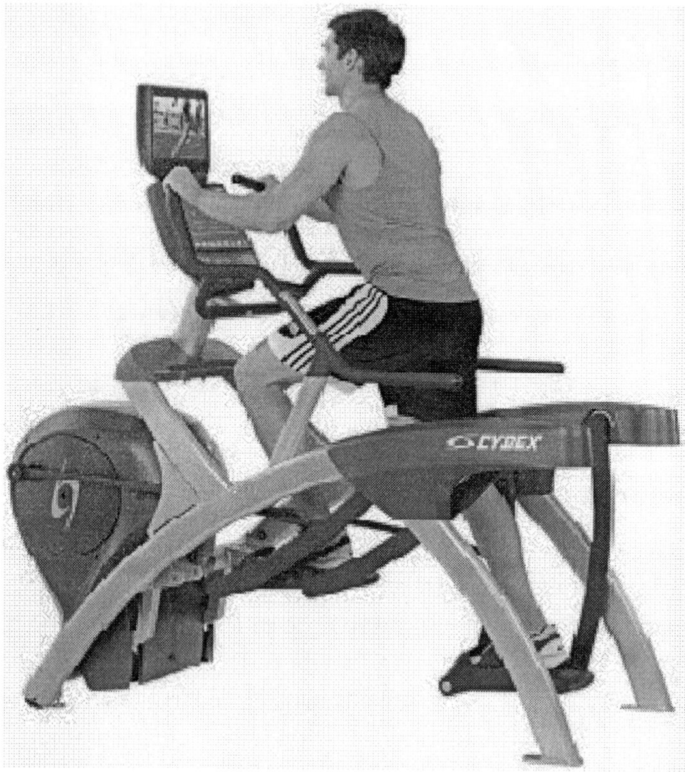

and general well-being, the strong scientific focus on metabolic processes as determinates of sporting performance, and the exaggerated condemnation of strength, training as a cause of musculoskeletal injury, impaired flexibility and diminished speed of movement.

Biomechanics, the applications of mechanics to the understanding of the statics and dynamics of living organisms, appeared to be relegated largely to the analysis of human movement, the etiology of injuries and the design of equipment for training or competition – an interesting mathematical and computational pursuit playing a somewhat peripheral role compared with the more overt physiological processes which underlie human performance. It is only fairly recently that biomechanics has assumed a prominent position alongside the more traditionally accepted aspects of exercise science. It is now recognized throughout the world as an integral part of exercise science, ergonomics, sports medicine and orthopedics, with numerous universities offering undergraduate and postgraduate courses in this field.

The contribution of biomechanics to enhancing sporting and industrial efficiency, performance and safety is now well accepted and it is now being applied with great vigous in territory that once seemed largely the preserve of bodybuilders, power lifters and weightlifters whose pursuit of hypertrophy and strength for many years seemed to be rather irrelevant to other sports.

The reigning belief was – and in some circles still is – that strength, power and all other motor qualities in a sport can be quite adequately developed by means of the sport itself, since this approach ensures that the principles of specificity is exactly adhered to.

Objective

It is the objective of this chapter to apply biomechanics to examine strength and power as motor qualities, and thereby to show how this knowledge may be applied in training to optimize strength and power in a wide range of sporting applications.

The emphasis is on the practical uses of this information, i.e on the value of applied biomechanics, rather than on the predominantly theoretical aspects which often fail to reach the coach and athlete. However, in striving to meet this objective, it does not ignore the fact the biomechanics, like any other component of motor action, does not operate in glorious isolation of the whole gamut of factors which determine human performance.

Scope of Biomechanics

Biomechanics as a discipline in its own right is relatively new, but its methods, principles and equations have been used for many years in many other applications. In simple terms, biomechanics is that discipline which borrows mechanics from the world of physics and applies it to living forms in order to understand how they function, with many of the fundamentals in this field being based upon the work carried out by Isaac Newton. This chapter falls into the

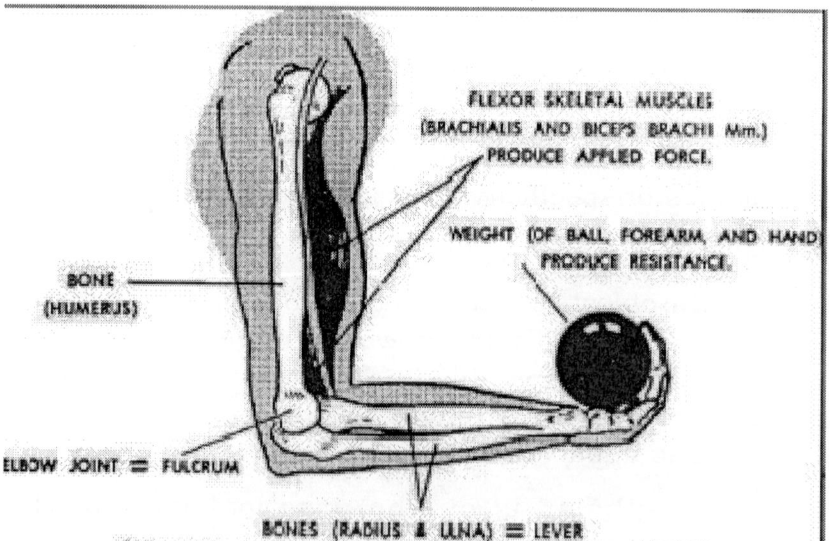

[arm-forearm flexion (3rd class lever system)].

realm of sports biomechanics, which is that specialization of biomechanics used to analysc how the human body functions in a wide specturn of sporting activities.

The strength and weaknesses of sport biomechanics, like that of any other scientific discipline, all lie in the scope and limitations of the paradigms and models used to understand and dissect activity in sports. The dominant paradigm is the widespread use of model which regard the human body as a physical machine and thereby enable us to involve the powerful physical and mathematical methods which have proved invaluable to the progress of applied mechanics in general. This has enabled scientists to scrutinize the human body in motion for beyond the capabilities of even the most skilled coach and helped sport to refine training methods, competitive techniques, rehabilitation technology and sporting equipment to a degree which seemed the stuff of science fiction less than half a century ago.

At the same time, many issues remain unresolved or controversial, which is a major reason why biomechanics needs to be applied to sport within integrated framework comprising all possible fields which relate to the structure of the human organism in physical action.

Sporting powers cannot be explained in terms of biomechanics, physiology motor control, psychology or any single one of the other factors which have become important specializations in the broad field of sports science. Instead, this prowess has to be considered as the result of the synergy of every one of those components acting in a given sport in a given situation for a given individual at any given time. Therefore, although the scope of this chapter lies solidly within the realm of biomechanics, it draws on other relevant components wherever this may be necessary in the interest of providing greater completeness.

In particular, neural processes are a super-ordinate feature of the biomechanics of strength and power, since they constitute the cybernetic command system which orchestrates the production of human movement. Thus, while it may appear adequate to apply analytical mechanistic methods such as free body diagrams for certain aspects of understanding sporting movement, it is also necessary to comprehend any implications and limitations of this approach in the context of overall control mediated by bioelectrical messages passing between the musculoskeletal and nervous systems of the body. In many respects, relying solely on the methods of biomechanics to analyse human movement is tantamount to analyzing a symphony concert by focusing entirely on the resulting sound and the musical instruments involved and ignoring the players and conductor.

For example, it is inadequate to assess the speed and power of athletes by relying entirely on meticulous force plate and high speed video laboratory tests or special fields tests without examining the underlying motor control processes. Performance capabilities suggested by outstanding vertical jumps, broad jumps or various agility drills are relatively meaningless if the athlete reacts slowly or inappropriately to sensory stimuli occurring during actual sporting conditions. This is one of the reasons why so-called 'plyometric' or stretch – shortening drills many be of little significant benefit to any athlete.

While these drills may improve speed and power in simple movements, they do not necessarily enhance reaction time, decision time or problem-solving capabilities in complex sporting actions under competitive conditions.

Thus, a basketball player who display a fairly modest vertical jump, but superior reaction and decision time, may be a far more proficient competitor than a team mate who has a remarkable vertical jump but poor reaction and decision times, or inefficient motor coordination. In other words, isolated biomechanical tests of strength, power and speed may suggest that a player is eminently suited to a given sport, but in the overall context involving vital neural and motor control processes, he or she may be seriously deficient.

Similarly, physiological tests may also yield an incomplete picture of sporting capabilities. For example, muscle biopsies that reveal a high proportion of 'fast twitch' fibres may indicate that an athlete is well suited to activities which require the exhibition of speed, strength or power but adverse joint leverage, inappropriate force time curve for given joint actions, and inefficient motor skill may mean that the athlete is a mediocre performer in a given activity, such as sprinting or jumping.

Thus, in striving to apply the method of bio-mechanics to sports training, relevant information from allied disciplines will be drawn upon wherever necessary to offer a fuller, more balanced picture of each specific situation.

Objectives of Strength and Power Training

The effective and safe prescription of strength and power training begins with an understanding of force-time and related curve concerning the patterns of force production in sport and resistance training. On this basis we may identify several major objectives of strength training, namely :

1. To increase maximal or absolute strength;
2. to increase explosive strength;
3. to increase the rate of force production;
4. to enable the muscles to generate large forces of a given period;

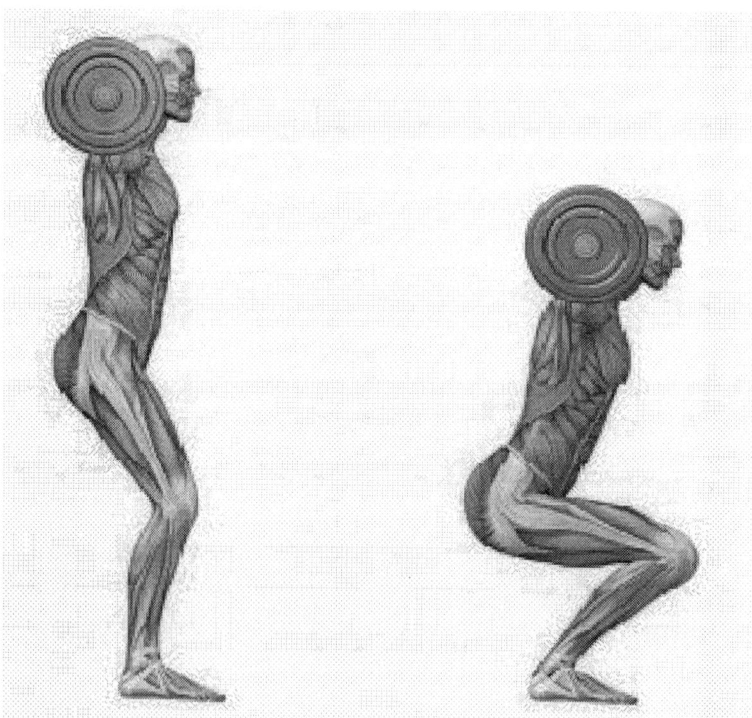

5. to enable the muscles to sustain small forces for a prolonged period; and

6. to increase muscles and connective tissue hypertrophy

Then, in using information to design a suitable training approach, factors such as the following have to be examine :

1. the type of strength fitness required.

2. the type of muscle contraction involved.

3. the speed of movement over different phases of movement.

4. the acceleration at critical points in the movement;

5. the rest intervals between repetitions, set and workouts;

6. active vs passive rest/ recuperation intervals.

7. the sequence of exercises;

8. the relative strength of agonist and antagonist, stabilizers and movers;

9. the development of optimal static and dynamic ranges of movement;

10. the strength deficit of given muscle groups;

11. the training history of the individual;

12. the injury history of the individual; and

13. the level of sports proficiency of the individual.

The last factor is of exceptional importance because the advanced athlete responds to a given training regime very differently from a novice. For instance, the exact sequencing of strength, strength-speed and hypertrophy methods in a workout of microcycle is of little consequence during the first weeks or months of a beginner's training, but is very important to a more experienced athlete.

The Nature of Strength

Successful strength and power training depends on a thorough understanding of the factors that influence the development of strength. The next task is to determine which of these factors can be modified by physical training and which methods do so most effectively and safely. Some of these factors are structural while others are functional. Structural factors, however, only provide the potential for producing strength, since strength is a neuromuscular phenomenon which exploits this potential to generate motor activity.

It is well known that strength is proportional to the cross-sectional area of a muscle, so that larger muscles have the potential to develop greater strength than smaller muscles. However, the fact that Olympic weightlifters can increase their strength from year to year while remaining at the same body mass reveals that strength depends on other factors as well.

The most obvious observation is that a muscle will produce greater strength if large numbers of its fibres contract simultaneously, an event which depends on how efficiently the nerve fibres send impulses to the muscle fibres. Moreover, less strength will be developed in a movement in which the different muscles are not coordinating their efforts. It is also important to note research by Vvedensky which has shown that maximum strength is produced for an optimum, not a maximum, frequency of nerve firing. Furthermore, this optimal frequency changes with level of muscle fatigue.

Determinants of Strength

In general, the production of strength depends on the following major structural and functional factors:

1. the cross-sectional area of the muscle;

2. the density of muscle fibres per unit cross-sectional area;

3. the efficiency of mechanical leverage across the joint;

4. the number of muscle fibres contracting simultaneously;

5. the rate of contraction of muscle fibres;

6. the efficiency of synchronization of firing of the muscle fibres;

7. the conduction velocity in the nerve fibres;

8. the degree of inhibition of muscle fibres which do not contribute to the movement;

9. the proportion of large diameter muscle fibres that are active;

10. the efficiency of cooperation between different types of muscle fibre;

11. the efficiency of the various stretch reflexes in controlling muscle tension;

12. the excitation threshold of the nerve fibres

supplying the muscles; and

13. the initial length of the muscles before contraction.

With reference to the concept of synchronizing action among muscle fibres and groups, it is important to point out that synchronization does not appear to play a major role in increasing the rate of strength production. Efficiency of sequentially rather than simultaneity may be more important in generating and sustaining muscular force, especially if stored elastic energy and reflexive activity has to be contributed at the most opportune moments into the movement process. Certainly, more research has to be conducted before a definite answer can be given to the question of strength increase with increased synchronization of motor unit discharge.

Specificity in Training

Training for enhancing strength and power is not at all straightforward in that strength training displays definite specificity in many respects: all forms of strength training are different and produce significantly different effects on neuromuscular performance.

Fitness training for a given sport is not simply a matter of selecting a few popular exercises from a bodybuilding magazine or prescribing heavy squats, power cleans, leg curls, bench press, circuit training, isokinetic leg extensions or cross-training'. This approach may produce aesthetic results for the average non-competitive client of a health centre, but it is of very limited value to the serious athlete. It is not only the exercise which modifies the body, or, more specifically, the neuromuscular system, but the way in which the exercise is performed. In this regard, it is vital to remember that all exercise involves information processing in the central nervous and neuromuscular systems, so that all training should be regarded as a way in which the body's extremely complex computing systems are programmed and applied in the solving of motor tasks.

For many years, there have been two opposing theories of supplementary strength training in sport. One theory proposes that strength training should simulate the sporting movements as closely as possible with regard to movement pattern, velocity, force-time curve, type of muscle contraction

And so forth, whereas the other maintains that it is sufficient to train the relevant muscles with no regard to specificity. Separate practice of technical skills would then permit one to utilize in sporting movements the strength gained in non-specific training. While both approaches to strength training will improve performance, current scientific research strongly supports the superiority of the specificity principle in the following respects:

1. type of muscle contraction;
2. movement pattern;
3. region of movement;
4. velocity of movement;
5. force of contraction;
6. muscle fibre recruitment;

7. metabolism;
8. biochemical adaptation;
9. flexibility; and
10. fatigue

In the context of training, specificity should not be confused with simulation. Specificity training means exercising to improve in a highly specific way the expression of all the above factors in a given sport. While simulation of a sporting movement with small added resistance over the full range of movement or with larger resistance over a restricted part of the movement range may be appropriate at certain stages of training, simulation of any movement with significant resistance is inadvisable since it can confuse the neuromuscular programmes which determine the specificity of the above factors.

Even if one is careful to apply simulation training by using implements or loads that are similar to those encountered in the sport, there will usually be changes in the centre of gravity, moments of inertia, inertia, of rotation, centre of percussion and mechanical stiffness of the system which alter the neuromuscular skills required in the sport.

Fundamental Concepts

The development of strength and power would appear to be a fairly straightforward quest. Since the human constitutes an adaptive and self-regulating organism, the imposition of progressively increasing loads on the musculoskeletal system according to the well-known principle of gradual overload would be all that is required to achieve this aim. In this context, the load exerts a force on the body, which uses muscle action to stabilize or move that load, thereby giving rise to what we call strength. Once this concept of strength/force has been introduced, we can immediately draw from mechanics a number of other physical definitions which enable us to formulate a scientific framework for analysing sporting action.

Thus, strength may be defined as the ability of the body to produce force; energy may be understood as that physical quality which imbues an object with the ability to exert a force; work may be regarded as the energy involved in moving from one state or position to another; and power refers to the rate at which work is done at any instant.

Because force involves the movement of a limb about a joint or fulcrum, the concept of torque is frequently used in sport biomechanics. Torque is defined as product of a force with the perpendicular distance from the line of action of the force to the fulcrum about which it acts. Sometimes, since it is defined in the same way, torque is regarded as synonymous with the moment of a force, and in the context of this chapter either term may be used without contradiction.

Even in the most basic applications of resistance training, the concept of torque is of great practical value. For instance, the simple act of flexing the elbows will decrease the torque acting about the shoulder during dumbbell side raises, supine dumbbell flyes and bench press by bringing the load closer to the shoulder fulcrum, thereby enhancing the safety of these exercises. Similarly, keeping the line of action of the bar as close as possible to the body during the weightlifting clean or powerlifting deadlift reduces the torque acting about the lower lumbar vertebrae and the hips, thereby enabling a greater load to be lifted with a greater degree of safety. The common error of swinging the bar away from the body during the later stages of the pull during the Olympic snatch or moving the javelin further away from the shoulder during the wind-up for the throw are examples of the inefficient use of torque.

The obvious implication of an understanding of torque in the case of all joints of the body is that the expression of strength and power is not merely a function of changes in soft tissue structure or neuromuscular efficiency, but also of the optimal use of torque for any sporting movement.

For instance, although the presence of a high percentage of fast-twitch muscle fibres in an athlete may suggest that the latter may be well suited to sports which require production of power and speed, the existence of any inherently disadvantageous limb leverages or techniques which do not optimize torque production in specific complex joint actions may decree that any muscle fibre advantage is of little consequence. Occasionally, however, a disproportionate increase in strength for a given activity may tend to offset these negative factors and enable the athlete to perform very competently, albeit in a less efficient or economic manner.

Later, the issue of torque for activities involving several joints will be examined to caution us against the casual analysis of joint action according to the standard methods of functional anatomy. Hence, we are not necessarily justified in assuming that a given muscle produces the same joint action in a multijoint task because the anatomy charts show that it produces a certain joint action when only that joint is involved in the movement. Moreover, in multijoint tasks, a muscle may exert a profound effect over a joint which is not crossed by that muscle.

Contrary to how strength is commonly defined, strength is not the maximal force which a muscle can generate; that is actually maximal strength. To be consistent with the definition of force according to Newton's Laws, strength is simply the ability to generate force to overcome inertia or a load. Similarly, we can define concepts such as maximal torque and maximal power, as well as optimal torque and power.

Optimization of force, torque, speed and power or the production of 'just the right amount at the right time' of these motor abilities sometimes seems to be forgotten, especially in the so-called strength, heavy or contact sports. All too often, the solution to most performance problems in such sports seems to be a philosophy of 'the greater the strength and the greater the muscle hypertrophy, the better', despite the fact that one constantly witnesses exceptional performances being achieved in these sports by lighter and less strong individuals.

This identifies a fundamental factor in training for strength and power, namely the importance of developing optimal hypertrophy, strength and power to suit a given individual in a given activity, and avoiding the tendency to develop superfluous hypertrophy or redundant general strength. To identify such inappropriate conditioning, it is helpful to calculate relative strength (one's maximal load divided by body mass, in any given lift) and to see how this changes in relation to sport- specific changes in one's chosen sport. If performance remains much the same, while one's relative strength remains the same or decreases along with an increase in overall body mass or lean body mass, then this indicates that the increase in hypertrophy is redundant. If relative strength and maximum strength both increase, but performance remains static, then this suggests that technical skills and psychological factors need to be carefully scrutinized.

Since bodily motion is the result of muscle action and its underlying metabolic processes, one needs to distinguish between internal and external energy and work. Externally, assuming no losses by heat or sound, mechanical energy generally occurs in the form of potential energy and kinetic energy, where PE is the energy possessed by a body by virtue of its position and KE is the energy which a body has by virtue of its velocity.

Although external work is defined popularly as the product of the force and the distance through which it is exerted, this definition applies only if the force is constant and acts strictly along the path joining the starting and end points of the movement.

The mathematical definition based on integral Calculus generally is avoided in training texts, because, it that it may not be adequately understood the practitioner, while the popular definition usually attracts the condemnation of the scientist, because of its limited applicability and scope. For reason, a definition of work in terms of energy changes is given, namely :

Work = final energy - initial energy

= final — initial

Alternatively, we could draw a graph of how the force varies with displacement; then work would be given by the area under the curve between the starting and end points of the action.

Since some of the fundamental equations used to analyse sporting movements may be expressed in the form of suitable graphs, this same graphic approach may be adopted to enable us to visualize more simply the implications of biomechanics for training and competition.

In this respect, the following relationships will be seen later to play an especially important role in the biomechanics of strength and power in sport :

1. force vs. time;
2. force vs. displacement;
3. force vs. velocity; and
4. rate of force development vs. time.

Initial implications of Laws of Mechanics

Because of their fundamental importance, Newton's three Laws of Motion warrant repetition here :

1. Newton I : a body will persist in its original state of rest or motion unless acted on by an external agent.

2. Newton II : Newton stated it as 'The change of motion is proportional to the motive force impressed; and is made in the direction of the straight line in which that force is impressed'. In modern terms it may be

restated as: the rate of change of velocity is proportional to the resultant force acting on the body and is in the same direction as the force, or, if suitable units are chosen, force mass x acceleration.

3. Newton III : for every action there is an equal and opposite reaction.

Despite the familiarity of these laws, some of their implications appear to be forgotten in the practical setting, in particular regarding comparison between machine and free weight training. Some machine manufacturers advertise that their variable resistance machines are superior to free weights, because, in the latter case, the weight remains constant and does not change in response to altering joint leverages throughout range of any movement. Newton's first two laws show clearly that this claim is false, since a load may only be lifted if its weight is overcome by the lifter with an acceleration which exceeds that of gravity.

Furthermore, during the lift, proprioceptive feedback makes the athlete aware that the load is changing and enables him to intervene voluntarily in the loading process by accelerating or decelerating the bar to increase or decrease the force involved. This method is sometimes known as compensatory acceleration training and can be useful in altering muscle tension or movement velocity to achieve a specific training goal.

Although the role of CAT is well known during concentric movement, its vital role during eccentric movement is inadequately appreciated. In non ballistic eccentric motion in which muscle contraction continues throughout the movement, the muscles try to oppose the effects of the gravity to slow down and ultimately halt the downward motion of the bar. In ballistic motion, in which muscle action is intermittent, so-called antagonistic muscle action comes into play to slow down and halt the limb to ensure that the joint is not dislocated or soft tissues are ruptured.

Even during isometric action, compensatory processes are at play if no movement is to occur, since neural activation changes due to fatigue, altered mental focus or other physiological processes. This means that the athlete has to maintain adequate muscle tension for the entire duration of the isometric action, either by means of involuntary conditioned reflex action or by voluntary intervention.

The implication for the well-known 'principle of progressive overload' is that 'overload' should refer not simply to the use of progressively greater resistance over a given period, but also to the progressive increase in muscle tension, which may be produced by involuntary or voluntary processes. This change in tension may be produced in ways which relate directly to Newton II and which pose a question of fundamental importance to all strength training. It is relevant to examine this issue before we go any further.

Since force F = m x a, we may apply it to produce the same magnitude of force F in several different ways.

1. F = M x A, where the mass M is large and the acceleration is small.

2. F = m x A, where the mass is small and the acceleration A is large.

3. F = m x a, where both mass and acceleration are moderate.

This might immediately suggest, since the production of an adequate level of muscle tension is necessary for strength training, that all of these methods of 'force training' are entirely the same and it is just a matter of personal choice which method is used. So, the question is: does it make any real difference which method of strength training is used, as long as adequate muscle tension is produced?

If one attempts to answer this question in purely mechanistic terms, one might be tempted to reply 'no' and qualify one's reply with comments about initiating movement against heavy loads with high inertia, possible detrimental effects of sustained loads on the soft tissues of the body, and duration of loading.

Interestingly, practical experience from three different competitive aspects of strength training, namely Olympic weightlifting, powerlifting and bodybuilding, offers some preliminary information. Option 1, with very heavy loads, is most commonly encountered in powerlifting, whereas the hypertrophy associated with bodybuilding generally is a product of option 3 training, with moderate loads performed for about 8-12 repetitions. Option 2 is characterized by many actions in track-and-field events. Olympic weightlifting, which involves lifting heavy loads rapidly, appears to contradict evidence that velocity decreases with load, but this is because weightlifting is ballistic and relies on the quick movement of the lifter under the bar. It may be concluded that powerlifting is essentially strength generating, while weightlifting is maximum power generating in nature.

The practical evidence shows that the above three ways of generating force do not produce the same results and research reveals that this is because different neural, muscular and metabolic processes are involved in each case. Thus, strength and power training are not simply a matter of using some generalized form of resistance training to produce adequate physical loading and muscle tension; the principle of specificity of training is central to the entire issue.

Some coaches maintain that maximal muscle hypertrophy depends on tension time, with continuous tension times of 30-60 s per set of any exercise being commonly recommended. The observation that the extended use of isometric exercises of this magnitude of duration does not produce the degree of hypertrophy associated with dynamic exercise militates against this simplistic hypothesis. The fact that tension fluctuates from low to high values throughout a movement also militates against this idea. Clearly, both hypertrophy and strength increase depend on the existence of some minimum level of tension, but nobody has identified what this tension threshold should be in the case of hypertrophy. Moreover, it is well known that novices to resistance training respond to much lower intensities of loading both in terms of hypertrophy and strength gains. It is also known that the development of strength and hypertrophy do not necessitate the induction of fatigue during strength training, but that exercise to momentary failure and at higher percentages of one's IRM are morc in this respect.

Research has shown that the threshold training

stimulus necessary for increasing muscular strength in the average person should not be less than one-third of the maximal strength.

Thus, the development of strength requires that stimulus intensity be gradually increased. It was discovered that every stimulus has a changing strengthening threshold, the achievement of which fails to any further increase in muscular strength. The less trained the muscles, the further the strengthening threshold from the beginning. The rate at which strength increases from initial level to the strengthening threshold, expressed as a percentage of the current maximum strength, is independent of sex, age, muscle group and the level of the strengthening threshold. After the strengthening threshold has been reached, strength can be increased only by intensifying the training.

In this regard, according to Korobkov, Gerasimov and vasiliev, strength increases relatively uniformly during the initial stages of training, independent of how the load is applied training, whether large or small. Approximately equivalent increases in strength are obtained with loads of 20, 40, 60 and 80% of IRM. An increase the intensity of training in the initial stages does not always enhance the effectiveness of strength development, this becoming effective only later, as strength increases. This principle is corroborated by the training results of weightlifters.

Specific Definitions of Strength

Now that some of the fundamental biomechanical aspects of strength and power have been discussed, we can return to examine the phenomenon of strength more closely.

At the outset, it is vital to remember that strength is the product of muscular action initiated and orchestrated by electrical processes in the nervous system of the body. We have seen that strength is the ability of a given muscle or group of muscles to generate muscular force under specific conditions, while maximal strength is the ability of a particular group of muscles to produce a maximal voluntary contraction in response to optimal motivation against an external load. This strength is usually produced in competition and may also be referred to as the competitive maximum strength, CFmax. It is not the same as absolute strength, which usually refers to the greatest force that can be produced involuntarily by a given muscle group by, for example, electrical stimulation of the muscles or recruitment of a powerful stretch reflex by impulsive heavy loading. It should be noted, however, that absolute strength is sometimes used to define the maximum strength which can be produced by an athlete, irrespective of body mass.

It is vital to recognize a training maximum or training 1RM, which is always less than the competition maximum, CFmax in experienced athletes, because optimal motivation invariably occurs under competitive conditions. Zatsiorsky states that the training maximum is the heaviest load that one can lift without substantial emotional excitement, as indicated by significant rise in heart rate before the lift. It is noteworthy that, in the untrained person, involuntary or hypnotic conditions can increase strength output by up to 35%, but by less than 10% in the trained athlete. The mean difference between TFmax and CFmax is approximately 12.5% in experienced weightlifters, with a larger difference being exhibited by lifters in heavier weight classes.

The merit of identifying the different types of strength or performance maxima lies in enabling one to prescribe training intensity more efficiently. Intensity is usually defined as a certain percentage of one's maximum, and it is most practical to choose this on the basis of the competitive maximum, which remains approximately constant for a fairly prolonged period. The training maximum can vary daily, so, while it may be of value in prescribing training for less qualified athletes, it is of limited value for elite competitors. It is relevant to note that competitions involve very few attempts to reach a maximum, yet they are far more exhausting than strenuous workouts with many repetitions, since they involve extremely high levels of psychological and nervous stress. The high levels of nervous and emotional stress incurred by attempting a competitive maximum require many days or even weeks to reach full recovery, even though physical recovery would appear to be complete, so this type of loading is not recommended as a regular form of training.

In other words, any attempt to exceed limit weights requires an increase in nervous excitation and interferes with the athlete's ability to adapt, if this type of training is used frequently. In attempting to understand the intensity of loading prescribed by the apparently extreme Bulgarian coaches who are reputed to stipulate frequent use of maximum loads in training, one has to appreciate that training with a training maximum is very different from training with a competitive maximum.

Strength is a relative phenomenon depending on numerous factors, so it is essential that these conditions are accurately described when strength is being assessed. For instance, muscular strength varies with joint angle, joint orientation, speed of movement, muscle group and type of movement, so it is largely meaningless to speak of absolute strength without specifying the conditions under which it is generated. Sometimes, the term relative strength is introduced to compare the strength of subjects of different body mass. In this context, relative strength is defined as the strength per unit body mass produced by a given individual under specific conditions.

In determining whether an athlete requires a specific type of resistance training, it sometimes is useful to introduce the concept of strength deficit, which is defined as the percentage difference between maximum strength produced in a given action and absolute strength of which the athlete is capable in that same action. This deficit may be defined under static or dynamic conditions, with the deficit depending on the rate at which force has to be developed in a given joint action. In the laboratory situation, absolute strength may be estimated by subjecting the muscles concerned to the maximum electrical stimulation which can be tolerated.

Strength deficit reflects the percentage of maximal strength potential which is not used during a given motor task, but its accurate measurement is seldom performed in practice, because determination of maximum eccentric strength by electrical stimulation is a difficult and potentially harmful task, and even if this were not the case, most sporting actions involve many muscles and joints, so that measurements of deficits for separate muscle groups would not necessarily relate to performance deficits in complex tasks.

The closest one can approach involuntary recruitment of as many muscle fibres in a given task is to force the body to react by reflex action to a suddenly imposed load. Thus, in a jumping or pulling activity, an approximate measure of strength deficit may be made by comparing the vertical jump achieved from a static start with knees flexed with a vertical jump preceded by a sudden dip. If there is a small difference between the two jumps, this suggests that training focuses more on nervous stimulation via the use of 'shock' and ballistic methods such as plyometrics. If the deficit is large, then strength and hypertrophy training with 5RM to 8RM loads using methods such as CAT is more suitable, with a definite emphasis on the eccentric deceleration phase.

In general, if the strength deficit is large for a given muscle group, an increase in speed-strength produced by maximal or near-maximal neuromuscular stimulation. If the strength deficit is small, hypertrophy must be induced by submaximal loading methods as commonly used in bodybuilding, followed by maximal efforts against heavy loads.

Verkhoshansky has shown that the strength deficit increases as the external resistance and the time of motion decrease, indicating that training to decrease maximal strength becomes more import-art as the time available for a movement becomes longer. Conversely, training to increase rapidity of movement becomes more important as the external load decreases. This implies that identification of explosive strength deficit is especially important in devising strength training regimes for athletes whose movement's allow them little time to produce maximum force, in other words, for actions such as running, jumping, weightlifting and throwing.

Before concerning oneself about strength deficit, it is important to appreciate that superior performance does not depend simply on the ability to produce maximum force, since many sporting actions take place so rapidly that it is impossible to recruit an adequate number of muscle fibres. Presuming that technical skill is adequate, performance may also be limited by the inability to produce the optimal level of strength at any given instant or in a crucial phase of movement. In other words, rate of force development is another factor vital to sporting prowess. Thus, it is highly relevant to estimate deficits in maximal force production, as well as in the RFD.

Identification of a strength deficit for the most important muscle groups of an athlete enables the coach to design the specific type of strength training more accurately than relying on the more conventional approach of somewhat arbitrarily prescribing a certain number of sets and repetitions of several exercises with a given load. Development of the necessary type of sport-specific fitness entails far more than this: the training programme must also pay careful attention to many other factors including the method of executing each exercise and the manner in which force is displayed relative to time and space.

A more enduring type of strength fitness results from a well-sequenced combination of functional and structural resistance training. However, it is important to monitor regularly any change in relative strength to ascertain if increased hypertrophy is simply adding unproductive tissue bulk without a commensurate increase in functional strength. Other useful measures of training effectiveness are the analysis of injury or soreness patterns, and changes inflexibility, motor skills and reaction time.

Muscle Action

All sporting movement is the consequence of muscle action, so an understanding of the different types of muscle action is another basic component of biomechanics.

Traditionally, the following types of muscle contraction are defined: isotonic, isometric, iso- kinetic and isoinertial. In addition, movement may occur under concentric and eccentric conditions. Before these terms are unquestioningly applied to exercise, it is important to examine their validity. Isometric literally means 'same length', a state which occurs only in a relaxed muscle. Actually, it is not muscle length, but joint angle which remains constant. Contraction means 'shortening', so that isometric contraction, like all other forms of muscle contraction, involves internal movement processes which shorten the muscle. Isometric contraction may be defined more accurately to mean muscle contraction which occurs when there is no external movement or change in joint angle. It occurs when the force produced by a muscle exactly balances the resistance imposed upon it and no movement results.

The term isotonic, however, should be avoided under most circumstances, since it is very rare for muscle tension to remain the same while joint movement occurs over any extended range. Constancy is possible only over a small range under very slow or quasi-isometric conditions of movement for a limited time. Whenever movement occurs, muscle tension increases or decreases, since acceleration or deceleration is always involved and one of the stretch reflexes may be activated. European and Russian scientists prefer o use the term auxotonic, which refers to muscle contraction involving changes in muscle tension and length. Other authors use the term allodynamic, from the Greek allos meaning 'other' or 'not the same'. Both terms are more accurate than isotonic in this context.

Isotonic action is most likely to occur under static conditions, in which case we have isotonic isometric action. Even then, as is the case with all muscle activation, there is a rise time of tension build-up, an intermediate phase of maximal tension, and a final decay time of tension decrease. For any prolonged action, the tension oscillates irregularly over a range of values. If the load is near maximal, the muscles are unable to sustain the same level of static muscle tension for more than a few seconds and the situation rapidly becomes anisotonic isometric.

The word isokinetic is encountered in two contexts: firstly, some textbooks regard it as a specific type of muscle contraction, and secondly, so-called isokinetic rehabilitation and testing machines are often used by physical therapists. The term isokinetic contraction is inappropriately applied in most cases, since it is impossible to produce a full-range muscle contraction at constant velocity. To produce any movement from rest, Newton's first two Laws of Motion reveal that acceleration must be involved, so that constant velocity cannot exist in a muscle which contracts from rest and returns to that state. Constant velocity can occur only over a part of the range of action.

Similarly, it is biomechanically impossible to design a purely isokinetic machine, since the user has to start a given limb from rest and push against the machine until it can constrain the motion to approximately constant angular velocity over part of its range. The resistance offered by these devices increases in response to increases in the force produced by the muscles, thereby limiting the velocity of movement to roughly isokinetic conditions over part of their range.

One of the few occasions when isokinetic action takes place is during isometric contraction. In this case, the velocity of limb movement is constant and equal to zero. However, it should be pointed out that, even if a machine manages to constrain an external movement to take place at constant velocity, the underlying muscle contraction is not occurring at constant velocity.

Two remaining terms applied to dynamic muscle action need elaboration. Concentric contraction refers to muscle action which produces a force that overcomes the load being acted upon; therefore Russian scientists call it overcoming contraction. Eccentric contraction refers to muscle action in which the muscle force yields to the imposed load. Thus, in Russia, it is referred to as yielding contraction. As with isometric contraction, it has been suggested that unique neural commands may control eccentric contractions, especially since the neural drive to the muscles is reduced, despite maximal voluntary effort under high-tension loading.

Since superimposed electrical stimulation was found to increase eccentric torque by more than 20% above voluntary levels and electrically evoked torque alone exceeded voluntary torque by about 12%, it is obvious that the maximum eccentric torque obtained voluntarily does not represent the maximal torque-producing capacity. Interestingly, no corresponding differences were observed between superimposed and voluntary torques under isometric or concentric conditions, so that neural mechanisms may protect against the extreme muscle tension that could otherwise develop under truly maximal eccentric conditions. Comparison between EMG recordings during eccentric and concentric exercise, as well as the magnitude of the training-induced changes in the EMG, also suggest that muscular activity under eccentric loads may be impaired by mental processes.

A little appreciated fact concerning eccentric muscle contraction is that the muscle tension over any full-range movement is lower during the eccentrics phase than the isometric or concentric phases, yet eccentric activity is generally identified as being the major cause of delayed-onset muscle soreness. Certainly, muscle tension of 30-45% greater than concentric or isometric contraction can be produced by near-maximal eccentric muscle contraction as when an athlete lowers a supramaximal load in a squat or bench press, but this degree of tension is not produced during the average submaximal training conditions.

4

EXERCISE AND BODY COMPOSITION

Obesity is a major health problem. It affects a large proportion of the population and adversely affects health and longevity. It either is a cause or is correlated with health problems such as diabetes, coronary heart disease, and hypertension, and such physiological effects as depression, withdrawal, poor self concept, and self pity. Many agree that reducing the incidence of obesity would advance public health.

Our society is tremendously preoccupied with obesity. Data from a 1985 National Health Interview

Survey indicated that 45% of females and 27% of males were trying to lose weight. Weight reduction is a multibillion-dollar industry; programs specifically aimed at weight management have spread rapidly in recent years. Nevertheless, obesity persists in our society.

BODY COMPOSITION

Body weight consists of many components, the relative proportions of which vary among individuals. Total body weight, which includes bone, muscle, fat, blood, and so on, is conveniently divided into the lean body mass and fat mass. Lean body mass is the weight of all body tissue except fat. Fat mass is the portion of the total body weight that is composed of fat tissue. Body fat is stored in various organs of the body, such as the heart, liver, lungs, and brain. In addition, body fat is retained in adipose tissue, including the fat surrounding various internal organs as well as the subcutaneous layer of fat just beneath the skin. Some body fat is essential as an energy store, for protection of internal organs, as a component of nerves and cell membranes, and as insulation against heat loss. Essential body fat is 3% to 5% for adult males and 11% to 14% for adult females of their total body weight, respectively. The average college-age woman has between 20% and 25% of her total body weight made up of fat. The average college-age man has between 12% and 18% body fat. However, it must be indicated that persons who engage in strenuous physical activities on a regular basis tend to have lower body fat percentages. It is recommended that body fat percentage not go below 5% in men and 12% in women because a certain amount of body fat is necessary for good health.

BEING OVERWEIGHT VS. BEING OBESE

The difference between being overweight and being obese is an important distinction. Being overweight implies having excess body weight relative to bone structure and height. Some define it as having 10% in excess of the midpoint of the normal body weight range. Unfortunately, this does not consider the amount of body fat. The excess weight could be due to excess fat or to a higher proportion of muscle. Using the term overweight is not very precise. On the other hand, obesity clearly describes a condition of having an excessive amount of fat. Women and men are considered obese if they possess greater than 32% and 2~% body fat, respectively. It has been estimated that in America about 50 million adult men and 60 million adult women are obese. The problem of having too much body fat has reached epidemic proportions in the United States.

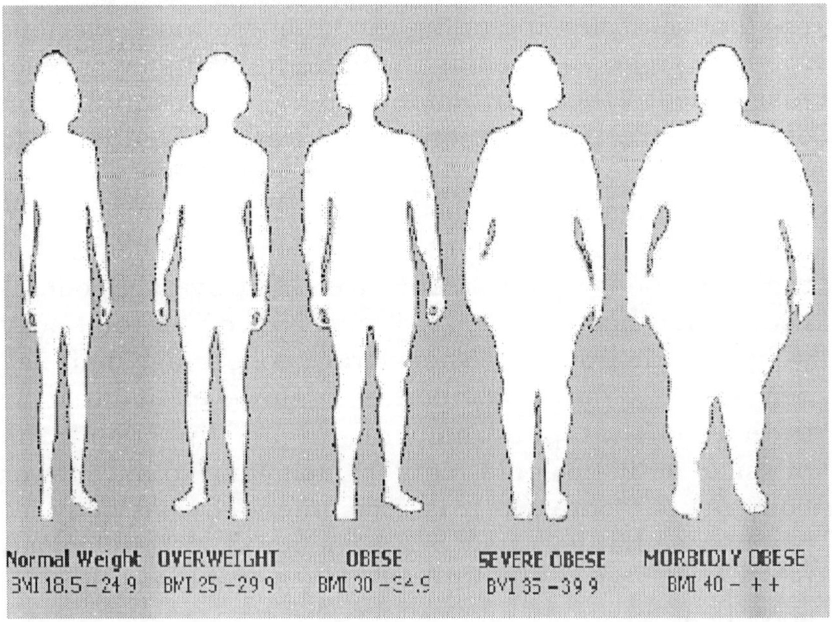

Recent studies also suggest that not only percent of fat but also regional fat distribution must be considered. Excess body fat in the abdominal region is associated with greater risk of cardiovascular disease and a greater incidence of Type II (non-insulin dependent) diabetes. In determining regional body-fatness distribution, measurements should also be made of the waist and hip circumferences. High waist-to-hip circumferences have been associated with Type II diabetes and hypertension. A great amount of abdominal fat and a high waist-to-hip ratio are characteristic of android-type obesity. This type of obesity involves hypertrophy (increase in size of adipose, fat, cells). Gynoid-type obesity is characterized by greater fat deposition on the buttocks, hips, and thighs, a low waist-to-hip ratio, and hyperplasia (increase in number of fat cells).

ASSESSING BODY COMPOSITION

An evaluation of body composition is essential prior to making specific recommendations about a person's need to lose or gain body weight. Among the several methods of assessing body composition are hydrostatic weighing, measurement of bioelectrical impedance, and measurement of skin fold thickness.

HYDROSTATIC WEIGHING

Hydrostatic (underwater) weighing involves placing a subject in a specially designed underwater tank to determine body density. Fat tissue is less dense than lean tissue. Therefore the more body fat pre-sent, the more the body floats (buoyancy) and the less it weighs in water. Body composition is calculated by comparing the weight of the submerged individual with the weight before entering the tank. If done properly, this technique is very accurate. Unfortunately, the tank and equipment are expensive and generally not available to most people. In addition, there are other drawbacks with this technique. It is time consuming (especially for large groups), and subjects must exhale completely and hold their breath underwater. Many students have real problems and fears with this.

BIOELECTRICAL IMPEDANCE

The second technique involves the measurement of resistance to the flow of electrical current through the body between selected points. This technique is based on the principle that electricity will choose to flow through the tissue that offers the least resistance or impedance. Fat is generally a poor conductor. Thus the higher the percentage of body fat, the greater the resistance to the passage of electrical energy. Very simply, this method predicts the percentage body fat by measuring bioelectrical impedance.

It should be mentioned that bioelectrical impedance measures can be affected by levels of hydration. If the body is dehydrated, the measurement will tend to overestimate percentage of body fat relative to measurements taken when there is normal hydration. The equipment available for taking these measurements is, again, fairly expensive and generally includes the use of computer software. A number of different methods for calculating body fat percentage using skin fold measurements have been developed. The most frequently measured skin fold sites are the triceps, subscapular, suprailiac, thigh, abdomen, calf, and chest.

Although skin fold measurement is a less accurate method than bioelectrical impedance or underwater weighing, most can gain expertise in performing this technique. Furthermore the calipers arc lcss costly and time consuming to use than the other equipment.

BODY MASS INDEX (BMI)

Once you have calculated the percentage of your total body weight that is made up of fat tissue, you may determine that you have to much fat. A relatively easy way to determine the extent of overweight or obesity is to use a person's body weight and height measurements to determine body mass index (BMI). BMI is a ratio of body weight to height. This technique represents a method for measuring health risks from obesity using height/weight measurements. Health problems associated with excess body fat tend to be associatcd with a BMI of more than 25. A BMI of 25-30 indicates that a person is overweight. A BMI of 30 or more indicates a state of obesity.

CALORIC BALANCE AND WEIGHT CONTROL

Caloric balance is the relationship between caloric intake and caloric expenditure (i.e. the number of calories taken in from food and drink compared to those expended by basal metabolism and voluntary activity). The energy-balance equation expresses this relationship mathematically

Caloric intake = Caloric expenditure

Λ calorie is simply a measure of the energy value of fat. A calorie by definition is the amount of heat necessary to raise the temperature of I g of water I degree C. In nutrition and exercise circles, the term calorie is frequently used for what is actually a kilocalorie.

A kilocalorie is the amount of heat needed to increase the temperature of 1 kg of water I degree C.

One Kcal equals 1000 cal. When caloric intake exceeds caloric expenditure, a person is in positive caloric balance. For example, a caloric intake of 2,800 Kcal per day while expending only 2,500 kcal per day leads to a positive 300-kcal balance per day. These 300 kcal that are not expended by the body are stored as adipose tissue, resulting in weight gain. If energy expenditure exceeds caloric intake, a person is in negative caloric balance, and a caloric deficit exists. An example would be a person who consumes 2,500 kcal per day while expending 3,000 kcal. The 500-kcal deficit leads to weight loss as the body primarily uses stored adipose tissue to meet its daily energy needs. People in physical-activity and weight-reduction programs need to know that a balance must be achieved between the number of calories taken in and the number expended, to stay the same weight. If more calories are consumed than expended, fat is stored in adipose tissue. One lb. of adipose tissue equals 3,500 kcal. Thus, if 3,500 more kcal are eaten than expended, 1 lb. of adipose tissue is gained.

Conversely, to lose 1 lb. of body fat, a 3,500-kcal deficit must occur. A deficit of 500 kcal per day, therefore, leads to the loss of approximately 1 lb. of adipose tissue in I week.

KEY POINT: a negative caloric balance of 3,500 kcal is required to lose 1 lb. of adipose tissue. It is recommended that the caloric deficit be achieved through a combination of caloric restriction and increased physical activity.

BASAL METABOLIC RATE

Total caloric expenditure, or the number of calories

used by the body, is determined by basal metabolism and voluntary metabolism. Basal metabolism is the energy expended when the body is at rest, it is the minimal amount of energy required to sustain the body's vital functions and maintenance of body temperature during a 24-hour period. Basal metabolic rate (BMR) is the rate at which calories are spent for these maintenance activities. BMR is most accurately determined in a laboratory through a measurement process known as indirect calorimetry, which measures a person's oxygen uptake to predict BMR. Measurement of BMR using this procedure is generally done as soon as the subject awakes; in a quiet, warm environment; and after a 12-hour fast. The term resting metabolic rate (RMR) is often used interchangeable with BMR, although the two are measured somewhat differently, with RMR having less stringent measure-ment restrictions.

FACTORS INFLUENCING BASAL METABOLIC RATE (BMR)

The greater the amount of body surface area, the higher the BMR. It is important to note that surface area, not body weight, is the influencing factor. Age: In general, the younger the person, the higher the BMR Gender: Men generally have a higher BMR than do women Diet: There is a dramatic and sustained reduction in BMR that occurs with very low calorie dieting Exercise: Consistent exercise tends to in-crease the BMR during the activity and for a period of time after the activity ceases.

SET POINT THEORY OF WEIGHT CONTROL

The set point theory provides and explanation of why it is so difficult to lose or gain weight. The body tends to maintain a certain level of body fat. This theory maintains that the body has a "set point" or some mechanism for maintaining a specific body weight. It operates like a thermostat that is set to control a house's temperature. When the temperature in the house drops below the set point, the furnace turns on. When the temperature warms to the setting, the furnace shuts off. For people, it may be that the body's fat level is set at a particular point, and attempts to reduce this level are met with resistance by the body. It is unclear how this set point is controlled; it may be that the fat cells tend to maintain a certain degree of fat stored within them and resist efforts to reduce their size. If you at-tempt to lower the set point through dieting alone, metabolic rate decreases to conserve calories. Exercise that elevates metabolism in combination with caloric restriction appears to be the only way to reduce the set point. In any case, the set point theory is just that, a theory that may explain why so many people are unsuccessful at keeping off the fat lost through dieting.

SUMMARY

Excess body fat is a risk factor for heart disease and diabetes. A certified fitness professional must be able to estimate body fatness and predict and ideal weight consistent with optimal health. Underwater weighing, skin fold measurement, and bioelectrical impedance are being used for this purpose. For body weight to be maintained, caloric intake must equal caloric expenditure. A caloric deficit of 3,500 kcal is needed to lose 1 lb. of fat. A balanced program of exercise and dietary reduction, rather than diet alone, is recommended for weight loss.

SKINFOLD METHOD

The third technique of assessing body composition by measuring the thickness of the skin folds has the widest use, compared to the other techniques. It is based on the idea that about 50% of the fat in the body is subcutaneous (under the skin). By measuring the thickness of this layer of fat, the total percentage of body fat can be calculated. Skin folds are measured at various body sites using skin fold calipers. Men and women tend to develop fat deposits in different body areas; skin fold measurements must be taken at these specified places.

Body Composition—Body Fat—Body Weight

Body Composition is the term used to describe the different components that, when taken together, make up a person's body weight. The human body is composed of a variety of different tissue types including lean tissues (muscle, bone, and organs) that are metabolically active, and fat (adipose) tissue that is not.

Body Weight Measurements

Standard body weight scales provide a measure of total weight, but don't determine the lean-to-fat ratio of that weight. Standing on most scales can tell you only if you weigh more than the average person, but not if that weight is fat or muscle. Based only on scale weight, a 250 pound athlete with 8 percent body fat may be considered "overweight" by a typical weight chart. Such charts are not a good indication of ideal body weight for general health or for athletic performance.

Body Composition — Body Fat Measurement

There are many methods of assessing a person's fat and lean mass. The most common methods include the following.

Underwater Weighing — Hydrostatic Weighing

One method of body composition analysis in which a person is weighed while submerged in a large tank of water is called underwater or hydrostatic weighing This method of determining body composition relies on Archimedes' Principle of displacement which states:

1. The density of fat mass and fat-free mass are constant

2. Lean tissue is more dense than water

3. Fat tissue is less dense than water.

4. Therefore person with more body fat will weigh less underwater and be more buoyant.

Underwater weighing has been considered the gold standard for body composition assessment, however new, more sophisticated methods may make underwater weighing obsolete in the future.

Skinfold Thickness Measurements

Because underwater weighting it is complicated and cumbersome and requires special equipment, most exercise physiologists use simple skinfold measurements to determine body fat percent. The American College of Sports Medicine says that when performed by a trained, skilled, tester, they are up to 98 percent accurate.

Bioelectrical Impedance

Bioelectrical Impedance is another method of assessing body fat percentage. There are a variety of body composition and body fat analyzers and scales available for home use that provide more than just total weight measurements. These devices determine total weight, the percent and amount of body fat, muscle mass, water, and even bone mass. While the readings can be affected by hydration levels, food intake, skin temperature, and other factors, if you follow the directions and take the reading under similar conditions, you will obtain the best results.

BMI — Body Mass Index

BMI or Body Mass Index, is another method of estimating a person's body fat percentage based upon simple weight and height measurements. While the BMI calculation is an indirect measurement, it has been found to be a fairly reliable indicator of body fat measures in most people. Although some studies still question the accuracy of the BMI method of body fat measurement, especially for athletes.

Ideal Body Weight and Body Fat Percent

The ideal weight and fat-lean ratio varies considerably for men and women and by age, but the minimum percent of body fat considered safe for good health is 5 percent for males and 12 percent for females. The average adult body fat is closer to 15-18 percent for men and 22-25 percent for women.

Athletes tend to be at low end of this scale due to their increased lean weight (muscle mass). While low levels of body fat seem to be related to improved performance, body composition alone is not a great predictor of sports success. A linebacker needs to have enough body mass (lean and fat weight) to generate high forces and avoid injury. Body fat among elite athletes vary largely by sport. There is little evidence of any benefit when men drop under 8 percent and women drop under 14 percent body fat.

How Low Is Too Low?

While the average body fat percent in the United States and Europe is increasing, extremely low body fat percent is also a health problem. The female athlete triad highlights the problem. Women athletes who lose too much fat risk injury, decreased performance and health issues.

The female athlete triad refers specifically to three related health problems often found in women athletes:

- Eating disorders and low energy availability.
- Amenorrhea and menstrual disorders.
- Decreased bone mass and increased risk of stress fractures and osteoporosis.

This attempt to reduce body fat by extreme measures not only leads to decreased exercise performance, but can lead to severe health complications. Nutrient deficiencies and fluid/electrolyte imbalance from low food intake can lead to increased risk of fractures, illness, loss of reproductive function and serious medical conditions such as dehydration, and starvation. The medical complications of this triad involve almost every body function and include the cardiovascular, endocrine, reproductive, skeletal, gastrointestinal, renal, and central nervous systems.

How Much Body Fat Is Too Much?

Just as too little body fat can cause physiological complications, too much body fat is also harmful. For men over 25 percent and women over 32 percent fat there is a dramatic correlation with illness and disease.

Isn't Body Composition Genetic?

Some aspects of your body composition are genetic (where you store fat), but most fat increase is related to lifestyle.

Can I Change My Body Composition?

Yes. To increase or decrease your percent of body fat you need to create the right balance between the calories in and calories out. The best way to do this is to decrease daily calories by about 500 and increase your exercise. Aerobic exercise along with strength training is ideal. If you are beginning a new exercise program, you are advised to first consult your physician.

BODY FAT MEASUREMENT

Determining your body fat percentage is useful for weight management, bodybuilding, sports training, and health risk assessment. You can find out:

1. Approximately how much body fat you have
2. If you have too much body fat
3. How your body fat may affect your health risk

How to Use Body Fat Knowledge

It's worth knowing that all body fat measurement methods have limitations. Some tools, like body calipers, may not sufficiently evaluate the fat that is stored around internal organs (visceral fat). This type of fat increases risk for heart disease and diabetes more than fat stored in tissue just under the skin. Further, individuals who are on the overfat side but who exercise consistently may be fitter and perhaps healthier than, for example, a skinny smoker who does not exercise.

Although you should feel free to monitor your body fat for fitness and weight management purposes, your doctor (perhaps with the assistance of a nutrition professional) is the best person to make health risk assessments. He or she will take all of your disease risk factors into account, such as blood cholesterol, glucose measurements, body fat, and fitness level.

Body Fat Charts

Defining absolute "healthy" body fat levels is less desirable than setting ranges of acceptable fat percentages. Women naturally carry more body fat than men, and a healthy range could be from 18 to 25 percent for relatively inactive women and 12 to 20 percent for athletes and fitness enthusiasts, although the distinction is contrived. For men, 12 to 18 percent for non-athletes and 5 to 12 percent for fitness enthusiasts are the normal ranges, even though some charts have higher maximums. For men and women over age 40, the percentages are usually adjusted upward, although this needs reviewing in my view.

Frankly, many of the professional body fat charts project an unfortunate spin on body fatness even though they are only meant as a guide. Some use categories like "underfat," "healthy," "lean," or "ideal." In my opinion, that suggests that being in the "underfat" or "lean" sectors is unhealthy. This is just untrue for many fit people. I don't accept that a 20 year-old woman with 15 percent body fat who runs more than six miles in 50 minutes and deadlifts 100 pounds should be categorized as underfat and by inference, unhealthy. The notation in these charts is plainly unhelpful and needs updating that's in line with current community standards of health and fitness.

One point to note is that women who get down to around 12 percent body fat experience hormonal disturbances that may result in loss of periods, bone loss, and disordered eating. This is called the "female athlete triad" in sports medicine. Endurance athletes and some women strength trainers may compete effectively at this body fat level, so this is not necessarily unhealthy. But it does require the management and advice of a sports medicine professional.

Body Mass Index or BMI

The body mass index is a body weight and height formula designed to provide a snapshot of your body fatness. It is calculated by dividing your weight in kilograms by your height in meters, squared. The easiest way to calculate this is to use an online calculator like this one from the US Heart Blood and Lung Institute. It allows you to calculate your BMI using pounds, feet, and inches as well as in kilograms and meters.

The BMI categories of are as follows:

- Normal weight = 18.5 to 24.9
- Overweight = 25 to 29.9
- Obese = 30 or greater

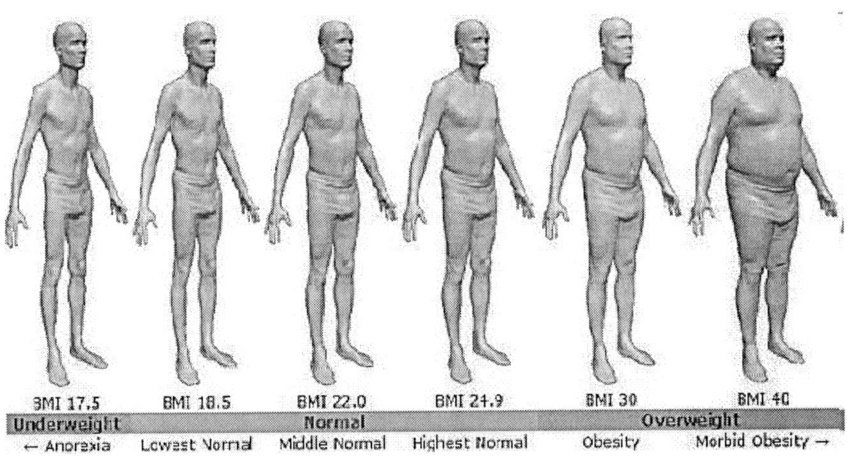

The BMI gets consistently criticized by exercise professionals because, like the charts above, athletes or other heavily muscled people are not factored in. That tends to skew the results by placing bodybuilders and heavily built people in the overweight category.

In a sense, this criticism is unjustified because the BMI is only one tool in the hands of experienced health professionals. A keen eye plus a waist measurement is often all that is required to establish if someone is overweight.

5

FORCES AND TORQUES

When evaluating a new design, the stress analyst will usually measure not only the mechanical strains in the test structures, but the forces and torques that produce the strains as well. This is especially important when the objective is to determine the response of the design to known or anticipated loading conditions with an eye toward reducing weight and establishing safety margins. For measuring these non-strain loading parameters, the experienced analyst will generally opt to utilize commercially available transducers specifically designed for that purpose. But when the use of a ready-made transducer is impractical — or even impossible — strain gages can often be installed on some component of the test structure or loading fixture in a configuration that will enable the applied forces and torques to be measured directly. The physical arrangements and electrical circuits necessary for achieving these measurements are described below.

This single longitudinal gage configuration will respond to bending loads but is unaffected by torsional loads if the gage is mounted on the centerline. Care must be taken with how the load is applied, because transducers utilizing this configuration will also respond to any axial loads that may be present. Since this configuration produces a small amount of nonlinearity (approximately 0.1% for each 1000 microstrain) and is sensitive to changes in temperature, the following "half-bridge" configuration is generally preferred. When a half bridge cannot be used, the sensitivity to temperature for a single active gage configuration can be minimized by using the proper self-temperature-compensated strain gage and by zero-balancing before the load is applied.

The use of a three-leadwire circuit is recommended for all quarter-bridge installations used to make static

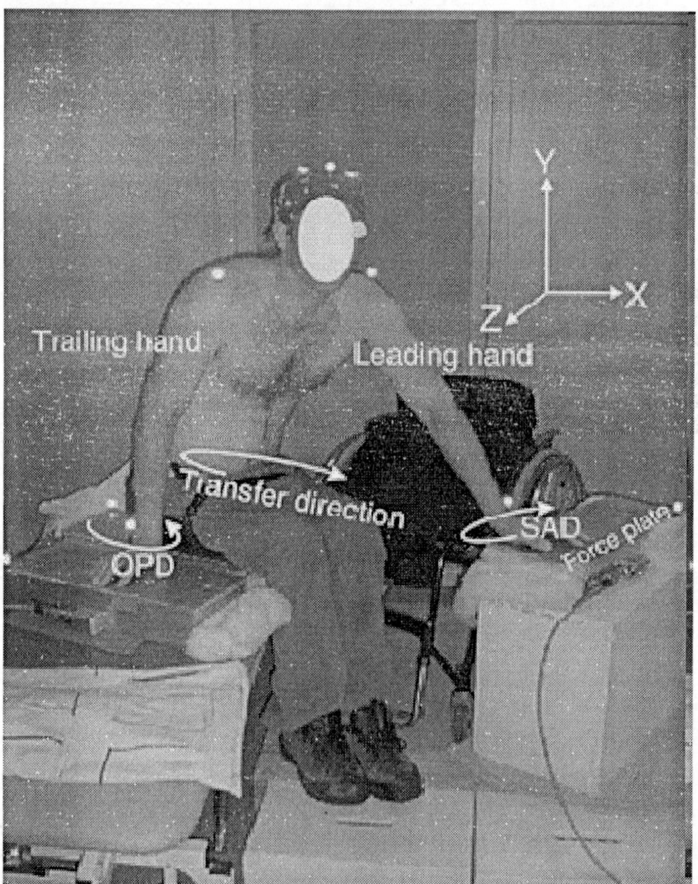

measurements.

Because the longitudinal gage and the transverse "Poisson" gage are in adjacent arms, the resistance changes of thermal origins will be cancelled in this version when both active gages and the specimen experience like changes in temperature. The bridge output is increased by a factor of approximately $(1 + \upsilon)$ and the nonlinearity is reduced to approximately $[(1-\upsilon)/10]\%$ per each 1000 microstrain of longitudinal strain.

In this configuration, two axial gages are used. The gage on the lower surface is located precisely under the gage on the top surface and they measure bending strains that are of equal magnitudes but of opposite signs. Any resistance changes in the active gages resulting from strains of like sign produced by axial loads will be cancelled because the two active gages are in adjacent arms of the Wheatstone bridge. Likewise, resistance changes of thermal origins will be negated when both gages and the specimen experience the same changes in temperature. And because the strains produced by bending loads are of equal magnitude but opposite sign, the bridge output is not only linear but is nominally double that produced by a single active gage under the same conditions.

This four-gage version is the most popular bending beam configuration. The linear bridge output is twice that of the preceding half-bridge version. Note that the two gages on the top surface are in opposite arms of the Wheatstone bridge, as are the two gages on the bottom surface.

The physical configuration of the gages is the same as that used for the bending half bridge. But because the two active gages are now electrically connected in opposite arms of the Wheatstone bridge, this configuration cancels bending strains with equal magnitudes and opposite signs. The magnitude of the bridge output resulting from axial loads is relatively high (because of the additive effect) but is nonlinear (approximately 0.1% per each 1000 microstrain produced in the column by axial loads). And because any thermal output from the active gages is additive for this configuration, temperature compensation is the poorest of any configuration shown here.

This "full-bridge" configuration with a longitudinal gage and transverse "Poisson" gage on both top and bottom surfaces is the most popular for axial loads. The output is not only higher by approximately a factor of $(1+\upsilon)$ than for the previous two-gage version but, is also less nonlinear (approximately $[1 - \upsilon)/10]\%$ per 1000 microstrain produced by axial loads). This version has good temperature compensation because gages are present in all adjacent arms of the bridge. Note that both gages on a given surface are in adjacent arms of the bridge.

Like the full-bridge configuration for bending loads, this torsional version has a linear output and good temperature compensation. All effects of both bending and axial loads are cancelled in this most popular design for torque measurement. However, very accurate gage orientation and placement of all four gages is crucial for success.

Fundamental Considerations

High-quality transducers utilizing strain gages as the primary sensing element incorporate sophisticated techniques to minimize thermal effects, nonlinearities, hysteresis, and other sources of error. These same techniques can be engaged when a portion of a structure or loading frame must be adapted to function as the spring element. For now, however, considerations will be limited to how the unique characteristics of the Wheatstone bridge itself can be utilized for measuring force and torque. And only the most significant unresolved errors or potential errors associated with the various configurations will be noted.

The output from the Wheatstone bridge can be expressed as:

$$\frac{E_0}{E} = \frac{R_1}{R_1 + R_2} - \frac{R_4}{R_3 + R_4}$$

where E_0 is the bridge output voltage, E is the bridge excitation voltage, and R_1, R_2, R_3, and R_4 are the resistances of the gages in the bridge.

Note that changes of resistance in adjacent gages (R_1 and R_4, for example) have the same (or numerically additive) effect on bridge output when the changes are of opposite sign. When the changes in adjacent arms are of the same sign, they have opposite (or numerically subtractive) effects. Conversely, the effects of resistance changes in opposite arms (R_1 and R_3, for example) are reversed: changes in resistance with like signs in opposite arms have the same effects on the output and changes with unlike signs in opposite arms have opposite effects. These phenomena are used later to eliminate the effects of bending strains on the measurement of axial strains, the effects of axial strains on measurements of bending strains, eradication of thermally induced apparent strain, and even elimination of nonlinearity in the output from unbalanced Wheatstone bridges.

The bridge is balanced and produces no output when:

$$\frac{R_1}{R_1 + R_2} = \frac{R_4}{R_3 + R_4}$$

or when:

$$\frac{R_2}{R_1 + R_2} = \frac{R_3}{R_3 + R_4}$$

A change in resistance of one or more of the gages will unbalance the bridge so that an output signal is produced. Equation (1) can be used to determine the output of any unbalanced bridge simply by adding the resistance change of each affected resistor to the initial value of that resistor.

Sample Calculation

As a sample calculation of the output from a bridge, assume that *R*is an active strain gage that has undergone a change in resistance, , when the test specimen to which it is bonded has been subjected to stress. Equation (1) can then be rewritten as:

$$\frac{E_0}{E} = \frac{R_1 + \Delta R_1}{R_1 + \Delta R_1 + R_2} - \frac{R_4}{R_3 + R_4}$$

Assuming that all gages have the same initial resistance, then equation (2) reduces to:

$$\frac{E_0}{E} = \left(\frac{R_1 + \Delta R_1}{2R_1 + \Delta R_1} - \frac{1}{2}\right) = \frac{\Delta R_1 / R_1}{4 + 2(\Delta R_1 / R_1)}$$

Noting that the relative resistance change of a strain gage ($\Delta R/R$) is equal to the product of the gage factor (F) and the strain producing the resistance change (E), the bridge output for our single active gage example can then be expressed in terms of strain:

$$\frac{E_0}{E} = \frac{F_\varepsilon}{4 + 2F_\varepsilon}$$

While usually small in comparison to the number 4, the 2 term in the denominator gives rise to some nonlinearity for this configuration. The magnitude of this error is approximately 0.1% per each 1000 microstrain for bridges with single active gages. In most stress analysis applications this very small measurement error can be ignored, especially at low strain levels.

The preceding sample calculation yields the output from a quarter-bridge circuit measuring strains produced by bending a beam. The same can also be used with equal success for any number of other active gage configurations for measuring force and torque with Wheatstone bridge circuits.

The design of good transducers is a highly complex and difficult task that is not to be undertaken lightly. Whenever possible, the stress analyst is well advised to purchase a commercially available unit from "off-the-shelf". The preceding gage configurations are applicable only to the most elementary of spring elements. When the necessity arises for constructing a "home-grown" transducer based on them, then do not hesitate to do so. Just be aware of their unique capabilities and any inherent limitations they may pose.

TORQUE

Torque is the tendency of a force to rotate an object about an axis, fulcrum, or pivot. Just as a force is a push or a pull, a torque can be thought of as a twist.

In more basic terms, torque measures how hard something is twisted. For example, imagine a wrench or spanner trying to twist a nut or bolt. The amount of "twist" (torque) depends on how long the wrench is, how hard you push down on it, and how well you are pushing it in the correct direction.

Torque is also called moment or moment of force. This should neither be confused with the various other definitions of "moment" in physics nor with "momentum". In the context of mechanical engineering, the terms "moment" and "torque" are not necessarily interchangeable; rather, one or the other may be preferred in a specific context. For example, "torque" is usually used to describe a rotational force down a shaft, for example a turning screw-driver, whereas "moment" is more often used to describe a bending moment acting on a beam, shaft or any other structural or machine element.

The symbol for torque is typically τ, the Greek letter tau.

The magnitude of torque depends on three quantities: First, the force applied; second, the length of the lever arm connecting the axis to the point of force application; and third, the angle between the two. In symbols:

$$\vec{\tau} = \vec{r} \times \vec{F}$$

$$\tau = rF\sin\theta$$

where

$\vec{\tau}$ is the torque vector and τ is the magnitude of the torque,

is the lever arm vector (vector from the axis to the point of force application), and r is the length (or magnitude) of the lever arm vector,

is the force vector, and F is the magnitude of the force,

$\times$ denotes the cross product,

θ is the angle between the force vector and the lever arm vector.

The length of the lever arm is particularly important; choosing this length appropriately lies behind the operation of levers, pulleys, gears, and most other simple machines involving a mechanical advantage.

The SI unit for torque is the newton meter (N·m). In Imperial and U.S. customary units, it is measured in foot pounds (ft·lbf) (also known as 'pound feet') and for smaller measurement of torque: inch pounds (in·lbf) or even inch ounces (in·ozf).

History

The concept of torque, also called moment or couple, originated with the studies of Archimedes on levers. The rotational analogues of force, mass, and acceleration are torque, moment of inertia, and angular acceleration, respectively.

Explanation

The force applied to a lever multiplied by its distance from the lever's fulcrum, the length of the lever arm, is its torque. A force of three newtons applied two meters from the fulcrum, for example, exerts the same torque as one newton applied six meters from the fulcrum. This assumes the force is in a direction at right angles to the straight lever. The direction of the torque can be determined by using the right hand grip rule: curl the fingers of your right hand to indicate the direction of rotation, and stick your thumb out so it is aligned with the axis of rotation. Your thumb points in the direction of the torque vector.

Mathematically, the torque on a particle (which has the position r in some reference frame) can be defined as the cross product:

$$\tau = r \times F$$

where

r is the particle's position vector relative to the fulcrum

F is the force acting on the particle.

The torque on a body determines the rate of change of its angular momentum, where

L is the angular momentum vector

t is time.

As can be seen from either of these relationships, torque is a vector, which points along the axis of the rotation it would tend to cause.

Proof of the Equivalence of Definitions

The definition of angular momentum for a single particle is:

$$L = r \times p$$

where " × " indicates the vector cross product and *p* is the particle's linear momentum. The time-derivative of this is:

$$\frac{dL}{dt} = r \times \frac{dp}{dt} + \frac{dr}{dt} \times p$$

This result can easily be proven by splitting the vectors into components and applying the product rule. Now using the definitions of velocity $v = dr/dt$, acceleration $a = dv/dt$ and linear momentum $p = mv$, we can see that:

$$\frac{dL}{dt} = r \times m\frac{dv}{dt} + v \times mv$$

But the cross product of any vector with itself is zero, so the second term vanishes. Hence with the definition of force $F = ma$, (Newton's 2nd law) we obtain:

$$\frac{dL}{dt} = r \times F$$

And by definition, torque $t = r \times F$.

Note that there is a hidden assumption that mass is constant—this is quite valid in non-relativistic mechanics. Also, total (summed) forces and torques have been used — it perhaps would have been more rigorous to write:

$$\frac{dL}{dt} = \tau_{tot}$$
$$= \sum_i \tau_i$$

Units

Torque has dimensions of force times distance and the SI unit of torque is the "newton meter" (N m). Even though the order of "newton" and "meter" are mathematically interchangeable, the BIPM (Bureau International des Poids et Mesures) specifies that the order should be N m not m N. N·m is also acceptable. Because "mN" is the symbol for the "millinewton", it must not be used to refer to the newton meter. In applications that are not case-sensitive, it is also necessary to avoid "NM" and "nm", because "nm" is the symbol for the nanometer.

The joule, which is the SI unit for energy or work, is also defined as 1 N m, but this unit is not used for torque.

Since energy can be thought of as the result of "force dot distance", energy is always a scalar whereas torque is "force cross distance" and so is a (pseudo) vector-valued quantity. The dimensional equivalence of these units, of course, is not simply a coincidence: a torque of 1 N m applied through a full revolution will require an energy of exactly 2π joules. Mathematically,

$$E = \pi\theta$$

where

E is the energy

t is torque

θ is the angle moved, in radians.

Other non-SI units of torque include "pound-force-feet" or "foot-pounds-force" or "inch-pounds-force" or "ounce-force-inches" or "meter-kilograms-force" or "kilogrammeter" (kgm). For all these units, the word "force" is often left out, for example abbreviating "pound-force-foot" to simply "pound-foot". (In this case, it would be implicit that the "pound" is pound-force and not pound-mass.)

Extended units in relation with rotation angles

As a consequence of the previous equation, if you introduce the radian (rad) as part of the dimensional units in the SI units system, the torque could be measured using "newton meters per radian" (N m/rad), or "joules per radian" (J/rad), while the energy needed and spent to perform the rotation would be measured simply in "newton meters" or "joules".

In the strict SI system, angles are not given any

dimensional unit, because they do not designate physical quantities, despite the fact that they are measurable indirectly simply by dividing two distances (the arc length and the radius): one way to conciliate the two systems would be to say that arc lengths are not measures of distances (given they are not measured over a straight line, and a full circle rotation returns to the same position, i.e. a null distance). So arc lengths should be measured in "radian meter" (rad·m), differently from straight segment lengths in "meters" (m). In such extended SI system, the perimeter of a circle whose radius is one meter, will be two pi rad·m, and not just two pi meters.

If you apply this measure to a rotating wheel in contact with a plane surface, the center of the wheel will move across a distance measured in meters with the same value, only if the contact is efficient and the wheel does not slide on it: this does not happen in practice, unless the surface of contact is constrained and is then not perfectly plane (and can resist to the horizontal linear forces applied to the irregularities of the pseudo-plane surface of movement and to the surface of the pseudo-circular rotating wheel); but then the system generates friction that loses some energy spent by the engine: this lost energy does not change the measurement of the torque or the total energy spent in the system but the effective distance that has been made by the center of the wheel.

The difference between the efficient energy spent by the engine and the energy produced in the linear movement is lost in friction and sliding, and this explains why, when applying the same non-null torque constantly to the wheel, so that the wheel moves at a constant speed according to the surface in contact, there may be no acceleration of the center of the wheel: in that case, the energy spent will be directly proportional to the distance made by the center of the wheel, and equal to the energy lost in the system by friction and sliding.

For this reason, when measuring the effective power produced by a rotating engine and the energy spent in the system to generate a movement, you will often need to take into account the angle of rotation, and then, adding the radian in the unit system is necessary as well as making a difference between the measurement of arcs (in radian meter) and the measurement of straight segment distances (in meters), as a way to effectively compute the efficiency of the mobile system and the capacity of a motor engine to convert between rotational power (in radian watt) and linear power (in watts): in a friction-free ideal system, the two measurements would have equal value, but this does not happen in practice, each conversion losing energy in friction (it's easier to limit all losses of energy caused by sliding, by introducing mechanical constraints of forms on the surfaces of contacts).

Depending on works, the extended units including radians as a fundamental dimension may or may not be used.

Special Cases and Other Facts

Moment Arm Formula

A very useful special case, often given as the definition of torque in fields other than physics, is as follows:

$$|\tau| = (moment\ arm)\,(force).$$

The construction of the "moment arm" is shown in the figure below, along with the vectors *r* and *F* mentioned above. The problem with this definition is that it does not give the direction of the torque but only the magnitude, and hence it is difficult to use in three-dimensional cases. If the force is perpendicular to the displacement vector *r*, the moment arm will be equal to the distance to the centre, and torque will be a maximum for the given force. The equation for the magnitude of a torque, arising from a perpendicular force:

$$|\tau| = (distance\ to\ centre)\,(force).$$

For example, if a person places a force of 10 N on a spanner (wrench) which is 0.5 m long, the torque will be 5 N m, assuming that the person pulls the spanner by applying force perpendicular to the spanner.

Force at an angle

If a force of magnitude F is at an angle θ from the displacement arm of length r (and within the plane perpendicular to the rotation axis), then from the definition of cross product, the magnitude of the torque arising is:

$$\tau = rF\sin\theta$$

Static Equilibrium

For an object to be in static equilibrium, not only must the sum of the forces be zero, but also the sum of the torques (moments) about any point. For a two-dimensional situation with horizontal and vertical forces, the sum of the forces requirement is two equations: ΣH = 0 and ΣV = 0, and the torque a third equation: Σt = 0. That is, to solve statically determinate equilibrium problems in two-dimensions, we use three equations.

Torque as a function of time

Torque is the time-derivative of angular momentum, just as force is the time derivative of linear momentum:

$$\tau = \frac{dL}{dt}$$

where

L is angular momentum.

Angular momentum on a rigid body can be written in terms of its moment of inertia I and its angular velocity ω:

L = Iω

so if *I* is constant,

$$\tau = I\frac{d\omega}{dt} = I\alpha$$

where α is angular acceleration, a quantity usually measured in radians per second squared.

Machine Torque

Torque is part of the basic specification of an engine: the power output of an engine is expressed as its torque multiplied by its rotational speed of the axis. Internal-combustion engines produce useful torque only over a limited range of rotational speeds (typically from around 1,000–6,000 rpm for a small car). The varying torque output over that range can be measured with a dynamometer, and shown as a torque curve. The peak of that torque curve occurs somewhat below the overall power peak. The torque peak cannot, by definition, appear at higher rpm than the power peak.

Understanding the relationship between torque, power and engine speed is vital in automotive engineering, concerned as it is with transmitting power from the engine through the drive train to the wheels. Power is typically a function of torque and engine speed. The gearing of the drive train must be chosen appropriately to make the most of the motor's torque characteristics.

Steam engines and electric motors tend to produce maximum torque close to zero rpm, with the torque diminishing as rotational speed rises (due to increasing friction and other constraints). Reciprocating steam engines can start heavy loads from zero RPM without a clutch.

Torque is also the easiest way to explain mechanical advantage in just about every simple machine.

Relationship between torque, power and energy

If a force is allowed to act through a distance, it is doing mechanical work. Similarly, if torque is allowed to act through a rotational distance, it is doing work. Power is the work per unit time. However, time and rotational distance are related by the angular speed where each revolution results in the circumference of the circle being travelled by the force that is generating the torque. The power injected by the applied torque may be calculated as:

Power = torque × angular speed

On the right hand side, this is a scalar product of two vectors, giving a scalar on the left hand side of the equation. Mathematically, the equation may be rearranged to compute torque for a given power output. Note that the power injected by the torque depends only on the instantaneous angular speed - not on whether the angular speed increases, decreases, or remains constant while the torque is being applied (this is equivalent to the linear case where the power injected by a force depends only on the instantaneous speed - not on the resulting acceleration, if any).

In practice, this relationship can be observed in power stations which are connected to a large electrical power grid. In such an arrangement, the generator's angular speed is fixed by the grid's frequency, and the power output of the plant is determined by the torque applied to the generator's axis of rotation.

Consistent units must be used. For metric SI units power is watts, torque is newton meters and angular speed is radians per second (not rpm and not revolutions per second).

Also, the unit newton meter is dimensionally equivalent to the joule, which is the unit of energy. However, in the case of torque, the unit is assigned to a vector, whereas for energy, it is assigned to a scalar.

6

BIOMECHANICS OF WALKING AND RUNNING

"Locomotion is a particularly richly studied but frustrating aspect of biology," according to Loeb. This is especially true when one attempts to understand how the numerous subdivisions of the neuromuscular and musculoskeletal systems interact to produce locomotion. At lower levels of organization, the structure and function of the system components become progressively more complex, making it difficult to discern general principles. One way of approaching the study of locomotion is to sequentially progress from a level of whole body dynamics toward a level of muscle tendon dynamics. We believe this approach can be particularly useful in that information from the higher levels of organization can guide the quest to understand fundamental mechanisms of locomotion at increasingly complex lower levels of organization. Thus, we will first examine the pattern of centre of mass movements during locomotion in humans and other legged animals. Next, we will consider how joint mechanics during locomotion are affected by both centre of mass dynamics and leg posture. After concentrating on the joint level, we will move to the level of muscle-tendon mechanics by examining the techniques that have been used to investigate muscle-tendon function during locomotion and the conclusions that have been reached to date.

Throughout this review, the locomotion of humans will be compared to the locomotion of other animals. A wealth of information shows that human locomotion is not unique. Indeed, at the level of the centre of mass, the dynamics of walking and running are similar in all legged animals that have been studied. The similarities in the dynamics of locomotion among diverse animals, including humans, suggest that there may also be similarities in the mechanisms by which locomotion is produced at other levels of organization within the neuromuscular system. Thus, by comparing diverse species, we can uncover common rules governing locomotion, and we can assess the applicability of data from animal models to biomedical issues in humans.

CENTRE OF MASS MECHANICS

Our discussion of centre of mass mechanics will be divided into four parts. First, we will discuss the pattern of ground reaction force that occurs during locomotion. Ground reaction force is the force exerted by the ground on the feet It reflects the acceleration of the body's centre of mass during locomotion. Second, the movements and mechanical energy fluctuations of the centre of mass that occur as a result of ground reaction force will be discussed. Third, we will discuss the transition from a walking gait to a running gait, an event that is marked by a sudden and distinct change in the pattern of movement of the centre of mass. By understanding the reasons for the transition from one gait to another, we can gain insight into the key factors that shape locomotion. Fourth, we will describe behavioural models for locomotion that give insight into how the musculoskeletal system produces the distinctly different ground reaction force and centre of mass movements in walking as compared to running.

Ground Reaction Force

The distinct difference between walking and running gaits is apparent in the ground reaction force patterns for the two gaits. In human walking, there is always at least one foot in contact with the ground, and there are short phases of "double support" when both feet are in contact with the ground. In contrast, running is a series of bouncing impacts with the ground that are usually alternated with aerial phases when neither foot is in contact with the ground. This difference leads to a substantially higher magnitude vertical component of the ground reaction force for running as compared to walking. The pattern of the horizontal component of the ground reaction force is similar, however, for both walking and running. In the first half of the stance phase, the horizontal ground reaction force is negative, indicating that it is pushing backwards on the person. In the second half of the stance phase, the horizontal ground reaction force is positive, pushing forward on the person. The ground reaction force pattern for walking and running gaits is similar in humans and in a wide variety of other animals with a range of body shapes, body masses, and numbers of legs.

Mechanical Energy Fluctuations of the Centre and Mass

The difference in the ground reaction force pattern between walking and running translates into dramatically different patterns of mechanical energy fluctuations for the centre of mass during the two gaits. During walking, the body vaults over a rclativcly stiff stance limb and the centre of mass reaches its highest point at the middle of the stance phase. As a result, the gravitational potential energy of the centre of mass is

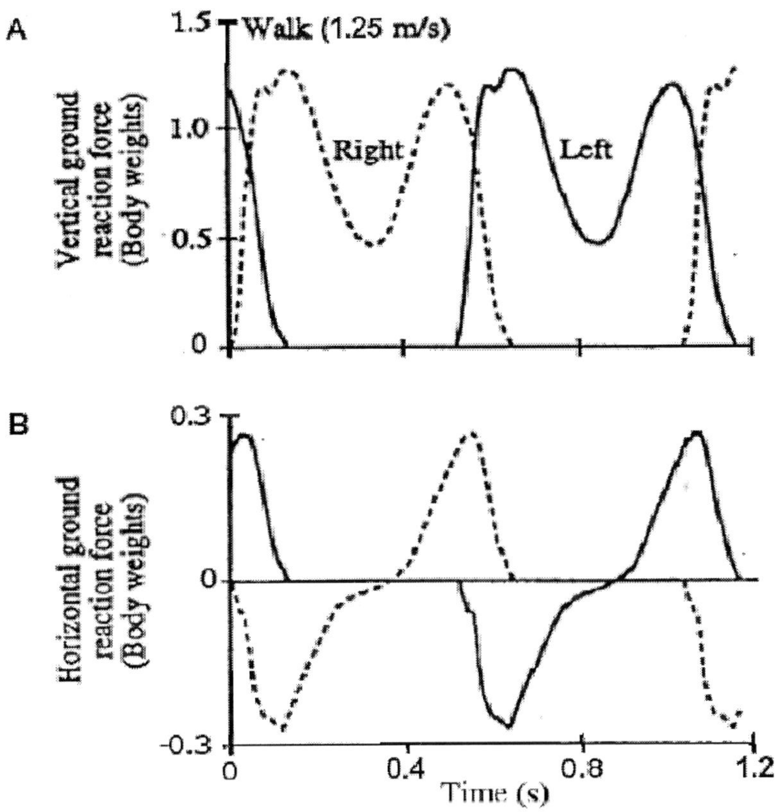

Representative ground reaction force as a fuction of time for walking (1.25 m/s) in a human. The dashed line represents the stance phase of the right foot, and the solid line represents the stance phase of the Left foot. (A) vertical component. (B) horizontal component. In both parts, the ground reaction force is expressed us a multiple of body weight.

maximized at the middle of the stance phase. In contrast, the stance limb is compliant in running so that the joints undergo substantial flexion during the first half of

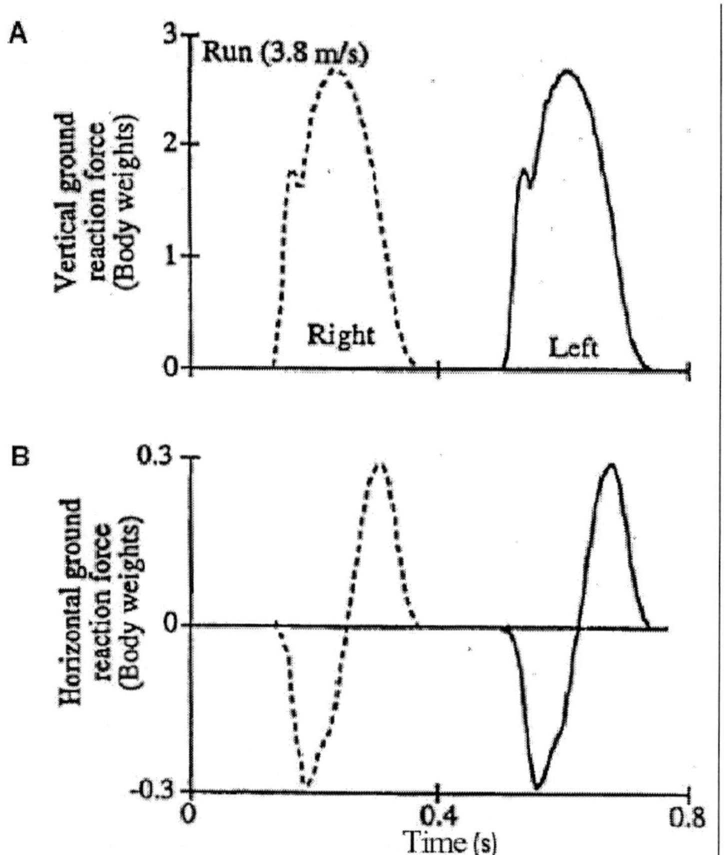

Representative ground reaction force as a function of time for running (3.8 m/s) in a human. The dashed line represents the stance phase of the right foot, and the Solid line represents the stance phase of the left foot. (A) vertical component. (B) horizontal component. In both parts, the ground reaction force is expressed as a multiple of body weight.

An inverted pendulum model and a stick figure representation of a single stance phase of human walking. The model consists of a mass and a rigid strut that connects the point of foot-ground contact and the centre of mass of the human. This figure depicts the stick figure and the model at the beginning and the stance phase (left-most position), the middle of the stance phase (centre position), and the end of the stance phase (right-mart position).

stance and extension during the second half of stance. This compliance causes the vertical displacement and gravitational potential energy of the center of mass to reach their minimum values at mid-stance in running. The pattern of movement of the centre of mass has been proposed as the defining difference between a walking gait and a running gait.

Unlike the gravitational potential energy fluctuations, the pattern of kinetic energy fluctuations is similar for walking and running. In both gaits, the kinetic energy of the centre of mass reaches its minimum value at mid-stance since the horizontal

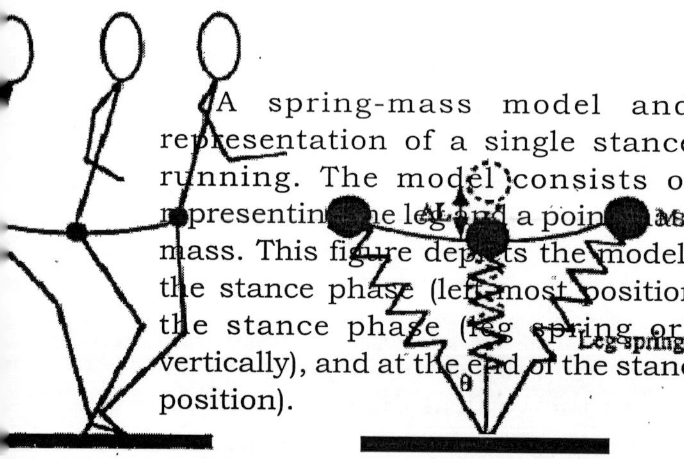

A spring-mass model and a stick figure representation of a single stance phase of human running. The model consists of a Linear spring representing the leg and a point mass equivalent to body mass. This figure depicts the model at the beginning of the stance phase (left-most position), at the middle of the stance phase (leg spring oriented is oriented vertically), and at the end of the stance phase (right-most position).

ground reaction force tends to decelerate the body during the first half of the stance phase. During the second half of stance, the kinetic energy of the centre of mass increases due to the accelerating effect of the horizontal ground reaction force. Although the pattern of kinetic energy fluctuations is similar, the magnitude is much larger for running than for walking.

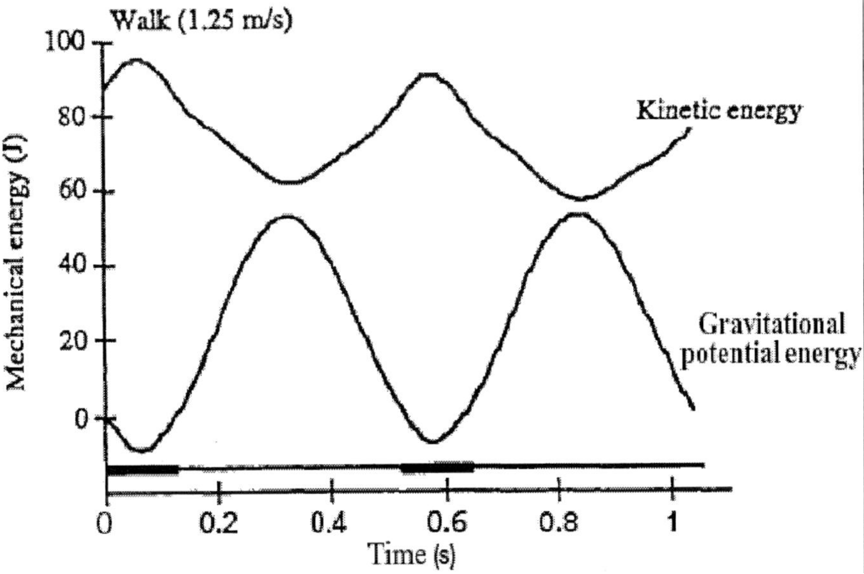

During moderate speed walking (1.25 m/s), the kinetic energy fluctuations of the centre and mass are approximately 186 out of phase with the gravitational potential energy fluctuations, allowing substantial pendulum-like energy exchange. *T k* thick horizontal line at *t k* bottom of the group represents the phases when both feet are in contact with the ground ("double support" phases), and the thin horizontal line represents the phases when only a single foot is in contact with the ground ("single support" phases).

The kinetic energy and gravitational potential energy of the centre of mass are approximately 180' out of phase in walking. At mid-stance in walking, the gravitational potential energy is at its maximum and the kinetic energy is at its minimum: Because these energies are approximately a half-cycle out of phase with each other and their fluctuations are similar in magnitude, substantial pendulum-like exchange occurs between them. During the first half of the stance phase of walking, the centre of mass loses kinetic energy but gains gravitational potential energy. In this phase, kinetic energy can be converted to gravitational potential energy. During the second half of the stance phase, the centre of mass loses gravitational potential energy but gains kinetic energy. Thus, during this phase, gravitational potential energy can be converted to kinetic energy. A similar energy transfer mechanism occurs as a pendulum swings or as an egg rolls across the ground. As a result, the energy transfer mechanism used in walking is often referred to as the “inverted pendulum mechanism” or the "rolling egg mechanism." The pattern of mechanical energy fluctuations is similar in other walking animals as it is in humans. As a result, many other animals, including mammals, birds, reptiles, and arthropods, also conserve substantial mechanical energy by the inverted pendulum mechanism during walking.

In human walking, as much as 60-70% of the mechanical energy required to lift and accelerate the centre of mass is conserved by this energy transfer mechanism. Mechanical energy savings are maximized at moderate walking speeds, and fall toward zero at very low and very high, walking speeds. At the walking speed where energy conservation is maximized, the magnitudes of the fluctuations in kinetic energy and gravitational potential energy are similar. Nevertheless, the maximum energy recovery by the inverted pendulum mechanism is approximately 70%, substantially less than the theoretical maximum of 100%. At the speed where energy transfer is maximized, the metabolic energy cost per unit distance is lower than at any other walking speed. It has been suggested that metabolic energy cost is minimized because the muscles have to do the least mechanical work at the speed where energy transfer is optimal.

The speed at which energy transfer is maximized during walking depends on body size. The optimum speed for energy transfer is lower for a small child than for an adult. While a two-year-ld child's optimum speed is about 0.6 m/s, an adult's optimum speed is about 1.6 m/s. A similar difference in optimum speed occurs among animal species due to their different body sizes. For example, a small lizard maximizes energy recovery at a much lower absolute speed than a sheep. In spite of this difference in optimum walking speed, energy transfer by the inverted pendulum mechanism reduces the mechanical work required for lifting and accelerating the centre of mass by a similar fraction in animals of all body sizes. A 0.005 kg lizard or a 70 kg sheep reduce the mechanical work required to lift and accelerate the centre of mass by about 50% through the inverted pendulum mechanism of energy exchange. Similarly, the mechanical work required to lift and accelerate the centre of mass is reduced by about 60-7096 for a two-year-old child or an adult human. Thus, body size has a profound effect on the optimum walking speed but has little effect on energy conservation by the inverted pendulum mechanism.

In running, there cannot be substantial pendulum-like exchange between kinetic energy and gravitational

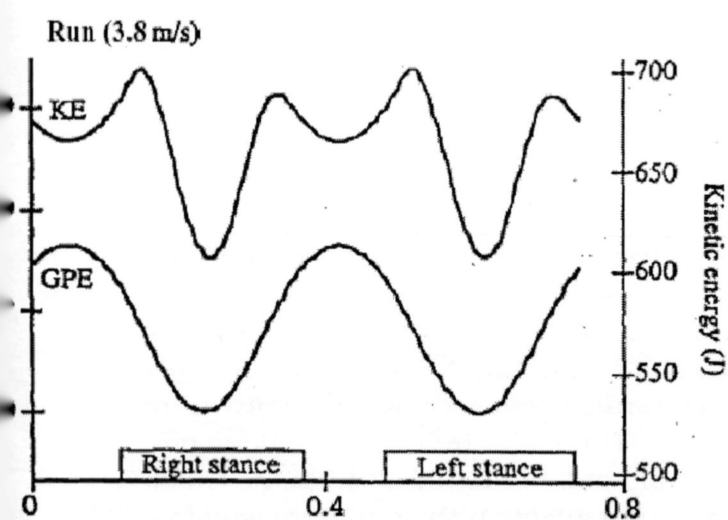

kinetic energy
approximately in
tential energy
h limb are noted

ns are nearly in
tic energy and
their minimum
e ground contact
netic energy and
es less than 5%
t and accelerate
g. Substantial
mechanical energy, however, is conserved through the storage and return of energy in elastic tissues. Because the movements of the centre of mass during running

are similar to a bouncing ball, running is often referred to as a "bouncing gail-'* A similar pattern of mechanical energy fluctuations occurs during fast gaits used by other animals. For example, trotting dogs, hopping kangaroos, running quail, and trotting cockroaches all have a similar pattern of mechanical energy fluctuations as running humans. Although the pattern of limb movements and gaits varies among these animals, all show the characteristic pattern of kinetic energy and gravitational potential energy being nearly exactly in phase with each other. All of these gaits are referred to as bouncing gaits.

Gail Transitions

It is clear that walking and running are distinctly different in terms of their patterns of ground reaction force and patterns of mechanical energy fluctuations Indeed, simply watching a person gradually increase her forward speed and break from a walk to a run makes it obvious that there are distinct differences between walking and running. What determines the speed range where each of these distinctly different gaits is used? It is likely that by understanding the triggers for the gait transition, we will reach a better understanding of how the neuromuscular system and the physical characteristics of the body shape locomotion.

The transition from walking to running is not a smooth and continuous event. Rather, there is a distinct transition from one gait to the other that can be observed in both the kinematic and kinetic patterns. For example, the transition from walking to running involves sudden changes in ground contact time, duty factor, ground reaction force, and movements of the centre of mass. It is not yet clear exactly what triggers the transition from walking to running or vice-versa in humans or other animals.

It was long believed that humans and other animals choose their gait transition speed based on minimization of the metabolic energy cost of locomotion. In humans, the most economical gait at low speeds is a walk. As walking speed is increased, a speed is eventually reached where running requires less metabolic energy than walking. A similar pattern exists for quadrupedal animals. Walking is most economical at low speeds, trotting is most economical at moderate speeds, and galloping is most economical at the highest speeds. However, the speed where an animal prefers to switch gaits is not the speed that would minimize metabolic energy cost. Horses switch from a trot to a gallop at a speed substantially below the optimal speed for minimizing metabolic energy cost. Thus, galloping actually requires more metabolic energy than trotting at the speed where a horse chooses to switch from a .trot to a gallop. Similarly, humans switch from a walk to a run at a speed that is not energetically optimal. These findings suggest that another factor, perhaps biomechanical, actually triggers gait transitions.

Based on the inverted pendulum mechanics of walking, it is reasonable to think that gravity is an important factor in determining the speed where the walk-run transition occurs. In walking, the gravitational force on the centre of mass must be at least equal to the centripetal force needed to keep the centre of mass moving in a circular arc as it vaults over the stance limb. The required centripetal force is equal to mv^2/L, where m = body mass, v = forward velocity, and L = leg length.

The ratio between the centripetal force and the gravitational force $(mv^2/L)/(mg)$ is the Froude number (v^2/gL). Based on the mechanics of an inverted pendulum system, it has been predicted that humans and other animals should be able to use a walking gait only at speeds where the Froude number is less than or equal to 1. This is so because the gravitational force is sufficient to keep the centre of mass moving in a circular arc when the Froude number is less than or equal to 1. Experimental evidence has shown that humans and other bipeds (e.g., birds) with a large range of leg lengths prefer to switch from a walk to, a run at a similar Froude number but at different absolute speeds. Furthermore, when humans walk at different levels of simulated reduced gravity, they switch from a walk to a run at a similar Froude number but at very different absolute speeds. These observations suggest that the ratio of centripetal force to gravitational force is important in determining the gait transition speed. Nonetheless, it is puzzling that the gait transition occurs at a substantially lower Froude number than the-theoretically predicted Froude number of 1.

Most gait transition studies to date have examined gait choice when humans or other animals move steadily at speeds near the transition speed. However, neither humans nor other animals naturally choose to move in this way in their every day lives. Generally, humans and other animals prefer to use speeds near the middle of each gait and rarely will choose other speeds for an extended period of time. Thus, they tend to make rapid transitions from one gait to another, which occur in concert with abrupt changes in speed. In the extreme case of accelerating from a standstill, humans and other animals seem to immediately choose the appropriate gait for the speed to which they are accelerating. For example, a human sprinter runs, not walks, out of the blocks. Similarly, a dog immediately gallops at the beginning of a sprint regardless of its starting speed. These observations suggest that in the future it will be important to examine gait choices in more natural locomotor patterns including acceleration and deceleration.

JOINT MOMENTS, WORK AND POWER

So far, we have discussed the mechanics of locomotion at the whole body level, including the ground reaction force, mechanical energy of the centre of mass, and the behaviour of the overall leg. During locomotion, muscles generate moments and perform mechanical work at the joints, producing the ground reaction force and the movements of the body. The next section will concentrate on the current understanding of joint dynamics during walking and running. The focus of this section will be the moments and mechanical work produced by muscles at each joint. Understanding locomotion at the level of muscle action at each joint provides a bridge for understanding the link between the movements of the centre of mass and the actions of individual muscle-tendon units. Little published information is available about muscle moments and mechanical work at each joint during locomotion in diverse animal species. Thus, it is difficult to assess the similarities and differences between humans and other animals at this level of organization.

Net Muscle Moments

The muscles of the body operate by exerting moments

about joints. To begin to understand how the neuromuscular system produces walking and running, researchers often examine the "net muscle moment" or "generalized muscle moment" about a joint. A net muscle moment includes h e moments produced by all of the muscles, tendons, ligaments, and contact forces at the joint. The moment produced by muscle-tendon forces is thought to be much higher than the moment produced by the ligaments or other joint forces over the range of joint angles that occur during locomotion. As a result, the net muscle moment gives a reasonable approximation of the net moment produced by all the muscles at a joint. An inverse dynamics approach can be used to determine the net muscle moments during locomotion. This involves using force platform, kinematic and anthropomorphic measurements in concert with a rigid linked segment model. The Newtonian equations of angular and translational motion are applied to each segment starting distally and moving proximally. This type of approach has revealed that the net muscle moment during the ground contact phase of walking is the largest at the ankle and is substantially lower at the knee and hip. At the ankle, the net muscle moment tends to extend the joint throughout the ground contact phase. Electromyographic (EMG) measurements have revealed that both extensor muscles and flexor muscles are active during the ground contact phase, occasionally simultaneously. The observation that the net muscle moment tends to extend the anklc shows that the ankle extensor muscles are creating a larger moment than the ankle flexor muscles. The net muscle moment about the ankle is very small during the swing phase.

The net muscle moments at the knee and hip during the ground contact phase of walking are much smaller and more variable than at the ankle. The ground reaction force vector is closely aligned with the knee and hip. As a result, small net muscle moments at the knee and hip are required in order to exert a given force on the ground. The exact pattern of net muscle moment at the knee and hip varies between subjects and is matched by variation in the EMG patterns of the major limb muscles. This observation has led to the proposal that different individuals use different motor strategies for walking. It has been suggested that these individual patterns are consistent with a strategy that minimizes the total muscle effort for each individual.

Walking kinematics are far less variable than the net muscle moments or the muscle activation patterns at the knee and hip. A comparison of strides that have dramatically different net muscle moment patterns at the knee and hip shows that the limb kinematics are remarkably similar. This observation led Winter to propose the idea of a "support moment" equal to the sum of the net muscle moments at the ankle, knee, and hip. Data on walking humans show that the support moment is substantially less variable than the net muscle moment at each individual joint. Thus, it seems that changes in muscle activation and net muscle moment at one joint are offset by changes at another joint. This conclusion is further supported by the observation that humans with various injuries can still walk in a kinematically normal manner by changing the pattern of muscle activation.

As one would expect, the peak magnitude of the net muscle moment at each joint is higher during running than during walking. The leg is compliant during running, and the major leg joints undergo substantial flexion and extension during the ground contact phase. In contrast, during walking, the limb behaves more like a stiff strut, and the joints undergo smaller angular displacements, remaining relatively extended throughout the ground contact phase. As a result of the postural difference, the muscles must generate larger joint moments in order to exert a given force on the ground during running than during walking. The net muscle moment tends to extend the joint at the ankle, knee, and hip during running. The peak net muscle moment is larger at the knee than at the other joints. Indeed, this is a major difference between running and walking. The magnitude of the peak net muscle moment at the knee is much larger during running than walking. The knee is substantially more flexed at the middle of the ground contact phase of running, and as a result, a higher net muscle moment is required in order to exert a given ground force during running compared to walking.

In contrast to walking, running involves little variability in the pattern and magnitude of the ground reaction force or the net muscle moments. It has been speculated that the net muscle moments are less variable in running than in walking because the muscles are operating closer to their force limits.

Joint Power and Work

The net power output at a joint can be calculated from the product of the net muscle moment and the joint angular velocity. When the net muscle moment and the angular velocity are both in the same direction, there is net power production at the joint. Conversely, when the net muscle moment and the joint angular velocity are in opposite directions, there is net power absorption at the joint. The net muscle mechanical work can be calculated from the integral of the power with respect to time.

It is important to realize that the net power output measured at a joint is not necessarily produced by muscles that cross that particular joint. This is because there are many muscles in the body that cross more than one joint. These muscles can transport power produced by muscles acting across one joint and allow them to contribute to the power output at another joint. The extent to which this transfer occurs during human walking or running is not clear, but there is evidence that energy transfer by biarticular muscles is substantial during cat locomotion.

7

FACTORS AFFECTING PREFERRED RATES OF MOVEMENT IN CYCLIC ACTIVITY

Many human movements are characterized by the continual repetition of a fundamental pattern of motion. For cyclic activities, the average speed of progression is defined by the product of the average of progression is defined by the product of the average distance travelled per cycle of motion and the average rate of cadence at which the cycle of motion is being repeated. In normal human movements, these speed and distance factors are usually freely determined or self-selected by the performer and are rarely fixed or pre-established. In addition, humans have an incredible ability to intentionally alter speed, distance and cadence to meet the demands of the environment. Nilson and Thortensson observed that over a normal range of walking speed subjects were able to walk with a lowest possible stride rate of 25 strides min-1 at the lowest speed and a highest possible rage of 143 strides. min-1 at all speeds. Within a range of running speeds, subjects could run with rates as low as 33 strides. min-1 to as high as 214 strides min-1. given this ability to alter cycle cadence and distance factors, how is the preferred cadence chosen, and how does it relate to different optimally criteria? The mechanisms that underlie the selection process leading to a particular condense distance combination chosen by a performer for a given activity at a given speed are not clear, although numerous factors have been considered.

While much information has been gained about the neurophysiology of rhythmic movements, especially in lower verterbrates and invertebrates, relatively little attention has been directed to understanding how cycle distance and cadence are determined and controlled by the neuro-muscular skeletal system in humans. Nevertheless, it is useful to gain some understanding of how cycle distance and condense are related, even though available evidence applies primarily to walking.

Laurent and Pialhous had subjects walk overground while imposing only stride rate or stride length by means of auditory or visual cues and allowing all other gait parameters to vary freely. Results revealed that when one parameter was steadily increased the other parameter remained almost constant despite the lack of constraint imposed on all other parameters. Moreover, Laurent and Pailhous found that stride rate and length were each strongly correlated with speed, but were relatively independent of each other. The authors proposed that speed, not rate or length, is the critical parameter around which locomotion is organized. Indeed, Diedrich and Warren found that subjects make the transition from a walk to a run at a critical speed, rather than at a critical stride rate of length, when rate and length are experimentally manipulated.

Even if speed is the parameter around which locomotion is ultimately organized, the flexibility with which stride rate and length can be altered implies that the central nervous system must have mechanisms for actively controlling these variables.

Because of the lack of dependence between stride rate and length, it has been suggested that ratc and length are modulated by two distinct neural control schemes, frequcncy medullation for rate and amplitude modulation for length. Bornnard and Pailhous also proposed that stride rate and length are controlled differently by the nervous system. Changes in stride rate are associated with changes in the global stiffness of the lower limb during the swing phase, but not during the stance phase, suggesting that rate is altered by changing the tonic activity of the lower limb muscles during seeing. Changing the tonic activity of most of all of the muscles limb as it swings about the hip joint.

Bornnard and Pailhous further suggested that transient changes in stride length are linked to phasic activation of appropriate leg muscles. Patla et al. have shown that transient increases in stride length are indeed produced by phasic increases in the activity of others.

While stride rate and length may follow fairly fixed patterns during unrestrained walking and running, the CNs has the ability to dissociate rate and length if required or desired. Hogan proposed a physiological mechanism that would allow such a dissociation. When antagonistic muscles are simultaneously active about a joint, the net joint moment is related to the difference between antagonistic muscle forces and joint stiffness is associated with the sum of muscle forces. If the CNS actively modulates the co-activation of antagonistic muscles, stride rate and length can be varied independently within limits. As co activation is metabolically costly, one might hypothesize that the preferred movement patterns require the least co-activation. This leads to the possibility that cyclic activities are organized to minimize demands placed on the neuromusculo-skeletal system.

The review focuses specifically on the rate or cadence at which cyclic movements are produced and potential factors that influence preferred or self-selected cadences. A wide variety of factors that may be associated with or that directly affect preferred cadence have been examined over the course of decades of research has focused on an equally wide variety of movements or activities. While the majority of studies have investigated walking, running and cycling, there is a more limited number of investigations on other cyclic activities such as hopping, stair climbing, rowing, swimming and wheelchair propulsion that can offer additional insights into cadence determination. Our purpose is to broadly review the existing research literature to consider those factors that may play an important role in establishing preferred cadences and to determine whether selected factors appear to be especially important in influencing fundamental preferred cadences of numerous cyclic activities.

Maximizing Mechanical Efficiency

Mechanical efficiency, which has been defined in several ways has also been proposed as a key element in the processes underlying the selection of preferred rates of movement., Even from the early 1920s it has been known that there is a rate of movement that is most efficient for a given power output. An examination of the notion of maximizing efficiency of human movement is not independent of the principle of minimization of the energy cost since an expression of energy cost forms the denominator of an efficiency ratio.

More specifically, changes ingross efficiency as cadence is manipulated under controlled power conditions are necessarily inversely related to changes in energy cost. Movement efficiency has been investigated in numerous cyclic tasks including running. Hill, using an elbow flexion task, observed that the efficiency of muscular contraction increased rapidly to a maximum of approximately 36% and then fell more slowly as the duration of contraction increased. Peak efficiency occurred for contraction durations of approximately 1s. Hill subsequently cited cycling as an activity consistent with this 1s optimum contraction duration

Benedict and Cathcart had previously reported an most efficient cadence of 70 r.p.m. for cycling. The significance of Hill's observation, however, is muted when one recognizes that contractions of individual muscles during pedaling rarely last for more than half a pedal cycle. Because of the shape of the observed muscle efficiency function, Hill also noted that high rates of movement of short duration are likely to result in a substantial loss of efficiency, whereas movement cycle of longer duration suffer from only a small decline in efficiency. This suggests that high cadences may have a more deleterious effect on performance than low rates.

Cavagna and Franzetti examined the effect of cadence on mechanical power required to sustain constant-speed walking. They noted that maintaining walking speed with long stride lengths and a low cadence increases the magnitude of ground contact forces, whereas use of short stride lengths in combination with a high cadence requires that the limbs be accelerated more frequently. They further suggested that an optimum condition might exist at intermediate cadences that would reduce inefficiencies created by either extreme, and used a mechanical power assessment to test this notion.

Two components of mechanical power were quantified as cadence was varied under controlled walking speeds: external power required to lift and accelerate the centre of mass of the body and internal power used to accelerate the limbs relative to the center of mass. As predicted, external power declined and internal power increased as stride rate increased. The sum of these two power component, which provided an expression of total mechanical power required to sustain walking speed, exhibited a minimum at intermediate cadences of approximately 34,43 and 52 strides. min-1 for walking speeds of 4.6, 5.5 and 6.6 km. h-1, respectively. Assuming that mechanical power is somewhat reflective of demand placed on the musculature, overall muscular effort would be minimized at these minima.

Hull and colleagues applied a similar concept when using a joint moment cost function to examine the relative demands of generating pedal forces and accelerating the limbs under different cycling cadences. Their quasi-static moment component was a function of external forces applied to the foot via the pedal, and is analogous to Cavagna and Franzetti's external power expression. Their kinetic moment component was related to limb accelerations, which is analogous to internal power. The relationships of these variables with respect to cadence or stride rate are strikingly similar in shape and interpretation. Both approaches predict an optimal rate of movement. Curiously, Cavagna and Franzetti reported that their calculated mechanically optimal cadence for walking was 20-30% less than self-selected cadences, while Redfield and Hull predicted a mechanically optimal cadence approximately 10% higher than typical preferred cycling cadences. Thus, there appear to be other factors not accounted for in these models that influence the determination of self-selected cadences.

Gresser and Brooks examined the effect of peddling cadence and power output on multiple expressions of efficiency. Twelve subjects rode a stationary ergometer at cadences 40,60,80 and 199 r.p.m. at power output 0,200,400,600 and 800 kgm. min-1. The results demonstrated that efficiently tended to increase as power output increased, although the responds varied depending on the efficiency definition that was used.

More importantly, increase in cadence resulted in a decrease in efficiency, regardless of the efficiency expression. Gaesser and Brooks argued that delta efficiency, which is defined as the ratio of a change in power output and the associated change in energy cost, proved the best indicator of true muscular efficiency. Results from Sidossis et al. tend to contradict those of Gaesser and Brooks. In as assessment of the effect of power output. On gross and delta efficiency, Sidossis and colleagues observed that cadence had little effect on gross efficiency. Delta efficiency, however, increased significantly from 20.6 to 23.8% as cadence was increased from 60 to 100 r.pm Sidossis et al. speculated that the improved delta efficiency reflects an increase in muscular efficiency under higher cadence commotions.

Citing fundamental muscle research that demonstrates peak muscular efficiency is achieved when fibre shortening velocity reaches one-third of the maximum velocity of shortening.

Widrick et al. argued that acceleration of the limbs, particularly at high cadences, contribute significantly to the muscular effort required to maintain a given cadence and power output. Further, they suggested that exclusion of internal mechanical power from a total power expression may confound subsequent conclusions regarding optimal rates of limb movement. Subjects preluded at 40, 60, 80 and 100 r.p.m. under three external power output conditions established using a Monark bicycle ergometer. Their results demonstrated that internal mechanical power increased systematically as condense increased for each nominal external power output condition.

Thus, total mechanical power also increased as cadence increased. Using energy expenditure estimates computed from aerobic demands for each cycling condition and total mechanical power results, widrick and colleagues computed mechanical efficiency. Optimal pedaling cadences, defined as the maximized, ranged from 82 r.p.m. at 49 w to 101 r.p.m. at 147 W, values that are clearly quite comparable with preferred cycling cadences.

The potential relationship between preferred and most efficient rates of movement, Corlett and Mahadeva developed an instrument to quantify mechanical power during a manual tyre-pumping task. Combining this assessment with measures of oxygen consumption they were able to quantify the energy expenditure per stroke for different pumping rates. Interestingly, the energy cost per stroke declined as rate of pumping increased from slow to intermediate rates. Energy cost per stroke did not change with further increases in rate.

Further, preferred rates of movement coincided with the minimum stroke rate of which the energy cost per stroke reached a plateau. Although efficiency was not quantified in this study, this minimum stroke rate corresponds to a rate at which efficiency would be greatest.

From this brief review of mechanical power and efficiency, it can be seen that preferred cadences in several cyclic activities may correspond well with cadences at which efficiency is maximized. Unfortunately, the existing research literature related to human movement efficiency is difficult to interpret because of inconsistencies in the definitions of both mechanical power and energy expenditure expressions used in efficiency ratio calculations. Additionally, mechanical power and energy expenditure can be difficult to quantity and/or control experimentally for many activities. In part because of these difficulties, the number of different activities investigated in efficiency studies is limited.

Minimization of Movement Energy Cost

It is intuitively appealing to speculate that submaximal, steady-state cyclic movements are organized such that body mass-specific rate of energy consumption or aerobic demand is minimized when self-selected or preferred cadences are used. Data for both walking and running lend support to this supposition. Numerous investigators have measured energy cost as stride rate, and thus stride length, were manipulated systematically during constant to speed treadmill walking or running. /results have shown consistently that energy cost rises. A 5 % increase or decrease in stride rate of walking resulted in an 8-10 % increase in aerobic demand, Hreljac & Martin. Self-selected cadence and stride length for most individuals usually do not deviate substantially from those that minimize energy cost at a given speed of walking or running. Morgan et al. found that only 20% of a foot of 45 recreational runners reflected a stride length from the most economical stride length and that deviated by more than a few centimeters from the most economical stride length and showed a difference in aerobic demand between preferred and most economical conditions that was greater than 0.5 ml. These results proved convincing evidence that most individuals self-optimize walking and running cadences, and suggest that minimizing energy cost may be an important factor contributing to cadence determination.

Similar responses of energy cost or aerobic demand to cadence changes have been shown for other activities as well. Seven competitive race-walkers were most economical at their preferred stride rate/stride length combinations and displayed progressively higher energy costs as cadence was either increased or decreased from the preferred rate. In addition, van der would et al. studied the effect of cadences ranging from 60 top 140% of preferred cadence on several cardio-respiratory measures during humdrum wheelchair propulsion on motor-driven treadmill.

Aerobic demand at the preferred cadence was approximately 10% lower than that for cadence were observed for both experienced and inexperienced wheelchair users at several speeds of progression, although the response of the inexperienced users was less uniform and consistent across speeds. Despite the fact that the preferred cadence or experienced wheelchair users increased systematically by more than 50% as speed of progression was increased from 0.55 to 1.39, the preferred cadence at each speed remained the most economical cadence.

Considering all of the energy cost or economy research considered thus far, preferred and most economical cadences appear to match well for multiple forms of gait and wheelchair propulsion. A common feature of both types of activities is the presence of distinct propulsion and swing phases, even though magnitudes of muscular and contact forces are substantially different for gait and wheelchair propulsion.

Unfortunately, minimization of energy cost is not generalizable to all cyclic activities. Cycling and arm cranking appear to be two tasks for which preferred and most economical cadences are different. Numerous investigators have examined the effect of pedaling cadence on aerobic demand or energy cost under a variety of power outputs and for subject groups differing in terms of fitness status and experience with the locomotion activity. In general, aerobic demand or energy cost reflects a curvilinear relationship with cadence such that minimum demand occurs at about 55-65 r.p.m. Although preferred cadences have been reported in only a few studies preferred cadences are normally much higher than the most economical cadences. Marsh and Martin reported most economical cadences ranging from 53 to 60 r.p.m. for each of three subject groups tested at power outputs ranging from 75 to 250 W. Preferred cadences were approximately 90-95 r.p.m. for the fit cyclists and fit runners and between 80 and 65 r.p.m. for a less-fit group of non-cyclists.

Similarly, Boning et al. reported most economical cadences ranging from 52 to 67 r.p.m. for a group of fit, amateur road-racing cyclists for power outputs of 50-200 W, respectively. Finally, Seabury et al. found most economical cadences of 44, 54 and 58 r.p.m. for power outputs of 80, 163 and 196 W for two trained distance runners and one recreational cyclist. Only two of the cycling studies cited above report most economical cadences exceeding 709 r.p.m. Coast and Welch found that the most economical cadence steadily increase from approximately 50 r.p.m. at 100 W to 78 r.p.m. At 300 W for five trained cyclists, suggesting that exercise intensity may significantly impact the most economical cadence. Although preferred cadences were not measured, they were still likely to be well above most economical cadences for all but the highest power outputs.

Only results from Hagberg et al., who studied seven road-racing cyclists at power outputs of about 330 W, have shown a match between the most economical and preferred cadences.

Arm cranking appears to reflect an economy response similar to that observed for cycling, although the phenomenon for arm cranking has received substantially less attention. Powers et al. tested recreational runners at three arm-cranking cadences under four power outputs. Aerobic demand was lowest at 50 r.p.m. for each power output condition and increased systematically as condense increased. Unfortunately. Powers et al. did not report preferred cadences for their subjects, but other investigators have. Pelayo et al. reported an average preferred cadence for their subjects, but other investigators have. Pelayo et al. reported an average preferred cadence of 91 r.p.m. for a group 20 sedentary subjects exercising at 80% of their maximal arm-cranking aerobic demand, and Weissland et al. found preferred cadence increased from 74 to 81 r.p.m. as exercise intensity increased from 65 to 100% of maximal capacity.

Thus, preferred cadences appear to be comparable with, or perhaps slightly lower than, those reported for cycling. Weissland et al. also investigated submaximal aerobic demand under three subject-specific cadence conditions: Preferred cadence and cadences either 10% greater or 10% lower than preferred. Aerobic demand was significantly higher under the highest cadence condition relative to preferred cadences. Although aerobic demand difference between the preferred and -10% cadence conditions were not statistically significant, aerobic demand tended to be lower under the preferred cadence condition. Both Weissland et al. and Palayo et al. observed systematic increases in heart rate as cadence increased. Considering all three arm cranking studies cited here, the evidence suggests that the most economical cadences for are cranking are lower than the preferred cadences and that the economy response for arm cranking is similar to that observed in cycling. Nevertheless, much more evidence is needed before any definitive conclusions can be drawn.

Mechanical Optimization of Muscular Effort

One approach in the search for an explanation for preferred rates of movements is to use optimization or meddling strategies. These strategies use modifiable characteristics, such as cadence, and kinematic constraints to define muscle action. Such strategic have been used to predict optimal cycling cadence. In cycling, there is an important link between pedalling cadence and performance. Cyclists use the gears of the bicycle to select a particular cadence suited to the riding demands. The traditional approach has been to collect empirical data whereby metabolic cost or riding at particular combinations of cadence and power output have been determined.

Hull and colleagues have taken a different approach to identifying essential factors that determine optimal pedalling cadence. They argued that physiological cost, which is of considerable importance with respect to overall performance, is directly associated with muscular effort and that mechanical markers can provide a reasonable representation of lower-extremely muscular effort. In their earlier efforts, Hull and colleagues developed a five-bar linked segment model that could be used to simulate net joint moment profiles under many different pedalling conditions. Inputs for their model included scaled pedal-force profiles, measured mark positions, lower-extremity kinematic data predicted from crank position and anthropometric constraints, and pedal angles derived from a sinusoidal function. In an effort to delineate muscle function more effectively, net joint moments were subsequently divided into a quasi-static component, which was a function of external forces applied to the foot via the pedal, and a kinematic moment related to limb accelerations.

Redfield and Hull specifically explored the relationship between net joint moments and pedalling condense. Net joint moments were simulated for cadences of 63,80 and 100 r.p.m. at a power output of 200 w. They found that as cadence increased, the kinematic moment increased and the quasi-static moment decreased. The increased kinematic moment was attributed to the increased accelerations of the limbs at higher speeds, whereas the decreased quasi-static moment was a function of the inverse relationship between pedal force and cadence when power output is maintained.

When these components are added, a parabolic-like curve representing the total moment. From these Rustles, Redifield and Hull showed that the total joint moment is high a relatively low cadences because of a high quasi-static contribution., At relatively high cadences the total moment is also high because of high kinematic moment contributions. Thus, total joint moment is minimized, suggesting that muscular effort is minimized, at intermediate cadences.

Redifield and Hull refined and extended their simulations of optimal cycling cadence by applying a muscle stress-based function that had been used previously in gait research. Their muscle stress based cost function improved prediction of both propulsive and recovery phase pedal forces as well as net joint moments, compared with their previous moment-based modelling efforts. Hull subsequently used the muscle stress function to predict the optimal cadence for a 200 W power output and found a minimum in this cost function in the range of 95-100 r.p.m., a value that was consistent with their earlier work using the moment cost function. Interestingly, the close match between the optimal cadences predicted from the muscle-stress and net joint moment cost functions led Hull et al. to conclude that the moment-based function offered the advantage of greater case of computation without sacrificing accuracy in predicting optimal cadence.

A crucial feature of any simulation research is the extent to which its results can be supported by empirical data. A fundamental assumption made by Hull et al. was that pedal forces scale in inverse proportion to the scaling of crank angular velocities as pedalling cadence changes. Mac Lean and Lafortune showed that while the normal component of the pedal force scaled in proportion to crank velocity during the propulsive phase or downstroke, the reverse was true during the upstroke or recovery phase. Further, shear forces applied to the pedals increased during the downstroke and became smaller in the upstroke as cadence increased.

They concluded that scaling of pedal forces in inverse proportion to crank velocity was not acceptable. Thus, use of this assumption may compromise the validity of model predictions.

In a separate presentation, Mac Lean and Lafortune compared optimal cadence determined using five net joint moment-based cost functions with the cadence at which group mechanical efficiency was maximized, the latter being assumed to reflect the optimal cadence criterion. Using a group of 10 experienced cyclists riding at 200 W over five cadences from 60 to 120 r.p.m., they found that only one of their five moment-based cost functions. The remaining moment based cost functions yielded optimal cadences that were substantially higher, on average about 100 r.p.m, and much nearer to values reported by Hull and colleagues. Mac Lean and Lafortune suggested that it is not surprising that minimizing the net knee moment will minimizing the net knee moment will minimize physiological cost and maximize gross mechanical efficiency because of the many muscles acting about the knee in cycling.

Other issues surrounding optimization of cycling cadence, including seat height, foot position, etc., have been explored and are reviewed by Gregor et al. There remains conjecture regarding the relationships between muscle characteristics and selection of optimal rate, and these have yet to be resolved. Currently, there are few or no published empirical data that substantiate the supposed relationship between muscle moments, muscles stress and condense selection. Clearly, this needs to be a focus of ongoing research.

Pendular Properties of Swinging Limbs

Kugler and colleagues noted that limb motions is locomotion are auto-oscillatory and possess mechanically conservative characteristics of a pendular-like mode of organization; in other words, the limbs represent complex pendulum systems. During cyclic activity of an anatomical system, a certain amount of mechanical energy is dissipated from the system with each cycle of motion. Thus, muscular effort is required to sustain limb pendular-like movements.

It has been hypothesized that a resonant frequency for any complex pendulum system can be predicted if the anthropometric and inertial characteristics of the limbs are known. Further, it is suggested that the resonant frequency relates directly to the fundamental rate that minimizes the energy cost associated with sustaining the motion. Holt et al. proposed that walking can be modelled as a force-driven harmonic oscillator and that the resonant frequency of the FDHO model corresponds to the preferred rate of walking. Results for 24 young adults supported their hypothesis that the resonant frequency of a harmonic oscillator can accurately predict that chosen by subjects when appropriate adjustments are made to the formula based on an optimization criterion of minimum force.

They concluded that the physical attributes of the lower extremity, more specifically its inertial characteristics, specify the most economical stride rate. In subsequent research, Holt et al. confirmed that preferred stride rate was not different from that predicted from their FDHO model. Subjects walked under eight stride rate conditions as aerobic demand, lending additional support to the association between preferred stride rate and gait economy. Although the FDHO model has not been applied to activities other than gait, recent research has successfully predicted preferred stride rates for backward walking and for 3 to 12 year-old children, effectively extending the generalizability of the phenomenon.

The association between the energy cost of walking and running and the inertial characteristics of the lower extremity has been demonstrated in several segment loading studies in which segment inertia has been modified artificially. In contrasting proximal and distal applications of load, more distally positioned load on the segment produces a larger increase in the moment of inertia of the leg about the hip and a greater increase in the aerobic demand of gait than proximal loading. Less attention has been paid to the effect of load distribution on the temporal features of walking and running. Consistent with the pendular phenomenon, Marting reported a small but statically significant decrease in stride rate and increase in swing time when 0.50 kg was added to each foot during treadmill running at 3.33. Recent data from our laboratory have also shown predictable effects of shank and foot loading on walking stride rate in able-bodied and unilateral below-knee amputes. Thus, while the FDHO made and pendular mechanics are theoretically sound and appear to apply well to cyclic activities in which the extremities are being oscillated, the magnitude of the effect on cadence is not well substantiated.

Minimization of Neuromuscular fatigue

Recently, a number of investigators have explored the role of muscle fatigue in determining the optimal cadence for cycling during both steady-state and exhaustive exercise. Sargeant has defined muscle fatigue as the failure to generate or maintain the required or expected force or power output, resulting from muscle activity, and reversible by rest. In a series of papers, Takaishi, Moritani and colleagues have estimated neuromuscular fatigue, using characteristics of the electromyograph signal, to help explain differences between preferred and most energetically optimal cadences in cyclists and non-cyclists. Takaishi et al. had eight non-cyclists pedal at rates ranging from 40 to 80 r.p.m., at 75% of maximal aerobic power.

Not surprisingly, metabolic cost was minimized at the lower cadences, and increased significantly as cadence approached 80 r.p.m. In contrast, the slope of the integrated EMG curve over the course of an exercise bout at a given cadence was significantly lower for the higher cadences. Over time, an increase in the firing frequency of previously recruited motor units. At such, the slope of the EMG is directly related to the intensity of the activity.

Takaishi et al. also found that the slope of the EMG was lower at higher cadences in six trained cyclists, whereas metabolic cost was minimized at 60-70 r.p.m. In both cases, the cadences at which the slope of EMG was found to be lowest were similar to the preferred cadences of the subjects. As the slope of EMG was lower at higher cadences chose by competitive cyclists are selected to help minimize peripheral neuromuscular fatigue. They further noted that the lower EMG slopes at the higher cadences suggests that fewer type II muscle fibres would be needed to meet the demands of the cycling task.

In support of this contention, Ahlquist et al. found that glycogen depletion was much grater in type I muscle fibres after cycling at 50 r.p.m. than at 100 r.p.m. at a power output equivalent to 85% of maximal aerobic power. Glycogen depletion was not different in type I fibres between the two cadence conditions. The lower pedal forces required at a higher cadence for a fixed power output would require lower muscle forces, and not require the recruitment of as many type II fibres. Patternson and Moreno noted that the resultant pedal forces were minimized at 90 r.p.m. and 100 r.p.m. in a group of 11 recreational cyclists. These values were also very close to the preferred cadence at both power outputs. During steady-state cycling, greater recruitment of type II fibres at lower cadences would presumably lead top more rapid fatigue.

At higher cadences, the greater reliance on type-I fibres would help prevent the onset of fatigue. Nevertheless, metabolic energy cost will still be higher under high cadence conditions due to the greater number of repetitions performed due to the greater number of repetitions performed per unit of time.

Takaishi et al. also noted that non-cyclists showed large increases in the iEMG of the vasti muscles at higher pedalling rates, whereas the trained cyclists did not demonstrate such an increase. The authors suggested that the lack of increase in iEMG for trained cyclist at higher cadences was related to pedalling skill developed by the trained cyclists. In subsequent research, Takaishi et al. demonstrated that while the vasti iEMG did not increase substantially for trained cyclists as cadence increased, biceps femoris activity. In addition, normal pedal forces decreased for both trained cyclists and trained non-cyclists are cadence increased; however, the normal pedal forces were lower for trained cyclists than trained non-cyclists at all but the lowest condense. The investigators suggested that the trained cyclists had developed a pedalling technique that involved pulling up the leg, via knee flexion, during the recovery portion of the pedal cycle at higher condenses.

The speculated technique would allow for the lower pedal force seen in the cyclists, and presumably result in lower muscle stress in the vasti group, and a lower dependence on type II muscle fibres.

Some papers in the literature would seem to contradict the findings of the above mentioned studies. Carnevale and Gaesser found that time to exhaustion was greater at 60 r.p.m. than 100 r.p.m. in a group of seven untrained subjects at multiple power levels. Similarly, Mc Naughton and Thomas reported time to exhaustion was greater at 50 r.p.m. than at 90 or 110 r.p.m. for untrained subjects. These results are consistent with the general finding that metabolic cost in minimised around 50-60 r.p.m. while the work of Carnevale and Gaesser, and of Mc Naughton and Thomas is certainly relevant, it cannot be directly compared with the studies by Takaishi et al. The former investigations used power outputs designed to bring about volitional exhaustion in a 1 to 10 min range, while Takaishi et al used lower output levels that were designed to allow subjects to cycle for a least 15 min without suffering undue fatigue.

Carnevale and Geasser and Mc Naughton and Thomas also used untrained subjects, while Takaishi et al. used a combination of untrained non-cyclists, trained mono-cyclists, and trained cyclists. A final point not directly addressed by Carnevale and Gaesser was that while time to exhaustion was substantially greater for 60 r.p.m. vs. 100 r.p.m. at all lowest power output, the time to exhaustion difference between 60 and 100 r.p.m. all but disappeared as power output was increase. With regard to this, Hill al. suggested that the advantage of decreased metabolic cost at lower cadences may be offset as power output increases, due to the increased muscle force requirements per cycle.

While the data relating to the role of muscle fatigue in setting preferred rate of movement during different modes of cycling are as yet equivocal, the theoretical work of Sargeant may provide some additional insight. In a muscle of mixed fibre-type, the optimal rate of shortening will be a compromise between the power-velocity relationships of type I and type II fibres. During real-world cycling, maximal power output is achieved at approximately 120 r.p.m. Based on the combined power-velocity relationship of a theoretical whole muscle, and the ability of the CNS to selectively recruit motor units, Sargeant argued that at 80% of maximal power output, pedalling at 120 r.p.m. would result in a reserve of 20% available power, due to the muscle being at the shortening velocity corresponding to the peak of the power-velocity curve.

At 60 r.p.m. there would be no power reserve, as the muscle would be on the ascending limb of the power-velocity curve. Pedalling at 120 r.p.m. would also allow the smallest possible contribution from type II fibres to meet the demands of the cycling task. Sargeant additionally contends that having the smallest theoretical contribution form the type II fibres requires a progressive increase in cadence as power output is increased. Sargeant's mode also predicts that at lower cadence. This would allow a greater reliance on more economical type I fibres than a higher cadences. While the work of Sargeant is suggests that the preferred or optimal rate of movement during cycling, and other cyclic activities, may mechanical properties of the specific muscles most involved in producing the movements . At present, this notion has not been thoroughly investigated experimentally.

Minimizing movement variability

In addition to metabolic cost, mechanical minimization phenomena and limb inertial properties, movement stability or variability may be another factor that stability or variability may be another factor that determines the preferred or optimal rate of movement during cyclic activities. The reader should note that high movement stability and low movement variability are synonymous in the present context. Much, if not all, of the literature relating to movement stability during cyclic activities movement organization.

According to dynamical systems theory, behavioural patterns and their dynamics are shown to arise in a purely self-organized fashion from cooperative coupling among individual components. A primary focus of this theory is the study of preferred movement patterns are associated with high stability, and a loss of stability is usually indicative of an impending change in behaviour.

There is also evidence from more traditional motor behaviour circles that movement variability is an important and relevant issue in control of preferred rate of movement. Smoll, and Smoll and Szhutz found distinct individual differences in preferred cadences and movement variability in a cyclic upper-limb task. They noted that movement variability is correlated with preferred cadence, and is likely to be related to underlying biological variability. According to Smoll, movement by variability is indicative of the status of an individual performance, and is an essential component of a complete description of that performance.

Movement variability has previously been characterized as stochastic in nature. Research by Hausdorff and colleagues, however, has demonstrated that variations in the stride interval during steady- state walking exhibit long-range correlations, such that the fluctuations in stride intervals at previous times. The long-term correlations extend as far back as 100-strides. Interestingly, when subject walked in time with a metronome set at their preferred stride rate, the long-range corrections disappeared, and the variations in stride interval became random in nature. Hausdorff et al. proposed that chaotic variability is an intrinsic part of the normal locomotor control system.

The researchers also suggested that supraspinal

centres are responsible for the presence of the long-term correlations. From a control perspective, systems that possess long-range correlations are inherently. Movement variability/stability is clearly a relevant factor for cyclic movement control, and a possible determinant of preferred rate of movement.

One of the most complete accounts of the relationship between movement stability and preferred rate of movement is provided by Holt et al. Their paper is notable because they employed stability, metabolic, mechanical and inertial measures, allowing direct comparisons not usually possible in univocal studies. They determined three measures of movement stability for eight subjects at their preferred speed and they walked on a treadmill at preferred stride rate, optimal stride rate predicted by an force-driven harmonic oscillator model of the lower limb, and of predicted stride rate.

The three stability measures were the standard deviation of the release phase between the lower limb joints, the standard deviation of normalized vector length of the phase planes for the head and back, and the magnitude of the spectral power near the predicted and preferred frequencies for the head and joints.

They additionally measured metabolic cast and mechanical energy conservation at each stride rate. Holt and colleagues found that movement stability was generally maximized and metabolic cost minimized at the preferred and predicted stride rates, which were not significantly different from each other. Holt et al. noted that the metabolic cost curve was steeper at low stride rates than a high rates, but the reverse was true for the stability curve. The investigators suggested that preferred stride rate may be a compromise between metabolic cost and movement stability.

Maruyama and Nagaski measured the variability of many temporal aspects of the stride using variable error and coefficient of variation in seven subjects during treadmill walking at speeds ranging from 0.5 to 1.7 and stride rates ranging from 30 to 80 strides. The two major findings by Maruyama and Nagaski were that stride variability for all stride phases decreased as speed increased, and variability was minimized at or near the preferred stride rate at any given speed. In a similar study using 22 subjects walking overground, Sekya et al. found that spatial variability of stride length was minimized near the preferred stride rate and preferred speed.

At the speed most closely approximating the commonly reported energetically optimal speed, temporary variability was minimized at a stride rate of 58.2 strides and spatial variability was minimized at a stride rate of 60.4 strides. The preferred rates at the same speed were 57.1 strides. Maruyama and Nagaski and Sekiya et al. concluded that preferred stride rate is optimized in terms of metabolic cost and movement stability.

Brisswalter and Mottet used variability and metabolic core measures in an analysis of the walk-to-run transition in 10 subjects walking and running on a treadmill. During the preferred transition speed. After the transition, variability was much lower, consistent with the findings of others. Brisswalter and Mottet also expected variability to be lower for walking below the transition speed, and lower for running above the transition speed, and lower for running above the transition speed; however, this was not the chase. Variability was lower for running than walking at all common speeds.

Therefore, below the energetically optimal transition speed, walking is more economical, but also more variable than running. In addressing this paradox, and authors noted the difficulty in associating gross energy cost with movement efficiency, and suggested that metabolic cost alone is not adequate to relate movement efficiency and variability.

Another factor not addressed by Brisswalter and Mottet is that at the common speeds, stride rate was higher for running than for walking, and variability tended to decrease with increase in rate of movement perhaps making the finding of lower variability at all running speeds less surprising. One should keep in mind that the paper by Briswalter and Mottet dealt with speeds near the preferred transition speed, and did not include data on preferred speed or stride rate for walking or running.

In a paper dealing with the walk-to-run transition, Diedrich and Warren presented an account of movement stability over a range of walking and running speeds. The walking stability function had a minimum at 1.66 m and 61.8 strides. The data from Diedrich and Warren compare favourably with the results from Maruyana and Nagasaki. At a speed of 1-67m Maruyama and Nagasaki reported minimum variability at 62.0 strides, and preferred rate 62.0 strides.

Patla examined EMG variability at fast, normal and slow stride rates in seven subjects walking on a treadmill at preferred speed. He used a pattern recognition technique to estimate variability. Surprisingly, muscle activity patterns were found to be more variable for the normal stride rate than the slow or fast rates. The author suggested that the attentional demand necessary to walk in a non-preferred manner could account for the lower variability under these conditions.

The finding of increased variability for muscle activity at the preferred rate is in direct contrast to the notion that kinematic variability is minimized at the preferred rate.

All of the studies reviewed so far have dealt exclusively with adults. A few papers in the literature have dealt with movement variability during locomotion in children. Jeng et al. determined inter-limb and intra-limb stability in 45 children aged 3-12 years walking on a treadmill at their preferred stride rates and 255\% of preferred stride rate. In most cases, inter-limb and intra-limb stability was maximized under preferred stride rate conditions.

The experts also noted that by ate 7 years, children exhibit a self-optimization pattern similar to adults. Jeng et al. also observed that 5 to 6 year-olds demonstrated an ability of modulate stride rate not seen in 3 to 4 year-olds, but as a consequence the giant of the 5 to 6 year-old became more variable. Variability subsequently decreased in the 7 to 12 year-olds. The dramatic differences between the 5 to 6 and 3 to 4 year-olds are possible due to morphological changes that occur between ages 3 and 6; however, they may also be indicative of a transition from a rigid form a control to a more adaptive form of control.

A more adaptive form of control would by its very nature require more variability in the system. Clark and Philips have also suggested that infants also go through a period of stability acquisition during the first 3 months of independent walking. Although the picture is far from complete, locomotion development in children may undergo at least two distinct phases of stability acquisition. One is associated with the initial development of the walking skill, and a second is associated with an increase, in the adaptability of stride rate to meet the demands of the environment.

The literature on movement variability at different rates of movement in cyclic outside the locomotion arena is sparse. Recently, Dawson et al. reported changes in temporal variability during rowing on an ergometer and on the water in five competitive rowers, over a range of stroke rates. The authors discovered that rowers increase stroke rate primarily by decreasing the duration of the stroke phase changed very little. As stroke rate increased, variability generally decreased for both the recovery phase and the stroke phase. The decreases in variability were most dermic for the recovery phase, which exhibited considerably higher variability than the stroke phase at the lower rates. Dawson et al. did not determine preferred stroke rate for the rowers in their study. They did note, however, that preferred strike rate is usually in the range of 30-40 strokes. This would suggest that movement variability is minimized at or near preferred stroke rates in competitive rowers.

Based on the studies reviewed, movement stability would appear to be a contributing factor to be selection of he preferred cadences during locomotion. Specifically, the results of Holt et al. indicate that stability may cooperate with metabolic cost in setting the preferred stride rate. The findings of Dawson et al. suggest that minimizing variability may be a factor in cadence selection for other activities as well. Many more studies will be needed on other cyclic activities before any far-reaching generalizations can be made regarding the role of movement stability/variability in rate of movement selection.

Limb Stiffness

Recently, Farley , McMohan, and co-workers have used a simple springs-mass model of the human body to demonstrate that limb stiffness by determine rat of movement in bounding and running gaits. According to this model, the human body is represented as a massless and a point mass. It has been shown that the stiffness of the leg spring remains nearly constant as running speed increase in human and several other animal species.

As running speed increases, the leg spring in swept through a larger angle, increasing the effective stiffness of the overall system, and causing the body to bounce off the ground at a faster rate. During hopping, or at a constant running speed, however, the stiffness of the leg spring appears to be modulated to produce a different hopping rate.

8

AN INTRODUCTION TO KINESIOLOGY

Kinesiology is referred to as the scientific study of the human body when it performs various activities in his day-to-day life. It is generally considered as a science or source of study of human organs pertaining to their movements and underlying principles of dynamics of physics. Activity of human body and limbs change accordingly to the time of requirements. This we feel in the change of ability, potentiality movement and its kinds of activity. Complex types of activities are found more in the field of sport. To import the activities to the players or sport persons it require energy,

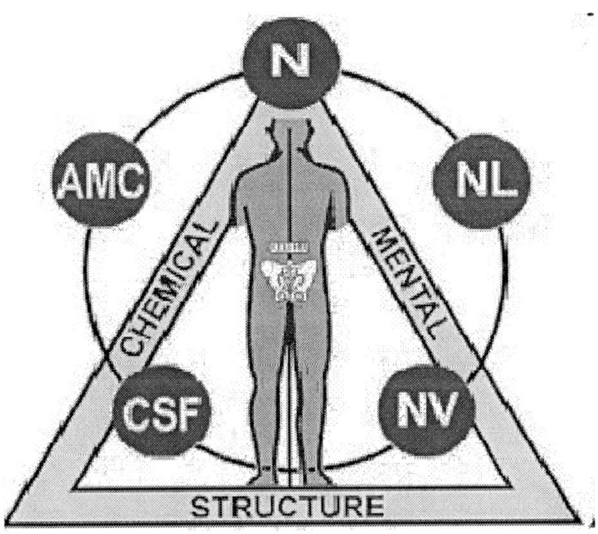

swiftness, ability and situations. In the field of sport, knowledge of kinesiology is use to make them skills of techniques more dynamic. In the industries employees and labours are required to undergo a vigorous work. Hence for increasing production of the industry it is necessary to increase production to the industry it is necessary to increase work capacity of the labour and technicians which is based science of activities.

Kinesiology, also known as human kinetics, is the science of human movement. It focuses on how the body functions and moves. A kinesiological approach applies scientific based medical principles towards the analysis, preservation and enhancement of human movement in all settings and populations. A coach or physical education teachers should have adequate and relevant knowledge of kinesiology.

Human Activities

There are various view points in the field of kinesiology from which the study of human activities are done. Those view points are as follows:

1. Starting Position;
2. Centre of Gravity;
3. Line of Gravity;
4. Planes of the Body;
5. Rotation; and
6. Circumduction

1. Starting Position

There are two kinds of starting positions in human body which are as follows:

(i) Fundamental Starting Position; and (ii)

Anatomical Starting Position

(i) Fundamental Starting Position

In this position, the person usually stand erect. The legs are usually kept quite closure but should be parallel to each other. Both ankles should be kept touching each other while toes should remain kept away from each other. The hands should be kept alongwith the body.

This type of body position is usually taken in the gymnastics while performing forward and backward roll.

(ii) Anatomical Starting Position

In this position, the legs are kept in the same position as described in the fundamental starting position. The body should be kept in erect posture, hand and palm kept facing front side. The hands should be kept stretched from the elbow.

Generally, this gesture is made prior to the training for learning of various activities.

2. Centre of Gravity

The position of the centre of gravity of the human body has been measured in a wide range of conditions, but in many cases a high degree of accuracy was not possible because of the crude nature of the equipment. Much less work has been carried out on the movement of the centre of gravity in quasi-static conditions, but similar remarks apply to the accuracy of the results. For the erect human body the swaying motion associated with long durations of standing is readily observed, but measurements of this movement are rare.

3. Line of Gravity

This is yet another form of imaginary line which is

assumed passing from middle of the body centre of gravity of the body.

A tennis player will keep the line of gravity centered sothat the CG can be shifted quickly in any direction without loss of balance.

The football player who knows he will be pushed from the frontshould shift his line of gravity forward (lean forward) so that he can give in a backward direction without losing his balance.

An individual in tug-of-war will lean backward (move the line of gravity back) in order to absorb a strong forward pull from the opponent.

The greater the mass of a body, the greater will be its stability.

Heavy, solid individuals are more likely to maintain balance than shorter individuals.

(i). The greater the friction between the supporting surface and the parts of the body in contact with it, the more stable the body will be.

In basketball, fencing, football, field hockey, and lacrosse, for example, the wearing of cleats and rubber-soled shoes aids in locomotion and provides for stability for positions held momentarily between quick and forceful movements.

(ii) An individual maintains better balance in locomotion when focusing on stationary objects versus disturbing stimuli.

4. Planes of the Body

When describing parts of the body, we use terms to define position and direction. An organ or entire body

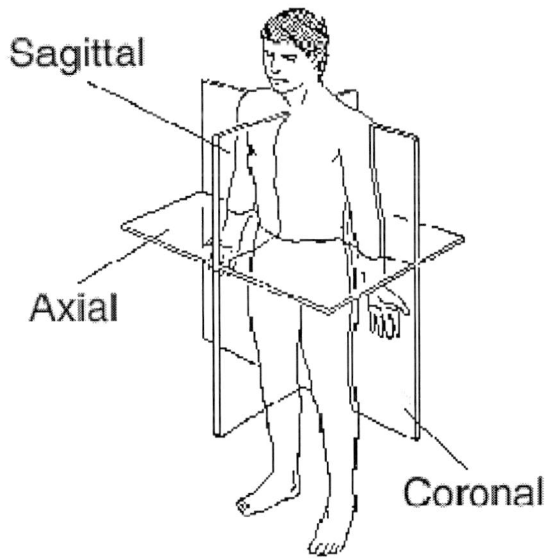

can be described by three planes known as the sagittal, frontal and transverse plane.

1. The transverse plane divides the body into top (superior means situated above or directed upward) and bottom (inferior means situated below or directed downward), cranialis describes everything that lies in a direction toward the head, caudalis describes everything that lies in a direction of the rump.

2. The frontal plane divides the body into front (ventralis / antrior means at or near the front); and back (dorsalis / posterior means at or near the back).

3. The sagittal plane divides the body into left (sinister) and right (dexter).

Medialis – describes everything that lies near the sagittal plane and lateralis describes everything that lies away from the sagittal plane.

(A) Sagittal Plane

A sagittal plane of the human body is an imaginary plane that travels vertically from the top to the bottom of the body along the Y axis, dividing it into left and right portions.

From a broader perspective, it is one of the planes of the body used to describe the location of body parts in relation to each other - for example, the extent of prognathism. The other reference planes used in anatomy are:

The coronal (or frontal) plane divides the body into dorsal (anterior) and ventral (posterior) commonly known as the back and front portions.

A transverse (or horizontal) plane divides the body into cranial and caudal (top and bottom) portions in medical terminology known as the superior and inferior portions of the body.

(B) Lateral or Frental Plane

In this plane line passes through there lateral side of the body due to body divided into front half of the back half.

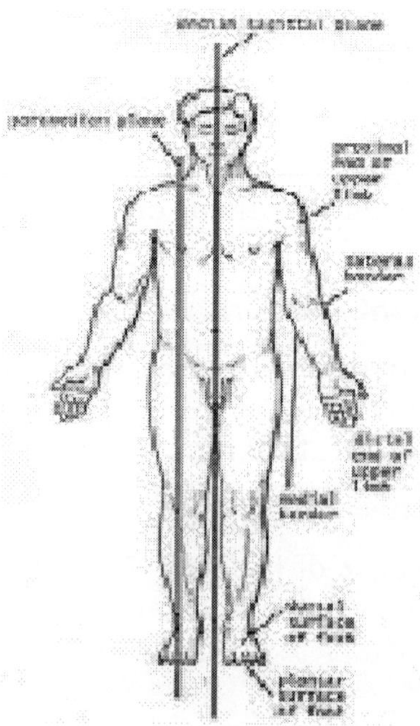

(C) Horizontal Plane

The transverse plane (also called the horizontal plane, axial plane, or transaxial plane) is an imaginary plane that divides the body into superior and inferior parts. It is perpendicular to the coronal and sagittal planes.

It is one of the planes of the body used to describe the location of body parts in relation to each other. The other two commonly used terms are the Coronal plane and the Sagittal plane.

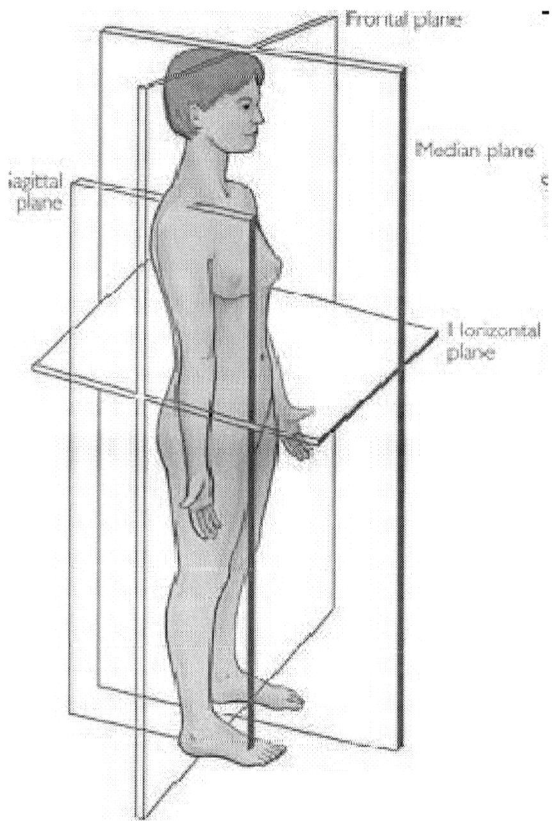

Examples

- The transpyloric plane
- The subcostal plane
- The umbilical plane
- The intertubercular plane (or transtubercular)
- The interspinous plane

5. Rotation

Around the axis of the joint, body organ moved toward right or left. They are of four types.

(i) Inward Rotation; (ii) Upward Rotation; (iii) Outward Rotation; and (iv) Downward Rotation

(i) Inward Rotation:

When bone or organ is moved towards body, it is referred to as the inward rotation.

(ii) Upward Rotation:

When joint is moved against the gravitational force it is referred to as the upward rotation.

During the early phase of upward rotation, the scapula and the clavicle move together around an axis through the sternoclavicular (SC) joint, the only joint where the scapula and shoulder girdle attach to the axial skeleton. The SC joint's antero-posterior (AP) axis is somewhat oblique and passes near the base of the scapular spine.

Around this axis, serratus anterior (SA) and upper trapezius (UT) produce upward rotation moments.

(iii) Outward Rotation:

When body rotation is done outwardly then it is referred to as the outward rotation.

(iv) Downward Rotation:

When rotation is performed towards the direction of gravitational force, then it is referred to as downward rotation.

6. Circumduction

Circumduction is defined as the movement pattern which is a combination of flexion, extension, adduction and abduction. It occurs at synovial joints where a circle can be described by the body part. True circumduction can only really occur at Ball and socket joints, such as the hip and shoulder. A sporting example of circumduction occurs when performing a serve in tennis or bowling a cricket ball.

9

ANATOMICAL PRINCIPLES OF KINESIOLOGY

Kinesiology is referred to as the scientific study of the human body when it performs various activities in his day-to-day life. It is generally considered as a science or source of study of human organs pertaining to their movements and underlying principles of dynamics of physics. Activity of human body and limbs change accordingly to the time of requirements. This we feel in the change of ability, potentiality movement and its kinds of activity. Complex types of activities are found more in the field of sport. To import the activities to the players or sport persons it require energy, swiftness, ability and situations. In the field of sport, knowledge of kinesiology is use to make them skills of techniques more dynamic. In the industries employees and labours are required to undergo a vigorous work. Hence for increasing production of the industry it is necessary to increase production to the industry it is necessary to increase work capacity of the labour and technicians which is based science of activities.

Anatomy

Bones provide attachment points and support for muscles. Bones are connected together by fibrous tissue called Ligaments. Tendons are also fibrous tissue and attach muscle to bone. Both have some elasticity and do not heal on their own if torn. An overstretched tendon is called tendonitis and is an inflamed tendon. Cartilage is also fibrous tissue but is not elastic. Cartilage is used to cushion the junction of two bones.

The body is divided into three anatomical planes the Frontal, Sagittal and Horizontal. The Frontal plane divides the body from front to back. The Sagittal plane divides the body down the center or vertically. The Horizontal plane divides upper and lower. The table below lists the anatomical term and the corresponding description.

ANATOMICAL TERM	DESCRIPTION
Anterior	front
Posterior	back
Medial	inside
Lateral	outside
Supine	face up
Unilateral	one side
Bilateral	both sides
Prone	face down
Superior	upper
Inferior	lower

Muscle Action

The three types of muscle contraction are Isometric, Isotonic, and Isokinetic. Isometric is defined as that type of contraction where muscle tension and muscle length remain constant.

This type of exercise provides muscle strength gains but only at the joint angle held during the exercise. Isotonic contraction is defined as that where the muscle tension remains constant and muscle length varies. Isokinetic contraction is defined as varying tension and length.

In each exercise there are four main functions of the associated muscles, Agonists (prime movers), Antagonists, Stabilizers and Assistors.

The Agonists is generally the muscle we are exercising. The Antagonist is the opposing muscle and acts in contrast to the agonist. The Stabilizer muscles are those that hold a joint in place so that the exercise may be performed. The Assistors help the Agonist muscle doing the work. The stabilizer muscles are not necessarily moving during exercise, but provide stationary support.

For example, when doing biceps curls, the biceps are the agonists, the triceps are the antagonists and various muscles including the deltoids are the stabilizer muscles. However, when doing a triceps push down, now the triceps are the agonists and the biceps are the antagonists.

Again the deltoid muscles are the stabilizer muscles. The agonist/antagonist relationship changes depending on which muscle is expected to do the work.

However, every muscle group has an opposing muscle group. The following table lists muscles and their opposing counterparts:

AGONIST (Prime Mover)	ANTAGONIST
Biceps	Triceps
Deltoids	Latissimus Dorsi
Pectoralis Major	Trapezius/ Rhomboids
Rectus Abdominis	Erector Spinae
Iliopsoas	Gluteus Maximus
Quadriceps	Hamstrings
Hip Adductor	Gluteus Medius
Tibialis Anterior	Gastrocnemius

In reference to Agonist and Antagonist, this above list could easily be reversed when exercising the muscles in the right hand column. Muscle balance is that relationship between the Agonist and Antagonist. It is important to have muscle balance to prevent injury. If the Agonist is much stronger than the Antagonist, the Agonist can overpower and injure the Antagonist.

Tendons are made up of fibrous tissue and connect muscle to bone. Tendonitis is an inflammation of the tendon due to overuse. A stretching or tearing of the tendon is referred to as a strain. A Strain is a muscle or tendon injury.

Ligaments are also fibrous tissue and connect bone to bone. There are less flexible than tendons. The function of ligaments is to restrict thc joint movement within normal parameters. When a ligament is over stretched or torn it is called a sprain.

Since ligaments don't have a vascular system, they may take a very long time to repair or may never return to their original length. This can cause abnormal joint movement and even cartilage and bone wear due to this unrestricted movement.

Joint Action

Joints provides a fulcrum point for muscles to do work. There are six types of joint action:

JOINT ACTION	MOVEMENT DESCRIPTION	EXAMPLE MOVEMENT
Flexion	decreasing joint angle	Biceps Curl
Extension	increasing joint angle	Triceps Extension
Abduction	movement away from body centerline	Lateral Raises (Deltoids)
Adduction	movement toward body centerline	Horizontal Flyes (Pectorals)
Rotation	rotation about and axis	Twisting the Arm
Circumduction	360 degree rotation	Arm circle around

Applied Kinesiology

Applied Kinesiology is a series of tests that locate weaknesses in specific muscles reflecting imbalances throughout the body. Then specific massages or

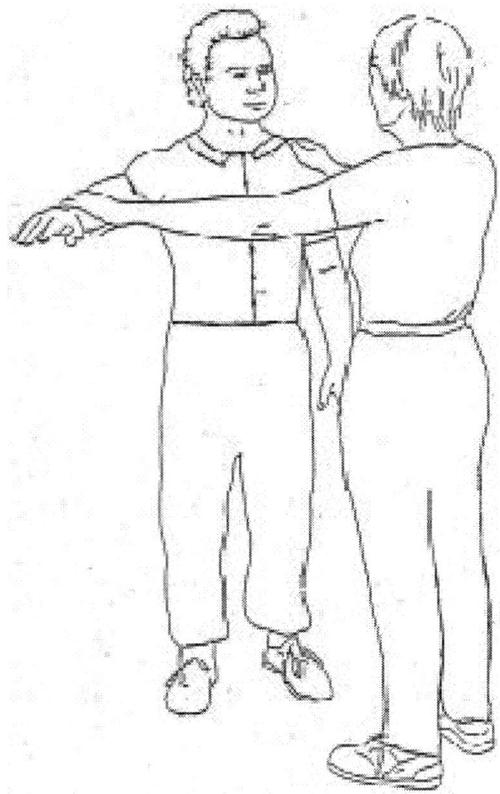

acupressure techniques are used in an attempt to rebalance what has been revealed by the kinesiology tests. Thus, kinesiology is used as both an assessment tool and as a limited therapeutic modality.

Purpose

Kinesiology claims to be a healing system that detects and corrects imbalances in the body before they develop into a disease, and which restores overall system balance and harmony. It is used to alleviate muscle, bone, and joint problems, treat all manner of aches and pains, and correct many areas of imbalance and discomfort.

Precautions

Since interpretation of the muscle tests is both complex and subjective, it should only be performed by a licensed health professional trained to look for "subclinical" symptoms (those which have not yet become a major problem). Kinesiology, itself, is more of a diagnostic technique and should not be thought of as a cure for any particular problem.

Description

Traditionally, the word "kinesiology" refers simply to the study of muscles and body movement. In 1964, however, American chiropractor George J. Goodheart founded what has become known as applied kinesiology when he linked oriental ideas about energy flow in the body with western techniques of muscle testing. First, Goodheart noted that all muscles are related to other muscles. He observed that for each movement a muscle makes, there is another muscle or group of muscles involved with that movement; one muscle contracts while another one relaxes. So when he was presented with a painful, overly-tight muscle, he would observe and treat the opposite, and necessarily weak, muscle to restore balance. This was then a very new technique.

Further, Goodheart argued that there is a definite and real connection between muscles, glands, and organs, and that by testing the strength of certain muscles he could learn about the health or condition of the gland or organ to which it was related.

Applied kinesiology is based on the idea that the

body is an interacting unit made of different parts that interconnect and affect each other. Everything we do affects the body as a whole; therefore, a problem in one area can cause trouble in another area. According to kinesiology, the muscles eventually register and reflect anything that is wrong with any part of the body, whether physical or mental. Thus, a particular digestive problem might show up in the related and corresponding muscles of the legs. By testing the strength of certain muscles, the kinesiologist claims to be able to gain access to the body's communication system, and, thus, to read the health status of each of the body's major components.

The manual testing of muscles or muscle strength is not new, and was used in the late 1940s to evaluate muscle function and strength and to assess the extent of an injury. Applied kinesiology measures whether a muscle is stuck in the "on" position, acting like a tense muscle spasm, or is stuck "off," appearing weak or flaccid. It is called manual testing because it is done without instruments, using only the kinesiologist's fingertip pressure. During the first and longest appointment which lasts about an hour, the kinesiologist conducts a complete consultation, asking about the patient's history and background.

During the physical examination, patients sit or lie down, then the kinesiologist holds the patient's leg or arm to isolate a particular muscle. The practitioner then touches a point on the body which he believes is related to that muscle, and, with quick, gentle, and painless pressure, pushes down on the limb.

Patients are asked to resist this pressure, and, if they cannot, an imbalance is suspected in the related organ, gland, or body part. This diagnostic technique uses muscles to find the cause of a problem, and is based on traditional Chinese medicine and its idea that the body has common energy meridians, or channels, for both organs and muscles.

Kinesiologists also claim that they are able to locate muscle weaknesses that stem from a variety of causes such as allergies, mineral and vitamin deficiencies, as well as from problems with the lymph system.

Once the exact cause is determined, the kinesiologist uses his fingertips to work the appropriate corresponding acupressure points in order to rebalance the flow of energy and restore health. Often he will recommend a complementary program of nutrition therapy.

Risks

There are no major risks associated with this gentle, noninvasive therapy. It is generally safe for people of all ages and has no side effects.

Normal results

If applied kinesiology does what it claims, patients should expect muscle testing to discover the cause of their physical complaint and to be told how to correct it.

Key Terms

- Acupressure - A form of acupuncture in which certain points of the body are pressed with the fingers and hands to release energy blocks.
- Alleviate - To make something easier to be endured.

- Complementary - Something that serves to fill out or complete something else.

- Deficiency - A shortage of something necessary for health.

- Diagnostic - The art or act of identifying a disease from its signs and symptoms.

- Flaccid - Flabby, limp, weak.

- Meridian - In traditional Chinese medicine, the channels which run beneath the skin through which the body's energy flows.

- Spasm - An involuntary, sudden, violent contraction of a muscle or a group of muscles.

Muscle Fiber Types

There are two types of muscle fibers, fast twitch (FT) and slow twitch (ST). Fast twitch fibers are used for explosive type movements and are easily fatigued. Slow twitch muscle fibers contain more mitochondria than Fast twitch. Mitochondria are cell structures that contain specific enzymes, which are required by the cell in order to use oxygen for energy production.

Fast twitch muscles fibers have less mitochondria and therefore less capacity for oxygen utilization in the production of energy within the muscle. This makes them better suited to anaerobic activities such as weight training, sprinting, jumping and other explosive type activities. FT fibers create energy anaerobically, that is, without oxygen. This system uses glucose as a prime energy source. The by-product of this anaerobic energy production is heat and lactic acid. Lactic acid accumulation in the muscle causes fatigue and soreness. The anaerobic energy system is a limited system for energy production.

Slow twitch fibers are used for endurance type activities and are particularly suited to aerobic type activities. These type fibers contain an increased number of mitochondria and therefore are capable of utilizing oxygen for the production of energy within the muscle. This system uses glucose or fat in combination with oxygen to produce energy. The by-product of this system is carbon dioxide, water and heat.

Each person has a specific ratio of FT to ST fibers. A person with a high ratio of FT fibers may find it easier to train for specific activities that involve explosive movements. Conversely, a person with a higher ratio of ST fibers might find it easier to train and excel at endurance type activities.

There is a third type of muscle fiber that exists only in humans. It is considered a FT fiber of type IIA. These fibers are less powerful than the type IIAB discussed above. What makes these type IIA FT fibers unique is that they can adapt somewhat to aerobic activities. These fibers provide the capability to alter our original genetic FT/ST ratio.

Energy Production

There are basically two types of energy systems that the body utilizes, Aerobic and Anaerobic. Each energy system produces Adenosine Triphosphate (ATP), which is used by the muscles to contract.

The Aerobic System can utilize carbohydrates,

proteins or fat to supply an unlimited amount of ATP as long as oxygen is present. The Aerobic system provides medium to very long duration energy production with low to moderate power (less than 85% of maximum output). The by-product of this system is heat, water and carbon dioxide.

The Anaerobic System can only utilize carbohydrates for ATP production. This system does not use oxygen in the metabolization of it's fuel source. The Anaerobic System provides short duration (45 - 70 seconds) and high power. The by-product of the metabolization of glucose (glycolysis) in this system is heat and lactic acid, the cause of muscle soreness immediately after exercise. Muscle soreness 24 to 48 hours after exercise is due to torn muscle fibers and connective tissue. This type of soreness can be reduced by adequate warm-up and cool-down stretching exercises.

Aerobic capacity is the ability of the body to collect and transfer oxygen from the air through the lungs and blood to the working muscles. This is related to cardio-respiratory endurance and is referred to as Maximal Oxygen Consumption or VO2 max. Aerobic Capacity reduces at about 10% per decade after 30 years of age.

The Anaerobic Threshold is defined as that point where the body can no longer meet the oxygen demand and it's anaerobic metabolism is accelerated. This point varies on an individual basis and is dependent on fitness level. For healthy individuals, this occurs between 50% and 66% of their maximal working capacity. This would be equivalent to running faster than half speed.

Cardiovascular and Respiratory System

Air is inhaled into the lungs where oxygen is exchanged through tiny gas permeable sacs within the lungs for carbon dioxide from the blood. The heart pumps the oxygen rich blood from the left atrium through the arteries then through tiny vessels called capillaries to the tissues of the body. At the cell level, oxygen is given up for metabolism and the carbon dioxide produced by this action is picked up by the blood. The oxygen depleted and carbon dioxide rich blood is then pumped back to the heart, through the veins to the right atrium to the lungs where the process is repeated.

Aerobic activity increases the strength of the heart muscle. The result is a greater volume of blood per stroke. This is referred to as Stroke Volume or the amount of blood ejected from each ventricle of the heart during one stroke. Cardiac Output is a measure of the amount of blood pumped through each ventricle in one minute. Vital Capacity is the volume of air that can forcibly ejected from the lungs in a single expiration. Aerobic activity provides a Training Effect on Vital Capacity, Stroke Volume and Cardiac Output.

An artery carries blood away from the heart while a vein carries blood towards the heart.

Bone Density Tests

Many consider osteopenia (a symptomless measurement of low bone density) to be an early sign of osteoporosis, but an article by New York Times science reporter Gina Kolata questions the significance of this diagnosis. In 1992, the World Health Organization (WHO) arbitrarily defined osteopenia as "bone density that [is] one standard deviation below that of a normal young adult"--i.e., a healthy 30-year-old white woman or man. Osteoporosis is defined as 2.5 or more standard deviations below normal. Low bone density is only one factor that predicts fracture risk, however. While half of all middle-aged men have osteopenia, according to the above definition, they have only 35% the risk of hip fractures, compared to women. Age, family history, and, perhaps most important, bone quality also contribute to osteoporosis. In addition, variation in bone density measurements further shadows the significance of a diagnosis of osteopenia. The incidence of osteopenia varies 28 to 45%, depending upon the machine used for diagnosis, according to a Merck study.

Osteoporosis epidemiologist Dr. L. Joseph Melton, who attended the WHO meeting, said, "It was just meant to indicate the emergence of a problem ... It didn't have any particular diagnostic or therapeutic significance. It was just meant to show a huge group who looked like they might be at risk." According to its own estimates, Merck says that 8 million women have been diagnosed with osteopenia and about a third are taking an osteoporosis drug. Osteoporosis drugs accounted for $3.98 billion in 2002 sales worldwide. Concern about low bone density has caused others to take a variety of calcium supplements. Since researchers are still trying to understand osteoporosis and the role of bone quality (not density), the effect of these interventions is uncertain.

Kolata, Gina. Is bone density a problem? The Sunday Herald-Sun (Durham, NC) 28 September 2003

Your Body Doesn't Lie

One of the simplest ways to gain information about the body's needs and condition is behavioral kinesiology (BK) as described by John Diamond, MD in his book Your Body Doesn't Lie. Dr. Diamond's system for checking the body at an energy level is based upon the work of Dr. George Goodheart. Dr. Goodheart discovered that "each large muscle relates to a body organ. A weakness in a muscle usually means that there is a problem at the energy level in the associated organ." Dr. Goodheart found that strengthening the muscle led to improvement in the corresponding organ. Full kinesiology testing involves most muscles in the body and over 100 test-touching points for full diagnosis and treatment. The technique in Your Body Doesn't Lie, however, uses one muscle (the deltoid) and the point over the thymus gland to determine how environment, diet choices, and emotional attitudes affect the body at an energy level. In addition to its immunological function, the thymus monitors and regulates the body's energy system, according to Dr. Diamond.

The BK basic test requires two people. The test subject stands erect with one arm relaxed at the side and the other arm held out parallel to the floor, elbow straight. The tester faces the subject and places one hand on the subject's extended arm just above the wrist and the other hand on the subject's shoulder. After instructing the subject to resist, the tester pushes down on the extended arm. "The idea is to push just hard enough to test the spring and bounce in the arm," writes Dr. Diamond, "not so hard that the muscle becomes fatigued." Testing the strength of the deltoid muscle in this way indicates the body's energy supply. If the muscle gives way, that supply is weak. If it remains strong, the energy supply is strong. Dr. Diamond recommends repeating the process while the subject touches the skin over the thymus area (the point where the second rib joins the breastbone) with the fingertips of the free hand. If the deltoid muscle in the extended arm weakens when challenged, either the thymus gland is underactive at that time or its energy supply is low.

The effect of food, supplements, and environmental factors on the energy system can be tested using this system. Test edible substances by holding a small sample in the mouth while doing the testing. If the substance is harmful to the body, the deltoid will weaken. Sometimes the deltoid may be unaffected until the subject touches the thymus area. A weak response while touching the thymus point indicates that the substance is detrimental to thymus function. Sometimes, a substance may cause the deltoid to test stronger than it had moments earlier when no stimulus was used, indicating that it is beneficial. Dr. Diamond also recommends that supplements be tested, noting that one brand may strengthen the indicator muscle while another brand may weaken it, possibly because of the colorings, fillers, and binders used. He has also noticed that "lower-potency, more natural substances are more likely to correct a specific muscle weakness than those of higher potency. The more refined supplements and vitamins may even weaken the patient generally."

Sounds and music, social environments, types of cloth, and personal hygiene products--anything to which we expose ourselves--can be tested as well.

Through his own investigation, Dr. Diamond has found that wearing sunglasses, wristwatches, hats, synthetic clothing, disposable diapers, or metal, weakens many people. Exposure to fluorescent light, cooking gas, smoking, household chemicals, auto exhaust, some sound waves (including the whistle given off by television sets), ionization, magnetic fields, X-rays, microwaves, some rock music, and digital sound (achieved through Pulse Code Modulation), also tend to stress and weaken the body's energy system.

When under stress, many people develop a state of cerebral hemisphere imbalance that Dr. Goodheart called 'switching'. If switching becomes the normal mode of operation, the results from BK testing flip. Substances that weaken the deltoid in most people appear to strengthen those with cerebral hemisphere imbalance, and beneficial substances weaken them.

It is as if his body no longer can distinguish what is beneficial and what is harmful. In fact, his body now actually chooses that which is destructive over that which is therapeutic.

The body "should be the final arbiter of treatment, not the textbook or even clinical experience. If the body's Life Energy (as measured by test-touching the thymus gland) is strengthened, then the substance may be given; if it is weakened, then it should not.

Through BK testing, Dr. Diamond has found that many patients test weak when asked to say "I want to be healthy." Since attitudes affect the energy system, a self-defeatist attitude can affect outcome.

Biomechanics

Biomechanics is the science concerned with the internal and external forces acting on the human body and the effects produced by these forces.

At the highest levels of sports in which techniques play a major role, improvement comes so often from careful attention to detail that no coach can afford to leave these details to chance or guesswork. For such coaches knowledge of biomechanics might be regarded as essential.

Linear Kinematics

Kinematics is the branch of biomechanics concerned with the study of movement with reference to the amount of time taken to carry out the activity.

Distance and displacement

Distance and displacement are quantities used to describe the extent of a bodies motion.

Distance is the length of the path a body follows and displacement is the length of a straight line joining the start and finish points e.g. in a 400m race on a track the length of the path the athlete follows (distance) is 400m but their displacement will be zero metres (they finish where they start).

Speed and velocity

Speed and velocity describe the rate at which a body moves from one location to another. These two terms are often thought, incorrectly, to be the same. Average speed of a body is obtained by dividing the distance by the time taken where as the average Velocity is obtained by dividing the displacement by the time take e.g. consider a swimmer in a 50m race in a 25m length pool who completes the race in 60 seconds - distance is 50m and displacement is 0m so speed is 50/60= 0.83m/s and velocity is 0/60=0 m/s

- Speed and Velocity = distance travelled ÷ time taken

Acceleration

Acceleration is defined as the rate at which velocity changes with respect to time.

- average acceleration = (final velocity - initial velocity) ÷ elapsed time

From Newton's 2nd law:

- Force = Mass x Acceleration
- Acceleration = Force ÷ Mass

If the mass of a sprinter is 70kg and the force exerted on the starting blocks is 700N then acceleration = 700 ÷ 70 = 10 $msec^2$

Acceleration due to gravity

Whilst a body is in the air it is subject to a downward accleration, due to gravity, of approximately $9.81 m/s^2$

Vectors and scalars

Distance and speed can be described in terms of magnitude and are known as scalars. Displacement, velocity and acceleration which require magnitude and direction are known as vectors.

Components of a vector

Let us consider the horizontal and vertical components of velocity of the shot in Figure 1.

Uniformly accelerated motion

When a body experiences the same acceleration throughout some interval of time its acceleration is said to be constant or uniform.

In these circumstances the following equations apply:

- Final velocity = initial velocity + (acceleration x time)
- Distance = (initial velocity x time) + (½ x acceleration x time^2)

Moment of force (torque)

The moment of force or torque is defined as the application of a force at a perpendicular distance to a joint or point of rotation.

Angular Kinematics

Angular distance and displacement

When a rotating body moves from one position to another the angular distance through which it moves is equal to the length of the angular path. The angular displacement that a rotating body experiences is equal in magnitude to the angle between the initial and final position of the body.

Angular movement is usually expressed in radians where 1 radian = 57.3°

Angular speed, velocity and acceleration

- Angular speed = angular displacement ÷ time

- Angular velocity = angular displacement ÷ time

- Angular acceleration = (final angular velocity - initial angular velocity) ÷ time

Linear Kinetics

Kinetics is concerned with what causes a body to move the way it does.

Momentum, inertia, mass, weight and force

- Momentum: mass x velocity

- Inertia: the resistance to acceleration - reluctance of a body to change whatever it is doing

- Mass: the quantity of matter of which a body is composed of - not affected by gravity - measured in kilograms (kg)

- Weight: force due to gravity - is mass x gravity ($9.81m/s^2$)

- Force: a pushing a pulling action that causes a change of state (rest/motion) of a body - is proportional to mass x acceleration - is measured in Newtons (N) where 1N is the force that will produce an acceleration of 1 m/s^2 in a body of 1kg mass

The classification of forces, external or internal, depends on the definition of the 'system'.

In biomechanics the body is seen as the 'system' so any force exerted by one part of the system on another is known as an internal force all other forces are external.

Newton's Laws of Motion

- First Law: Every body continues in its state of rest or motion in a straight line unless compelled to change that state by external forces exerted upon it.

- Second Law: The rate of change of momentum of a body is proportional to the force causing it and the change takes place in the direction in which the force acts

- Third Law: To every action there is an equal and opposite reaction OR for every force that is exerted by one body on another there is an equal and opposite force exerted by the second body on the first

Newton's law of gravitation

- Any two particles of matter attract one another with a force directly proportional to the product of their masses and inversely proportional to the square of the distance between them

Work, Energy and Power

Kinetic energy is mechanical energy possessed by any moving object.

An equation for Kinetic Energy can be derived from the work definition:

- Work = force x distance moved in the direction of the force

Kinetic Energy = ½ x mass x velocity^2 (result is in joulcs)

Power is defined as the rate at which energy is used or created from other forms

- Power = energy used ÷ time taken
- Power = (force x distance) ÷ time taken
- Power = force x velocity

Angular Kinetics

Translation and couple

A force that acts through the centre of a body result in only translation. A force whose line of action does not pass through the body's centre of gravity is called an eccentric force and results in translation and rotation.

Example - if you push through the centre of an object it will move forward in the direction of the force (translation) if you push to one side of the object (eccentric force) it will move forward and rotate.

A couple is an arrangement of two equal and opposite forces which cause a body to rotate.

Muscle Types

Muscle tissue consists of fibers (cells) that are highly specialized for the active generation of force for contraction. As a result of this characteristic, muscle tissue provides motion, maintenance of posture, and heat production. On the basis of certain structural and functional characteristics, muscle tissue is classified into three types: cardiac, smooth and skeletal.

Cardiac

Cardiac muscle tissue forms the bulk of the wall of the heart. Like skeletal muscle tissue, it is striated. Unlike skeletal muscle tissue its contraction is usually not under conscious control (involuntary).

Smooth

Smooth muscle tissue is located in the walls of hollow

internal structures such as blood vessels, the stomach, intestines, and urinary bladder.

Smooth muscle fibers are usually involuntary, and they are nonstriated (smooth). Smooth muscle tissue, like skeletal and cardiac muscle tissue, can undergo hypertrophy. In addition, certain smooth muscle fibres, such as those in the uterus, retain their capacity for division and can grow by hyperplasia.

Skeletal

Skeletal muscle tissue is named for its location - attached to bones. It is striated; that is, the fibers (cells) contain alternating light and dark bands (striations) that are perpendicular to the long axes of the fibers. Skeletal muscle tissue can be made to contract or relax by conscious control (voluntary).

All skeletal muscle fibres are not alike in structure or function. For example, skeletal muscle fibres vary in colour depending on their content of myoglobin (myoglobin stores oxygen until needed by mitochondria). Skeletal muscle fibres contract with different velocities, depending on their ability to split Adenosine Triphosphate (ATP). Faster contracting fibres have greater ability to split ATP. In addition, skeletal muscle fibres vary with respect to the metabolic processes they use to generate ATP. They also differ in terms of the onset of fatigue. On the basis of various structural and functional characteristics, skeletal muscle fibres are classified into three types: Type I fibres, Type II B fibres and type II A fibres.

Type I Fibres

These fibres, also called slow twitch or slow oxidative

fibres, contain large amounts of myoglobin, many mitochondria and many blood capillaries . Type I fibres are red, split ATP at a slow rate, have a slow contraction velocity, very resistant to to, fatigue and have a high capacity to generate ATP by oxidative metabolic processes. Such fibres are found in large numbers in the postural muscles of the neck.

Type II A Fibres

These fibres, also called fast twitch or fast oxidative fibres, contain very large amounts of myoglobin, very many mitochondria and very many blood capillaries. Type II A fibres are red, have a very high capacity for generating ATP by oxidative metabolic processes, split ATP at a very rapid rate, have a fast contraction velocity and are resistant to fatigue. Such fibres are infrequently found in humans.

Type II B Fibres

These fibres, also called fast twitch or fast glycolytic fibres, contain a low content of myoglobin, relatively few mitochondria, relatively few blood capillaries and large amounts glycogen.

Type II B fibres are white, geared to generate ATP by anaerobic metabolic processes, not able to supply skeletal muscle fibres continuously with sufficient ATP, fatigue easily, split ATP at a fast rate and have a fast contraction velocity.

Such fibres are found in large numbers in the muscles of the arms.

Body muscle make up

Most skeletal muscles of the body are a mixture of

all three types of skeletal muscle fibers, but their proportion varies depending on the usual action of the muscle. For example, postural muscles of the neck, back, and leg have a higher proportion of type I fibres.

Muscles of the shoulders and arms are not constantly active but are used intermittently, usually for short periods of time, to produce large amounts of tension such as in lifting and throwing. These muscles have a higher proportion of type I and type II B fibres.

Even though most skeletal muscle are a mixture of all three types of skeletal, all the skeletal muscle fibres of any one motor unit are all the same. In addition, the different skeletal muscle fibres in a muscle may be used in various ways, depending on need.

For example, if only a weak contraction is needed to perform a task, only type I fibres are activated by their motor units.

If a stronger contraction is needed, the motor units of type II A fibres are activated. If a maximal contraction is required, motor units of type II B fibres are activated as well.

Activation of various motor units is determined in the brain and spinal cord.

Although the number of the different skeletal muscle fibres does not change, the characteristics of those present can be altered.

10

GAIT ANALYSIS

Amputation is one of the most emotionally upsetting and traumatic events that a patient can undergo. However, with a team approach among the medical staff, the negative effects can be minimized, and positive benefits can be emphasized. Equipping the patient with a prosthesis not only greatly improves the patient's functional status but also helps his or her psyche.

People who have undergone amputations often adapt a unique way of ambulating with a prosthesis, but these adaptations also bring about challenges in diagnosing problems with their gait. By understanding the

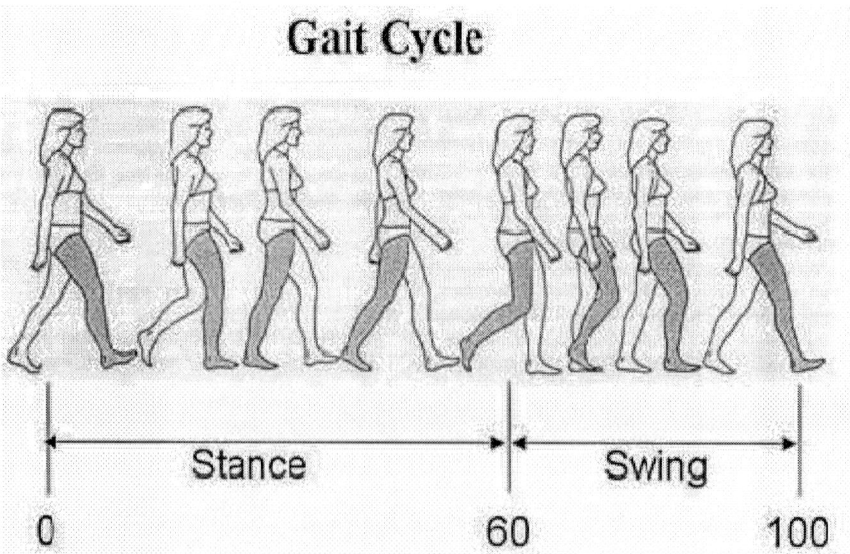

biomechanics of the patient's gait, most problems can be discerned by means of observation.

Frequency

Approximately 70,000 new major amputations are performed annually in the United States. Worldwide, 200-500 million major amputations are performed each year.

Major limb amputations of the lower extremities account for approximately 85% of all cases of amputations, and more than two thirds of these are due to vascular and infectious complications. Although people with diabetes make up about only 2-5% of the general population, they account for 40-45% of all patients who undergo amputations because of their propensity for peripheral vascular disease. The risk of amputation is correlated with a susceptibility to diabetes.

Amputations occur on the right side and on the left side in equal proportion.

Etiology

Amputations might be required for several reasons. Peripheral vascular disease predominates and is seen in about 65% of cases. It often occurs with diabetes. Patients with this disease are usually aged 60-75 years. Amputations due to trauma occur in 25% of all cases; most of these patients are aged 17-55 years.

In the pediatric age group, trauma causes about 75% of acquired amputations, usually from accidents with power tools such as lawnmowers. Malignancy with or without other disease is the third most common cause, leading to about 5% of amputations. Cancers such as osteogenic sarcoma are involved in about 25% of acquired amputations in those aged 10-20 years.

Congenital limb deficiency results in as many as 5% of all amputations, and 60% of the cases involve children. Congenital cases outnumber acquired cases with a ratio of 2:1 in the pediatric age group. GAIT CYCLE Section 3 of 8

Author Information Introduction Gait Cycle Adaptive Strategies Of Those Who Have Undergone Amputations Abnormal Transtibial Gait Abnormal Transfemoral Gait Summary Bibliography

Before any kind of pathologic gait can be examined and analyzed, the patient's normal gait and the terminology used in describing the different components of normal gait must be understood.

Gait is defined as the manner or style of walking. A full gait cycle is defined as the time interval between two successive occurrences of one of the repetitive events of walking. The gait cycle comprises 7 major components, as follows:

- Initial contact
- Opposite toe-off
- Midstance and heel rise
- Opposite initial contact
- Toe-off
- Feet adjacent

• Tibia vertical

Although any component can be used as the starting point in the gait cycle, starting with initial contact is advantageous. For example, if the left foot is the starting point or reference, the cycle continues until the left foot makes initial contact again. The distance covered during this cycle is called a stride length. A step length is one half the stride length.

The components of the gait cycle can be divided into 2 phases: (1) the stance phase and (2) the swing phase. The stance phase is when the foot is making contact with the ground. It covers the first 4 components of the gait cycle. The swing phase is when the foot is moving forward through the air and consists of the other 3 components of the gait cycle. Each of the 7 components of the gait cycle is examined in more detail below, with reference to the particular muscle activity in the lower extremity.

Initial contact

Initial contact, frequently called heel strike, is the first component of the gait cycle. On heel contact, the major role of the lower extremity is to absorb the impact forces created when the foot strikes the ground. The anatomy and morphology of the heel pad, along with control of the ankle as the foot moves from the heel to the forefoot, allows the absorption of the forces. On contact, the hip extensors, gluteus maximus, and hamstrings create internal extensor movement at the hip. These muscles concentrically contract and propagate an extension force at the hip joint. Concurrently, the knee demonstrates an internal flexor moment secondary to the contraction of the hamstrings to block hyperextension at the end of the swing phase. The ankle is usually kept in the neutral position on initial contact in preparation for the next phase.

Loading response

The loading response is the double support period between the components initial contact and opposite toe-off. The foot is lowered to the ground by means of plantarflexion of the ankle, which is simultaneously resisted by dorsiflexion produced by tibialis anterior. These actions maintain control of the foot and allow for its gentle lowering to the ground. At this point, the center of gravity is at its lowest point in the gait cycle.

Opposite toe-off

After the loading response occurs, opposite toe-off is the next component of the gait cycle. It is the beginning of midstance and the first period of single support. The forefoot impacts the ground at about the same time opposite toe-off occurs. The hips move steadily through extension with power, while the knee generates an external flexor movement. The quadriceps muscles eccentrically contract, absorbing energy and allowing the knee to act like a spring (prohibiting the vertical force from rising too rapidly). The direction of the ankles shifts from plantarflexion to dorsiflexion when the tibia passes over the stationary foot.

Midstance

Midstance is the period between opposite toe-off and heel rise. It signifies the moment when the swing-phase leg passes the stance-phase leg. During the period, the hip begins to lose its extensor movement with a decline in contraction of the gluteus maximus and hamstrings. The knee shifts its motion from flexion to extension and at the same time generates power. As the tibia moves forward over the ankle due to the inertia created by the trunk, it undergoes external rotation concomitant with forefoot supination. The ankle continues to shift from plantarflexion to dorsiflexion with the triceps surae muscle (gastrocsoleus complex) contracting eccentrically. The speed at which the center of mass of the body moves over the supporting stance-phase limb is regulated by the power created during plantarflexion of the ankle.

Heel rise

Heel rise is the next component of the gait cycle. As the name describes, the heel begins to lift from the walking surface. A progressive internal flexor moment is created at the hip, while an internal flexor knee moment is initiated when the quadriceps muscles stops contracting before heel rise. The knee action is thought to occur because the upper body moves faster that the tibia and because the triceps surae retards the forward motion of the tibia while the femur steadily moves forward. These motions create an external extensor moment opposed by an internal flexor moment at the knee. The ankle has an internal dorsiflexor moment as the soleus and the gastrocnemius begin to progressively contract.

Opposite initial contact

Opposite initial contact signifies the start of preswing. With the start of opposite initial contact, the

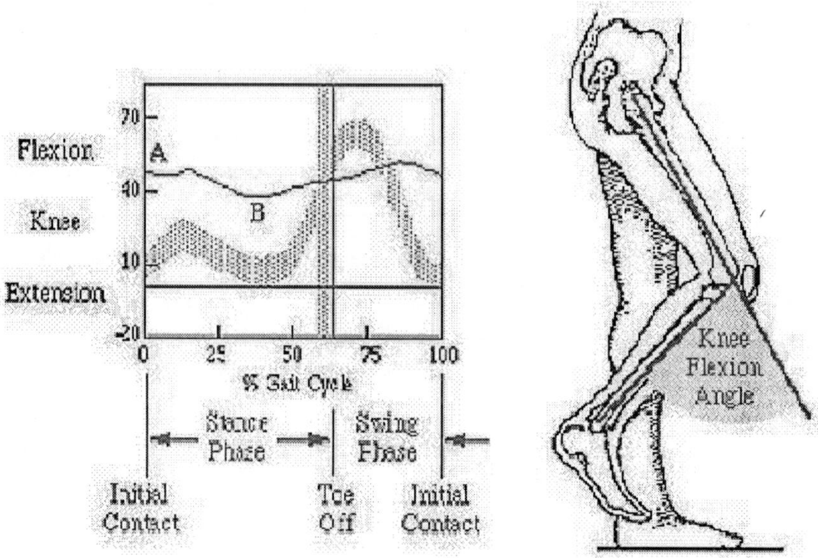

hip and knee begin to flex while the ankle is plantarflexing. Of note, the body now pivots on the forefoot instead of the ankle. This is the component of the gait cycle that creates the most power; the triceps surae and other secondary ankle plantarflexors create a corresponding internal plantarflexor moment in response to the external dorsiflexor moment. These muscles use an eccentric contraction.

Consequently, the triceps surae is used to impede the body's momentum instead of launching it forward. This allows favorable ankle stabilization and a decline in the amount of fall by the body's center of gravity. Ergo, the component of heel rise mentioned previously would be more appropriately named roll off. In addition, the adductor longus muscle acts as the primary hip flexor in this phase, and the rectus femoris muscle contracts eccentrically to stabilize knee flexion. All of these actions assist with forward acceleration of the leg into the swing phase.

Toe-off

The next component, toe-off, marks the end of the stance phase and the beginning of the swing phase. Muscle contraction changes from eccentric in stance phase to concentric in swing phase. Toe-off occurs at about the 60% point of the gait cycle.

An internal flexor moment occurs at the hip secondary to inertial forces and contraction of the adductor longus and iliopsoas muscles. The rectus femoris muscle contracts to prevent excessive knee flexion and the internal plantarflexion moment loses power at the ankle as the toe leaves the ground.

Feet adjacent

Feet adjacent is the next stage of the swing phase. A lot of power is generated at the hip by the rectus femoris, adductor, and iliopsoas muscles to move the leg forward through the swing phase.

Eccentric contraction of the quadriceps continues throughout the first half of the swing phase to regulate the rate and extent of knee flexion. Some of the kinetic energy created through contraction and inertia is transferred to the trunk as the swing leg is decelerated at the end of this phase.

Tibia vertical

The last component of the gait cycle is tibia vertical, which is signified by the tibia of the swinging leg becoming vertical. This is the period between midswing and terminal swing.

In this phase, the knee extends in preparation for the beginning of the stance phase. This extension is accomplished through 2 mechanisms: (1) Concentric contraction of the hip extensors causes a posterior rotation at the thigh, and (2) inertia created at the foot and shank allows it to continue forward.

Eccentric contractions of the hamstrings gradually decelerate the foot and shank until the knee arrives at an extended position. At this point, the swing phase leg not only is prepared for the next stance phase but also helped with trunk acceleration. As mentioned before, some of the kinetic energy created during the swing phase is transferred to the trunk upon deceleration.

This kinetic energy causes greater trunk acceleration than that due to the energy created during heel rise.

Adaptive Strategies of those who have Undergone Amputations

People who have undergone amputations have incorporated different muscles and adaptive strategies to ensure a smooth and well-coordinated gait pattern. An important concept must be remembered in analyzing any pathologic gait (including the gait of those who have undergone amputations): An individual's gait is optimized to use the least amount of energy to cover the greatest distance.

Several factors need to be accounted for when thinking about the energy costs of prosthetic ambulation.

One is the actual metabolic costs (peak exercise oxygen consumption [VO2] in mL/kg/m) of the person who has undergone amputation compared to that of intact people. That is to say, metabolic cost is measured based on the metabolic oxygen consumption in relation to the distance walked. Clinically, metabolic cost is a gauge of endurance. In the healthy intact person, walking is more efficacious at self-selected walking speeds. The metabolic cost rises at slower or faster rates of ambulation.

Comparatively, persons who have undergone amputations exhibit the same correlation of metabolic cost and ambulation speed with the metabolic costs exceeding the norm at any given walking speed. The increase in metabolic cost for persons who have undergone amputations means the gait is inefficient compared to that of healthy intact persons, who require less endurance for any given distance. Those who have undergone traumatic transtibial (TT) amputations use at least 25% more energy during gait, whereas someone who has undergone a vascular TT amputation has at least a 40% increase in energy expenditure. A person who has undergone a traumatic transfemoral (TF) amputation uses at least 68% more energy during gait, while a person who has undergone a vascular TF amputation uses at least 100% more energy.

A pathologic gait is an inefficient mode of locomotion that usually requires considerably more energy than a normal gait. Patients may adopt many kinds of abnormal movements to minimize their energy usage. Two methods of energy optimization exist: those involving energy transfers and those involving movements that minimize the displacement of the center of gravity.

The 6 optimizations, or determinants of gait, are as follows:

- Pelvic rotation
- Pelvic obliquity
- Knee flexion in the stance phase
- Ankle mechanisms
- Foot mechanisms
- Lateral displacement of the body

These optimizations can be combined to create a smoother gait and reduced energy expenditure by minimizing the downward and lateral motion of the center of gravity. With the healthy intact person incorporating these movements, displacement of the center of gravity is approximately 2.3 cm in each direction.

Patients with various amputations have adopted strategies for minimizing their energy consumption in ambulation. In persons who have undergone TT amputations, the timing and magnitude of the muscular work patterns in the intact limb are correlated with a normal gait. However, the prosthetic limb must make up for the energy absorption of the quadriceps and triceps surae muscles and for the eccentric power generation of the triceps surae.

During the stance phase, the prosthetic limb performs about 50% of the work of normal muscle. Energy absorption by the knee extensors and energy generation by the prosthetic foot are substantially reduced. To offset the loss of power from triceps surae with roll-off, the person who has undergone amputation changes the biomechanics of both the prosthetic limb in the stance phase and the intact limb during the swing phase. In the prosthetic limb, the primary energy absorbers and generators shift to the hip extensors during the stance phase. Also, during swing phase, the muscular work components substantially increase in the intact limb. The excess mechanical work is ultimately transmitted to the trunk during terminal swing-phase deceleration. The increase in the forward momentum of the trunk compensates for the loss of power generation with the prosthetic foot.

The person who has undergone TF amputation must deal with the loss of the foot, ankle, and the knee. The biggest apprehension of the person who has undergone TF amputation is the prevention of knee buckling. Besides the actual prosthetic hardware and knee alignment to add stability, the biomechanics of the gait are changed to provide additional stability. The person who has undergone TF amputation does not allow knee flexion in the first 30-40% of the stance phase. This limitation minimizes the likelihood of knee buckling. In addition, the hip extensors help maintain hip extension through closed kinetic chain mechanisms.

In the opposite initial contact part of the gait cycle, the ankle plantarflexors, particularly the triceps surae and the hip flexors, contract to generate power for the acceleration of the leg forward into the swing phase. Although the prosthetic limb is only approximately 30% of its normal mass with a TF amputation, the hip flexors

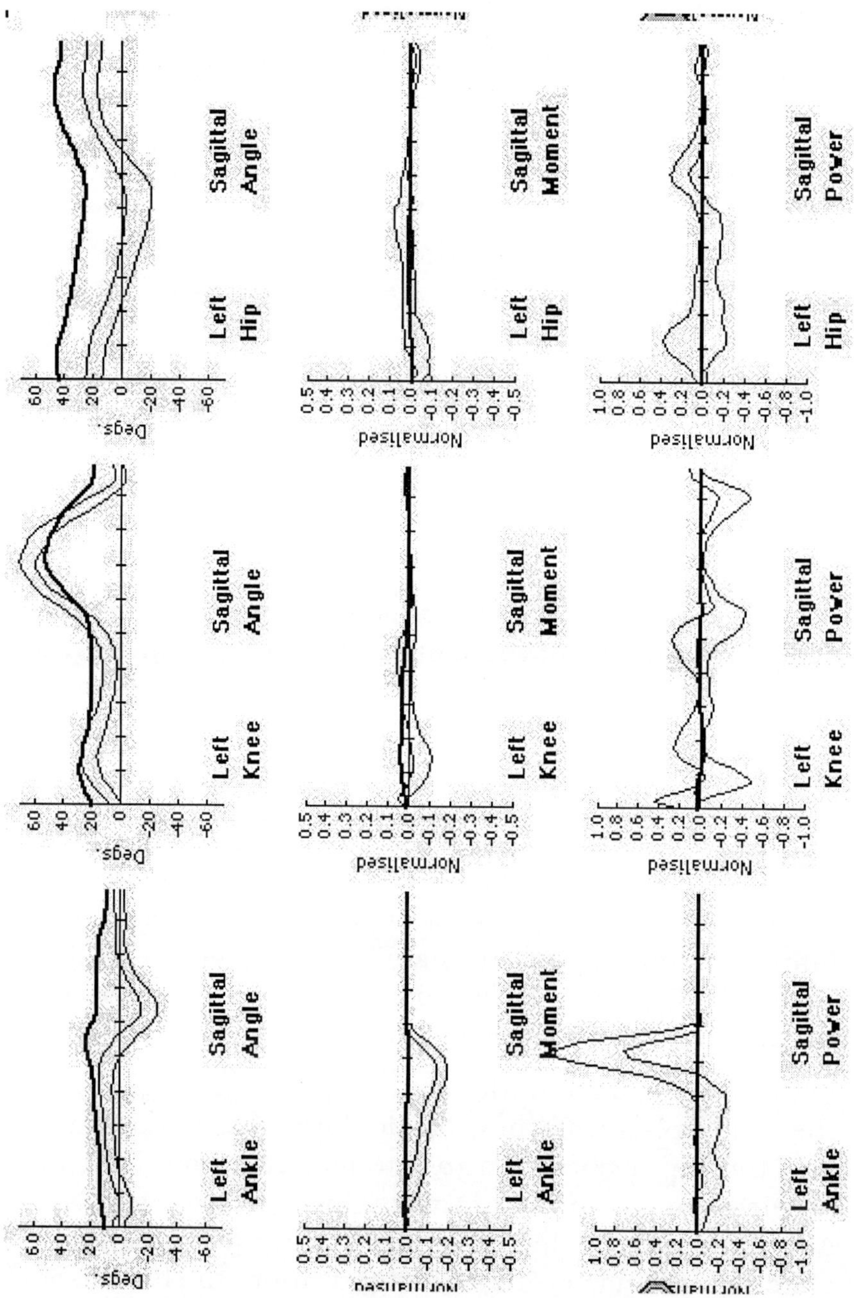

Left Hip Sagittal Angle
Left Knee Sagittal Angle
Left Ankle Sagittal Angle
Left Hip Sagittal Moment
Left Knee Sagittal Moment
Left Ankle Sagittal Moment
Left Hip Sagittal Power
Left Knee Sagittal Power
Left Ankle Sagittal Power
Degs.
Normalised

must generate the same power as a normal limb. The intact limb adjusts to compensate for the prosthetic limb in these cases.

During the stance phase in the intact limb, generated energy is augmented by the hip extensors and the ankle plantarflexors. In this way, person who has undergone amputation tries to offset the loss of power from the triceps surae in the prosthetic limb. During the swing phase, the biomechanics of the person who has undergone TF amputation mimics those of normal gait, including the energy-absorbing function of the quadriceps performed through the prosthetic hydraulic knee unit.

The common gait deviations of TT and TF prosthetic gait are briefly addressed in terms of the types of amputation and the times at which the deviations occur in the gait cycle.

Stance-phase problems can occur in the gait of individuals with a TT prosthetic. Inappropriate knee flexion can occur in the early stance phase, causing knee instability. Several problems could arise from this flexion, including excessive ankle dorsiflexion, socket flexion, and posterior foot placement. Knee hyperextension could also occur in the early stance phase, emanating from ankle plantarflexion or socket extension, weak knee extensors, anterior foot placement, or inadequate prosthetic foot selection.

Mediolateral knee thrust can also be observed in the stance phase. This is usually derived from inadequate side-to-side placement of the foot, excessive angulation of the socket, or wide mediolateral proximal socket dimensions that cause decreased knee control. If an individual who has undergone a TT amputation is noted to have a foot slap in his or her gait, it may be a result of excessive socket flexion or foot dorsiflexion, the uneven placement of the foot, or a deficient heel height for proper prosthetic alignment. Excessive forward progression of the tibia, or a drop-off gait can be caused by impaired rollover, shortening of the contralateral step length and swing time, and delayed heel-off.

External rotation can occur at 2 different phases of the gait cycle: heel strike or late stance. If external rotation occurs during heel strike, the etiology could be a solid ankle cushion heel (SACH) durometer that is too dense, an articulated foot plantarflexion bumper that is too hard, or misplacement of the suspension cuff-retention points. If external rotation occurs in late stance, it can be caused by inadequate excessive anterior placement of the foot, excessive foot plantarflexion, or excessive hardness of the forefoot.

Early heel rise could result from inadequate placement of the foot (posterior), flexion contracture in the hip or the knee that was not accounted for in fitting the prosthetic, or excessive softness of the forefoot. Contralateral early heel rise or vaulting is a pathologic gait that allows clearance of the prosthetic limb with decreased hip and knee flexion. Vaulting compensates for a prosthesis that is too long, inadequate suspension of the prosthesis, or a learned gait pattern.

Fewer gait problems are involved with the swing phase than with the stance phase. The objective of the swing phase is forward advancement of the nonweightbearing limb. When prosthetic limb clearance is poor, the gait becomes pathologic. Most predicaments occur because of poor suspension, a prosthesis that is too long, insufficient prosthetic knee flexion, or inadequate transfer of power from the residual limb to the prosthesis that decreases or delays knee flexion. A coordinated, smooth, swing phase is facilitated by energy-efficient limb clearance, which is enabled by synchronized motion at the hip and knee joints and by total joint displacement.

Foot drag is one of the most common problems of swing phase. It is usually caused by inadequate suspension of the prosthesis, a prosthesis that is too long, or lower-limb weakness in the hip abductors or ankle plantarflexors on the contralateral side. Any abnormal limb rotation is observed during the gait trial is usually caused by insufficient suspension of the prosthesis, misplacement of the suspension cuff-retention points, or overshooting (infringement) of the hip or knee flexors to evade foot drop.

Limited knee extension or flexion problems can always be traced back to mechanical contractures, problems with the suspension, or problems with the knee joint in relation to a thigh corset.

ABNORMAL TRANSFEMORAL GAIT

The gait deviations in persons who have undergone TF amputations differ from those of people who have undergone TT amputations in a couple ways. As alluded to previously, knee flexion in the stance phase is one of the most common problems related to gait instability with TF amputations. If a patient with a TF amputation is concerned about putting weight on the prosthetic leg because the knee flexion moment creates instability, an inefficient gait pattern results. For these patients, one of several unique models of prosthetic knees can be prescribed based on his or her individual needs.

Additional etiologies of knee flexion in stance are a hard SACH durometer, excessive foot dorsiflexion, excessive socket flexion, weak hip extensors, or decreased weightbearing. Prolonged knee extension in the stance phase is another problem that can occur with TF amputations. This extension can result in shortening of the contralateral step and an increase in the vertical displacement of the center of gravity.

If lateral hip thrust is the problem, immediate attention should be given to the wide dimensions of the mediolateral proximal socket that affect the stability of the hip. If the socket fits well, the patient could have weak hip abductors, or the hip adductors might not have been reattached at the time of surgery.

The most prevalent gait abnormality with TF amputations is ipsilateral trunk bending in the stance phase. Similar to the compensation for Trendelenburg gait, this abnormality could indicate weak hip abductors on the ipsilateral side or an inappropriately short prosthesis. Occasionally, a person who has undergone a TF amputation can have an awkward downward movement of the upper body over the prosthesis, especially during fast walking. This is referred to as a drop-off gait in the late stance. The foot of the prosthesis should be checked for excessive dorsiflexion whenever external rotation of the leg occurs, either during heel strike or in the late stance. The foot should be examined for excessively hard materials. As with TT amputations, TF amputations can be associated with some of the same problems in the stance phase; the etiologies of the abnormal biomechanics are similar.

In people who have undergone TF amputations, gait abnormalities in swing phase are limited in number. Stiff-knee gait patterns can be the consequence of excessive knee stability in the joint that makes the creation of a flexion moment at the knee difficult. Circumduction, or the swing of the limb in a wide arc, usually indicates inadequate suspension or excessive length of the prosthesis. Abnormal axis rotation at the knee that results in a whipping motion is usually due to incorrect alignment of the prosthesis at the knee.

Gait cycle

Walking is the most convenient way to travel short distances. Free joint mobility and appropriate muscle force increases walking efficiency. As the body moves forward, one limb typically provides support while the other limb is advanced in preparation for its role as the support limb. The gait cycle in its simplest form is comprised of stance and swing phases. The stance phase further is subdivided into 3 segments, including

- Initial double stance
- Single limb stance
- Terminal double limb stance.

Each double stance period accounts for 10% of the gait cycle (GC), while single stance typically represents

40% (60% total). The 2 limbs typically do not share the load equally during double stance periods. The swing phase for this same limb is the remaining 40% of the GC. Ipsilateral swing temporally corresponds to single stance by the contralateral limb. Slight variations occur in the percentage of stance and swing related to gait velocity. Duration of each aspect of stance decreases as walking velocity increases. The transition from walking to running is marked by elimination of double support period(s).

A stride is the equivalent of a gait cycle. The duration of a stride is the interval between sequential initial floor contacts by the same limb. A step is recognized as the interval between sequential floor contacts by ipsilateral and contralateral limbs. Two steps make up each gait cycle, which is roughly symmetric in normal individuals.

Gait Cycle Phasing

A consistent sequence of motions is performed at each of the lower extremity joints during locomotion. Each stride contains 8 relevant phases. Stance is comprised of 5 gait phases (ie, initial contact, loading response, mid stance, terminal stance, preswing), with the remaining 3 phases occurring during swing.

The first 2 gait phases (0-10% GC) occur during initial double support. These phases include initial contact and the loading response. Initial contact often is referred to as heel strike. While this term is appropriate in normal gait, many patients achieve heel contact later in the gait cycle, if at all. The joint motion during this phase allows the transfer of weight onto the new stance

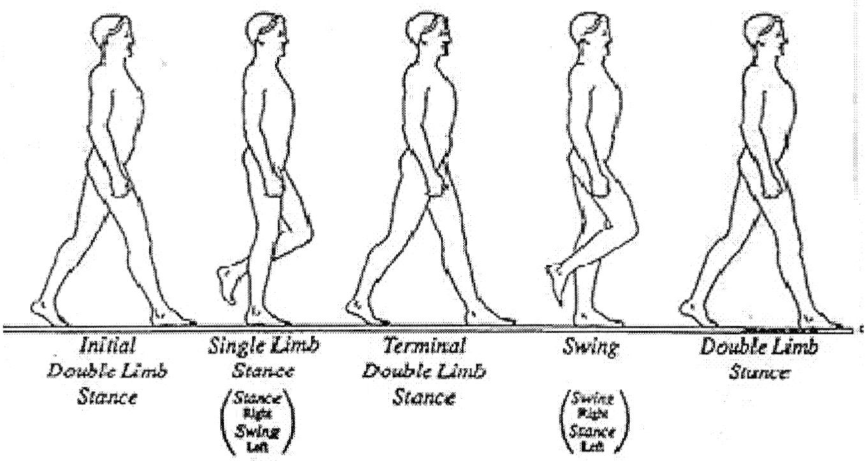

phase leg while attenuating shock, preserving gait velocity, and maintaining stability.

Swing phase by the contralateral limb corresponds with single support by the ipsilateral limb to support body weight in the sagittal and coronal planes. The first half of single support is termed mid stance (10-30% GC) and is involved with progression of the body center of mass over the support foot. This trend continues through terminal stance (30-50% GC). This phase includes heel rise of the support foot and terminates with contralateral foot contact.

The final stance element, preswing (50-60% GC), is related functionally more to the swing phase that follows than to the preceding stance phase events. Preswing begins with terminal double support and ends with toe-off of the ipsilateral limb.

Three unique phases characterize swing, including initial swing (60-73% GC), mid swing (73-87% GC), and terminal swing (87-100% GC). The swing phase achieves foot clearance and advancing of the trailing limb.

Shock Absorption

Shock absorption and energy conservation are important aspects of efficient gait. Altered joint motion or absent muscle forces may increase joint reaction (contact) forces and lead subsequently to additional pathology. In early stance, nearly 60% of one's body weight is loaded abruptly (less than 20 milliseconds) onto the ipsilateral limb. This abrupt impact is attenuated at each of the lower extremity joints. Loading response plantar flexion is passive, substantially restrained by eccentric work of pretibial muscles. The absorptive work by pretibial muscles delays forefoot contact until late in the initial double support period (7-8% GC).

At initial contact, external (ground reaction) forces applied to the contact foot produce a tendency toward knee flexion. Repositioning the knee (recurvatum) increases knee mechanical stability, but at the cost of increased contact forces and shock generation. A balance between knee stability and shock absorption is achieved by eccentric quadriceps contractions during loading response. The impact of loading is minimized at the hip during single support through hip abductor muscle contraction.

Energy Conservation

Ambulation always is associated with metabolic costs. These costs are relatively minor in normal adults performing free speed level walking. The self-selected walking speed in normal adults closely matches the velocity that minimizes metabolic work. This association does not apply with gait pathology. Walking velocity, energy cost per time, and energy cost per distance are considerations when the patient is making choices about walking versus wheelchair mobility. Gait velocity typically decreases with all neuromuscular pathology, and the reduction is related to the magnitude of the pathology. Energy cost per unit of time may not change substantially, even with severe involvement. Energy cost per unit of time is maintained by decreasing walking velocity considerably. Energy cost per unit of time does not change markedly following stroke, as compared to changes associated with aging; however, the energy requirement per distance traveled is more than 3 times normal.

In this same population, wheelchair use cuts energy cost per distance in half and decreases cost per minute slightly, while preserving ambulation velocity. Similar trends are observed when examining various energy cost parameters in individuals with spinal cord injury (SCI), myelomeningocele, and increasing levels of amputation. Energy cost to travel a prescribed distance increases (greater than 500% increase in myelomeningocele with bilateral knee-ankle-foot orthoses [KAFO]), while oxygen cost per minute is maintained by decreasing walking velocity substantially. Often the critical factor in selecting a wheelchair for mobility is the energy requirement to traverse a given distance. Most individuals self-select wheelchair mobility when cost per distance exceeds 300% of normal values.

METHODS OF ANALYSIS

Most commonly, observational gait analysis is appropriate to characterize most gait pathologies. This approach is sufficient to note gross abnormalities in walking; however, as walking complexity increases with organic pathology, objective analysis becomes necessary. The measurement systems that follow may be used individually or collectively. The choice of method is based on clinical need, financial considerations, and staffing at the specific laboratory. Typically, motion and force data are compiled simultaneously.

Motion

Instrumented motion analysis is a logical extension of observational gait analysis. The level of complexity involved in examining 3 joints each in 2 limbs is such that few individuals can perform this task consistently. Measurement of human motion is complex. Although most gait motion occurs in the sagittal plane, subtle rotations in the other planes are clinically important. Analysis of motion in the sagittal plane is confounded if that motion does not lie within the plane recorded by a single camera. Rotations of the limb are attenuated when the limb is internally or externally rotated with respect to the camera's plane. Three-dimensional motion analysis overcomes this drawback.

Position of joint centers of rotation is estimated by markers placed on the skin surface. Markers may be enhanced with passive markers or active light-emitting diodes. Motion of the limb segments about the joint centers is recorded. At least 3 markers are required per limb segment, and the position of each marker is recorded using multiple cameras. A calibration system is used to translate film to real-life dimensions. Angular position of each segment may be determined for each percent gait cycle interval. Angular velocity and acceleration of the limb segments are obtained by mathematical differentiation and smoothing of limb position data. Motion data may be combined with analysis of external forces that act on the body.

An alternative technique to quantify motion is through use of electrogoniometers. A triaxial electrogoniometer has parallelograms and potentiometers for the sagittal, coronal, and transverse planes. Electrogoniometers have several limitations, but the advantages of this method include convenience, ease of use, immediate availability of data, and decreased expense when compared to video acquisition techniques.

External forces

Calculation of joint moments (torque) and reaction forces between segments is dependent on knowledge of the inertial components of the respective segments (kinematics), body segment parameters, and external forces (kinetics) that affect the body.

The magnitude and distribution of segment masses with respect to joint axes are obtained from cadaveric data or mathematical modelling of limb segments. The contact (ground reaction) force applied at the distal segment is measured with a force platform. This thin plate typically measures forces and moments in 3 dimensions about the foot center of pressure. Oscillation of the center of pressure may be obtained in the same manner.

Moments and power

Integration of external force, center of pressure, unique body segment parameters, and motion data yields information on joint moments, joint power, and reaction forces between segments using standard inverse dynamics techniques. The role of muscle groups is inferred from the magnitude and sign of the moments and power at the respective lower extremity joints.

Dynamic electromyography

Muscle action cannot be measured directly. The electromyogram (EMG) allows indirect measurement of muscle activity. While single motor units are analyzed routinely in clinical electrodiagnostic studies, this level of analysis is not performed as part of a routine gait analysis. A typical kinesiological (dynamic) EMG represents the activity of multiple motor units. The stochastic nature of the waveform confounds simple analysis. The interference pattern recorded demonstrates both mechanisms used to increase force output and increase in the number and in the firing rate of motor units.

Kinesiological EMG contains important information about the timing and relative intensity of the signal. Timing of the signal is straightforward. Muscle electrical activity precedes force generation by 40-120 milliseconds. This electromechanical delay is associated with compliance of the tendon at the onset of the EMG signal and continued binding of actin-

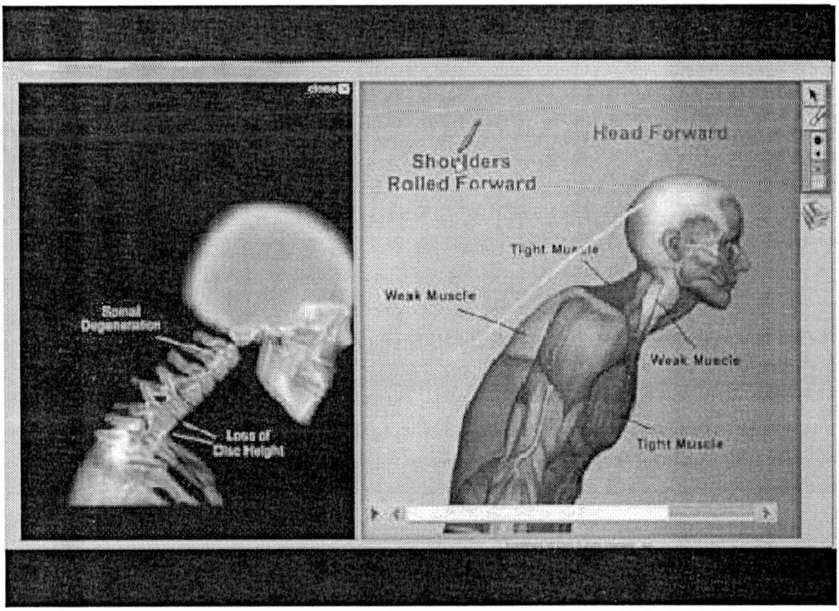

myosin crossbridges after termination of neural drive related to delays in calcium resequestration.

Muscle force cannot be estimated directly from the relative intensity of the signal. A linear relationship between EMG intensity and force output has been demonstrated only in isometric contractions. Presentation of the quantified EMG may be in absolute values (volts) or as a percentage of some normalized standard. Absolute voltage does not represent clinically significant effort, as the electrode type and placement substantially affect signal magnitude. Normalization of muscle force output allows for comparisons across muscles related to relative intensity. Gait EMG is expressed as a percentage of maximum muscle contraction. Another technique is to express gait EMG output as a percentage of gait maximum. This latter technique often must be used in persons who cannot give a maximum voluntary contraction as a result of decreased neural control. A disadvantage is that peak values of weak and strong muscle forces are defined as 100%.

Mechanical and metabolic efficiency

Mechanical work is the integral of force and velocity over time and the product of joint power and joint angular velocity. Mechanical work includes (1) changes in the mechanical energy of the body links; (2) energy expenditure for mechanical movement as the sum of the positive values, including general center of mass energy changes (external work); and (3) changes in energy in the links in their movement relative to the center of mass.

Limb movement requires energy for muscle contraction. Mechanical work does not equal metabolic work in most instances. For example, mechanical work in a cyclic motion with constant average speed (without dissipation of energy) is equal to 0 since the mechanical energy of the system has not changed (net 0 paradox). Metabolic energy is required for mechanical movement in this case. Energy metabolism is another means of assessing the cost of locomotion.

Energy expenditure may be determined by indirect calorimetry; however, in most recent literature, the O_2 gas volume is reported without conversion to calories. The volume of oxygen consumption per body weight enables intersubject comparisons and provides information on overall gait performance. Measurement of oxygen consumption (metabolic energy expenditure,

VO_2) generally is reported under standard conditions of temperature (0°C), pressure (760 mm Hg), and dry conditions (no water vapor). After 2-3 minutes of exercise at a constant submaximal workload, the rate of oxygen consumption reaches a level sufficient to meet tissue demand for oxygen. Parameters of physical work (cardiac output, heart rate, and respiratory rate) reach a steady state. Energy consumption for the activity at this time is reflected by the rate of oxygen consumption. The O2 rate determines the intensity and duration the exercise can be performed.

The rate of oxygen consumption is lowest at comfortable walking speeds in normal adults (approximately one third of maximal aerobic capacity). Slight increases in energy demands are demonstrated at slower walking speeds; more substantial increases are observed as walking speed increases above the upper limits of normal. Energy expenditure at each walking speed is not related to whether the patient is male or female.

NORMAL GAIT

Ankle/Foot

The arcs of motion at the ankle are relatively small; yet, they are essential for shock absorption and progression of the body's center of mass. The ankle plantar flexes throughout loading response. Dorsiflexion begins with single support, as the tibia rotates forward over the fixed foot. Rapid plantar flexion begins at terminal double support, with maximum plantar flexor position of 30° attained at toe-off. This action marks the initiation of swing with dorsiflexion throughout the 3

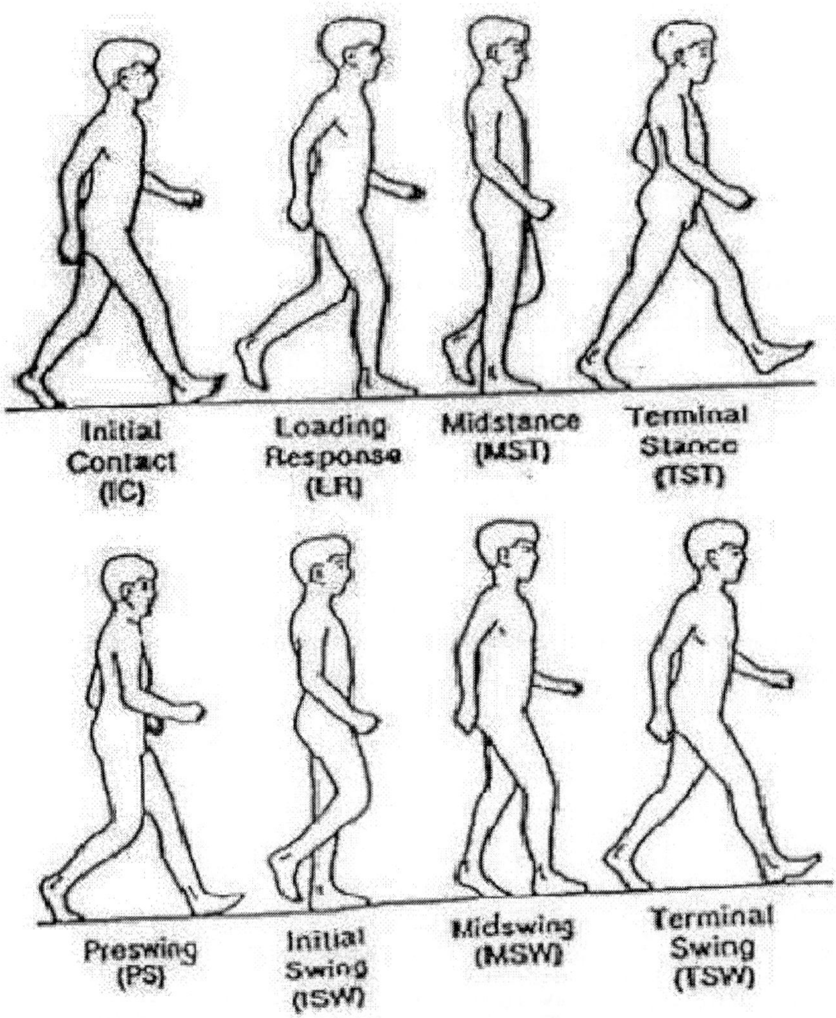

swing-phase segments.

Motor control at the ankle is understood most easily by commencing with swing phase muscle activity. Ankle dorsiflexors undergo brief eccentric contraction in preswing, followed shortly by concentric contraction at the initiation of swing. This contraction sequence increases mechanical efficiency and assures foot clearance. Continued pretibial muscle isometric contraction through swing maintains this neutral or slightly dorsiflexed posture. Subsequent loading response is notable for eccentric contraction of the pretibial muscles to control plantar flexion. A brief period of co-contraction of ankle plantar flexors and dorsiflexors occurs at the transition from initial stance double support to single support. This co-contraction interval increases limb stability and may smooth the transition from double to single support.

The orientation of the ankle and subtalar axes couples loading response dorsiflexion with eversion. Both are attenuated by eccentric contraction of the ankle inverters (ie, posterior tibialis). The plantar flexors begin force generation in single support, with peak activity late in terminal stance and preswing. The absorptive power demonstrated in single support is related to their role in restraining forward tibial rotation. The timing of the triceps surae and perimalleolar muscles is similar to that of the triceps surae (gastrocnemius plus soleus) that supplies most of the ankle plantar flexor moment. The ankle then is plantar flexed vigorously during preswing.

The role of the calf muscles during preswing is controversial. Some authors describe this gait phase as push-off and suggest that muscle force by the ipsilateral calf actively propels the limb (and body center of mass) forward. An alternative model is proposed by Perry, who states that the ipsilateral limb makes no active contribution to the push-off. A third model is that active plantar flexion occurs at the ankle (positive power) and does not serve to propel the body forward (no increase in walking velocity), but, instead, functions as part of a closed kinetic chain to initiate knee and hip flexion in preparation for swing. This phenomenon may account for the increased knee and hip power requirements in individuals who do not plantar flex actively in preswing (ie, transtibial amputees).

Knee

Most knee motion is limited to the sagittal plane. The knee travels from slight knee flexion at initial contact (5°) to nearly 20° of flexion by the end of loading response. The knee then extends (net flexion) through single support, with peak stance phase extension at 40% GC.

At the conclusion of terminal stance and preswing, knee flexion is rapid, continuing through initial swing until peak knee flexion (60°) occurs. This trend then is reversed, with knee extension continuing through terminal swing. Peak knee extension occurs slightly before the end of the swing phase, with minor flexion occurring in preparation for the subsequent stance phase.

The role of knee muscles, like that of ankle muscles, is understood most easily if one begins the analysis as the limb is in swing. In early swing phase, knee flexion is passive, resulting from active plantar flexion and hip flexion.

During swing, motion at the hip changes from flexion to extension, with the knee passively extended as a result of this change of hip joint direction. All 3 hamstrings (long head of the biceps femoris, semimembranosus, semitendinosus) are active in mid-to-late swing to decelerate the extending knee. The quadriceps is also active in terminal swing. This co-contraction of knee flexors and extensors prepares the limb for weight acceptance that follows shortly. The quadriceps continues to be active in loading support. The eccentric activity of these muscles attenuates the shock of weight acceptance, while preventing excess knee flexion (<20°).

Both the hamstring and quadriceps muscles are quiescent during mid stance while the knee is extended passively. The role of the remaining quadriceps muscle is different. The rectus femoris is active electrically for only a brief period corresponding with preswing and initial swing. Although this muscle crosses and extends the knee, its role in gait is to assist in flexion at the hip as swing commences.

Hip

The gluteus maximus timing and relative intensity are similar to those demonstrated by the other hip extensors (eg, hamstrings). During late swing, the gluteus maximus functions to reverse hip flexion to extension. The gluteus maximus, generally the body's single strongest muscle, resists external forces from loading response that would flex the hip excessively (eg, jack-knifing). A similar EMG profile and role are demonstrated by the adductor magnus. Unlike in the knee and ankle, there is a substantial amount of frontal plane motion at the hip. During single support, the mass of the torso tends to rotate the body about the stance limb hip joint axis (eg, contralateral lateral tilt). Typically, this motion is limited by eccentric activity of the gluteus medius, gluteus minimus, and, to a lesser extent, the tensor fascia lata.

Hip flexion marks transition from stance to swing. This motion advances the trailing limb and assists in foot clearance, which is accomplished by concentric contractions of the iliopsoas, rectus femoris, and sartorius muscles. Swing phase activity of the hip adductors brings the feet toward the line of progression, decreasing the energy demands of walking.

PATHOLOGICAL GAIT

Weakness

Insufficient force output by muscles may result from disuse, primary muscle disease, or neurologic impairment. Substitution of impaired motor function frequently is possible, and reduction of walking velocity

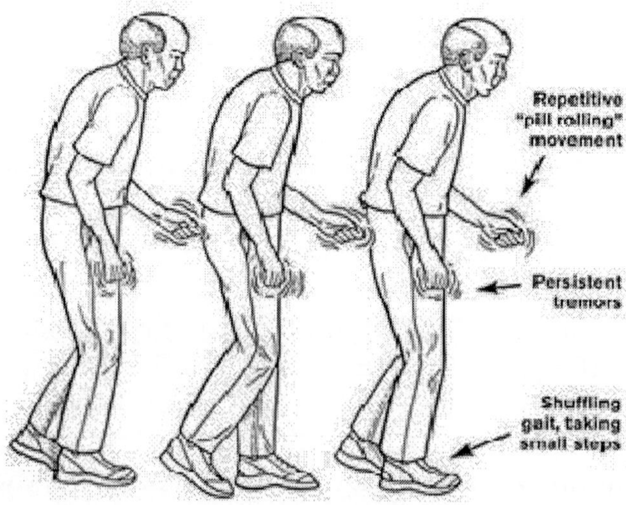

further reduces demand on muscles. Muscle force requirements are trivial in normal individuals. Less than 25% of normal strength (manual muscle test grade 3+/5) is needed for locomotion. In cases of disease, with decreased maximum muscle force, functional reserve is lost. Endurance is compromised, and community-level ambulation may not be possible. Selective loss of muscles (or muscle groups) is demonstrated by characteristic gait patterns. In each case, orthotic management is targeted at preventing excessive motion.

Uncompensated calf weakness results in diminished mid stance control of the forwardly rotating tibia. Substitution for calf weakness is difficult. The increased amount and rate of dorsiflexion increases the functional demands on the quadriceps to maintain limb stability. Alternatively, tibial advancement is curtailed with resultant genu recurvatum, decreasing the work of the quadriceps. Unfortunately, this gait alteration frequently initiates knee joint pathology. Other compensatory maneuvers include reducing step velocity and step length.

The consequence of pretibial muscle weakness is increased plantar flexion. With mild weakness, foot slap occurs during loading response. With more extensive dorsiflexion weakness, foot drop and toe drag are observed during swing phase. Compensation is achieved through circumduction of the ipsilateral limb, increased ipsilateral knee plus hip flexion, and hip hiking of the contralateral limb. Each of these tendencies assists in swing-phase toe clearance. Of these compensations, circumduction is the most energy efficient and most commonly observed technique for dorsiflexor insufficiency.

Quadriceps weakness diminishes knee control, and deficits in stance are most pronounced. External forces tend to hyperflex the knee, and a variety of compensations are employed to preserve stability in weight bearing. Compensations begin prior to weight acceptance (late swing) and continue through that limb's support activity. Late swing hip flexion leads to passive knee extension through momentum transfer. Stance phase increased knee flexion is attenuated by hip extension and premature plantar flexion. Alternatively, external rotation of the affected limb orients the external force vector medial to the joint axis, minimizing the tendency toward knee flexion.

Isolated hamstring weakness is an uncommon gait deficit. Isolated hip flexor weakness is uncommon. Clinical presentation includes decreased walking velocity or decreased hip range of motion (ROM). Reduction of hip extensor forces, which may be secondary to paralysis or muscle lengthening, leads to increases in anterior pelvic tilt during stance.

Hip adductor weakness results in pelvic instability during stance. External forces (ie, torso mass) lead to frontal plane rotation about the ipsilateral hip joint. This contralateral tilt normally is resisted by eccentric contraction of ipsilateral hip abductors (ie, gluteus medius, minimus). Shifting the torso over the ipsilateral hip joint in mid stance (Trendelenburg gait) minimizes the force required by the hip abductors. This gait pattern, which limits contact forces between femur and acetabulum, also is observed in hip joint pathology.

Spasticity

Spasticity results from lesions of the central nervous system (CNS). The primary lesion may be in the brain or spinal cord, although multiple lesions along the neuraxis also are possible. Spasticity may involve the upper and lower extremities. Although arm swing does have some effect on gait and is altered with spasticity, discussion of gait alterations resulting from upper extremity (UE) spasticity is beyond the scope of this analysis. In the lower extremity, a few common patterns emerge, including the equinovarus foot, valgus foot, striatal toe, stiff (extended) knee, flexed knee, adducted thighs, and flexed hip.

Equinovarus is the most common spasticity-related pathology seen in the lower extremity. Toe curling (clawing) may coexist. Contact is at the forefoot, with weight acceptance along the lateral aspect of the foot. Skin breakdown along the lateral border of the foot may be an associated problem. Equinovarus posturing limits single support dorsiflexion, prevents forward progression of the tibia, and leads to a hyperextension thrust of the knee and restrained forward translation of the body's center of mass. This abnormality compromises stability by decreasing the base of support and may prevent functional ambulation. Swing phase foot clearance is compromised. Musclcs that may contribute to this disorder include tibialis posterior, tibialis anterior, long toe flexors, mcdial and lateral gastrocnemius, soleus, extensor hallucis longus, and peroneus longus. Conservative management includes administration of neurolytic and chemodenervation agents. Tendon lengthening decreases force output with no change in neural drive.

Valgus foot results from inappropriate contraction of peroneal and triceps surae muscles. Stance phase stability is compromised by an abnormal base of support. This condition also may lead to genu valgum stresses and resultant pathology to medial knee joint structures.

Persistent great toe hyperextension (hitchhiker toe) is not uncommon. Selection of footwear is complicated. The usual offender is the extensor hallucis longus (EHL) muscle. This pathology often is managed successfully with motor point block of the EHL muscle. Diagnostic blocks often are helpful if co-contraction by the flexor hallucis longus is suggested.

Stiff knee, a frequent complication of stroke, is a severe hindrance during swing. Overactivity by iliopsoas, gluteus maximus, quadriceps, and hamstrings (as hip extensors) is a possible contributor to this condition. Functional deficits include increased effective limb length, with circumduction, contralateral vaulting, or hiking of the pelvis required for foot clearance. Energy consumption is increased, typically in patients with little functional reserve. Kinesiologic EMG analysis may be required to identify the contributing muscle(s) from the extensive aforementioned list.

Crouched gait is marked by excessive knee flexion in both swing and stance. Limb advancement is attenuated as part of this crouch pattern. Both hamstring and quadriceps muscles may be involved. Kinesiologic EMG may demonstrate prolonged activity of the medial hamstrings. Knee flexion contracture is common. Excessive hip flexion may interfere with multiple activities of daily living (ADL) and also may contribute to knee flexion deformity. Again, excessive hip flexion may interfere with limb advancement in swing, as well as decreased advancement of the center of mass over the flexed support limb. Initial treatment of both excessive knee and hip flexion is controversial. Therapeutic interventions include motor point blocks, chemoneurolysis, tendon lengthening, tendon transfers, and muscle release.

Thigh adduction (ie, scissoring) may interfere with daily activities, as well as with gait. Limb advancement is curtailed by severe hip adduction. Balance may be impaired as a result of a narrowing of the base of support. Muscles that potentially contribute to gait scissoring include the adductor longus and brevis, adductor magnus, and gracilis. Less frequently, the iliopsoas and pectineus are contributors. Diagnostic obturator nerve block helps establish whether contracture is present.

Contractures

Plantar flexor contracture of 15° is most common. This joint position minimizes joint capsule tensile forces. Contracture may be rigid or elastic.

Only the ankle orientation at initial contact and mid swing is altered with elastic contractures. Despite that fact, limb advancement may be slowed, because of the viscoelastic nature of tissues.

A rigid 15° contracture is associated with early foot flat and lack of early stance phase tibial advancement. Decreased toe clearance and foot drag are swing phase consequences. Dorsiflexion contractures are rare, although sometimes they are observed in lumbar-level myelomeningocele (present anterior tibialis and absent triceps surae).

Knee joint contractures are typically at 30° of flexion. This position correlates with the resting position of the swollen knee.

Only initial swing is affected by this posturing. Step length is shortened as a result of decreased knee extension in terminal swing, and metabolic demands are increased. Knee extension contractures (ie, capsule scarring) diminish limb advancement in early swing phase.

Hip flexor contractures result from shortening of hip flexor muscles or the joint capsule. A tight iliotibial band is a variant of this disorder. Each results in increased forward pelvic tilt. Loss of hip joint flexion due to hip extensor contracture is infrequent.

Pain

Pain does not inhibit normal motion directly; however, deformity and weakness may result from the person's attempts to attenuate pain through gait modifications. The positions of maximal joint capsule and ligamentous laxity typically are adopted.

Generally, joint reaction forces are magnified with increases in muscle forces crossing the joint, and increased joint contact force is associated with increased discomfort. One mechanism for reduction of joint pain is to limit the muscle force output at the painful joint. This protective response leads to muscle atrophy and weakness.

Sensory loss

Impaired proprioception inhibits walking because of diminished information about the limb segment positions in space. When sensory loss predominates (intact motor control), initial contact may be emphasized. Superimposed motor losses diminish the individual's ability to make rapid substitution efforts, resulting in decrements in walking velocity and stability.

Kinematic analyses of gait

- Kinematic measures
- Summary of gait kinematics
- Determinants of normal gait
- Center of gravity displacements during gait

• denotes sections that contain background material that is not included in course objectives.

Kinematic measures of gait

Kinematic variables describe the extent, speed, and direction of movement of joints or body segments

- Goniometric analysis
- Observational gait analysis
- Stride analysis
- step length
- stride length
- velocity
- cadence

Summary of Gait Kinematics

The kinematic interactions that occur during the gait cycle. The chart's rows distinguish between stance and swing phases. The columns are mapped to information about the relevant joints and segments.

The determinants of normal and pathological gait

Features of the movement pattern that minimize displacement in the body's center of gravity during gait:

- Pelvic Rotation
- Lateral Pelvic Tilt (Drop)
- Knee Flexion in Stance
- Knee Ankle Foot Interactions
- Knee Ankle Foot Interactions
- Physiological Genu Valgus

Saunders, J.B., Inman, V.T., & Eberhart, H.D. (1953). The major determinants in normal and pathological gait. Journal of Bone and Joint Surgery, 35A, 543-558.

Examples of how these kinematic features produce an efficient walking pattern:

During double limb support, that time when the center of gravity is at its lowest point, joint angles in both lower extremities are such that their effective lengths are maximized.

Additionally, the pelvis is rotated forward on the side where the limb is in loading response, and backward on the limb which is in preswing. This functional lengthening of the limbs minimizes the vertical drop in the center of gravity.

During midstance and midswing, when the center of gravity is highest, the stance limb's hip, knee, and ankle are all flexed 5 degrees. In addition, the pelvis is tilted downward laterally toward the swing limb.

This minimizes the center of gravity's upward excursion, keeping it lower than if the individual were standing erect.

The six "determinants" are logically appealing, because they help us focus on a relatively small number of critical factors from among the many degrees of mechanical freedom that are possible during walking.

However, very recent research questions whether the determinants are important, at least for the reasons that Inman and Saunders proposed:

CENTER OF GRAVITY DISPLACEMENTS

During ambulation, the body's center of gravity is propelled forward. However it also moves vertically and laterally; we presume a gait pattern to be energy efficient to the extent that it minimizes vertical and lateral displacements.

Vertical displacement of COG

Viewed in the sagittal plane, the vertical displacement of the center of gravity traces a smooth sinusoidal curve. This curve's amplitude in the normal adult male is approximately 5 cm or 2 inches.

The center of gravity moves vertically through two full oscillations during each gait cycle, so that the curve has two peaks and two troughs.

The low points or troughs in the sinusoidal pathway occur during the gait cycle's two periods of double limb support (loading response and preswing). The depth of the troughs is limited by:

- Pelvic rotation
- Knee-ankle-foot interactions

The high points or peaks occur at midstance and again at midswing. The height of these peaks is limited by:

- Lateral pelvic tilt (drop)
- Knee flexion in stance

Lateral displacement of COG

The center of gravity also oscillates laterally during ambulation. The total lateral displacement traces a sinusoidal curve with amplitude of approximately 6 centimeters or 2.5 inches. The greatest lateral excursion of the center of gravity occurs at the end of midstance.

Thus, only one full lateral oscillation of the center of gravity (to the right and left) occurs during a gait cycle. The amplitude of this lateral excursion is limited by a structural feature in the lower extremities, namely genu valgus.

Observational gait analysis

Although observational gait analysis is the therapist's primary clinical tool for describing the quality of a patient's walking pattern, it can be extremely unreliable.

Attempts to systematize observational gait analysis and to maximize its reliability (Krebs, Edelstein, & Fishman, 1985; Eastlack, Arvidson, & Snyder-Mackler, 1991) have led therapists to certain conclusions:

Binary scoring:

Rating of gait deviations as "mild," "moderate," or "severe" is unreliable; therapists display low rates of agreement in making these judgements. Agreement is much higher when therapists use a binary scale, one with only two categories, like "present" or "absent."

Focus on slow moving segments

Therapists agree more often regarding body segments which move slowly. Observational analysis is more reliable when it focuses on proximal segments instead of distal segments, and on stance phase events instead of swing phase events.

Focus on sagittal plane, then on frontal plane

Therapists are most reliable in judging gait patterns from the side and from behind or in front. They are extremely unreliable in judging movements which involve rotation of the LE joints.

Observational gait analysis checklist

The checklist, which we use in several laboratory sessions, is a "beginner's version" of ones you might find in various clinics.

Adapted from a checklist developed by the Professional Staff Association of Rancho Los Amigos Medical Center (1989), it requires you to make "yes-or-no" decisions about the presence of a short list of gait deficits.

The shaded regions are phases of the gait cycle during which you would not see the deficit listed. Thus, the checklist focuses your attention on the unshaded cells, which specify certain deficits during certain parts of the gait cycle.

Stride analysis

The stride analysis variables most commonly used to describe a gait pattern:

Step length is the distance between the point of initial contact of one foot and the point of initial contact of the opposite foot. In normal gait, right and left step lengths are similar.

Stride length is the distance between successive points of initial contact of the same foot. Right and left stride lengths are normally equal.

Cadence or walking rate is calculated in steps per minute.

Velocity, the product of cadence and step length, is expressed in units of distance per time. "Free speed" refers to the individual's comfortable walking speed.

Since individuals walk at different speeds depending on the situation, normal velocity values are somewhat arbitrary.

Walking base is the sum of the perpendicular distances from the points of initial contact of the right and left feet to the line of forward progression.

11

APPLIED KINESIOLOGY

Applied Kinesiology is a series of tests that locate weaknesses in specific muscles reflecting imbalances throughout the body. Then specific massages or acupressure techniques are used in an attempt to rebalance what has been revealed by the kinesiology tests. Thus, kinesiology is used as both an assessment tool and as a limited therapeutic modality.

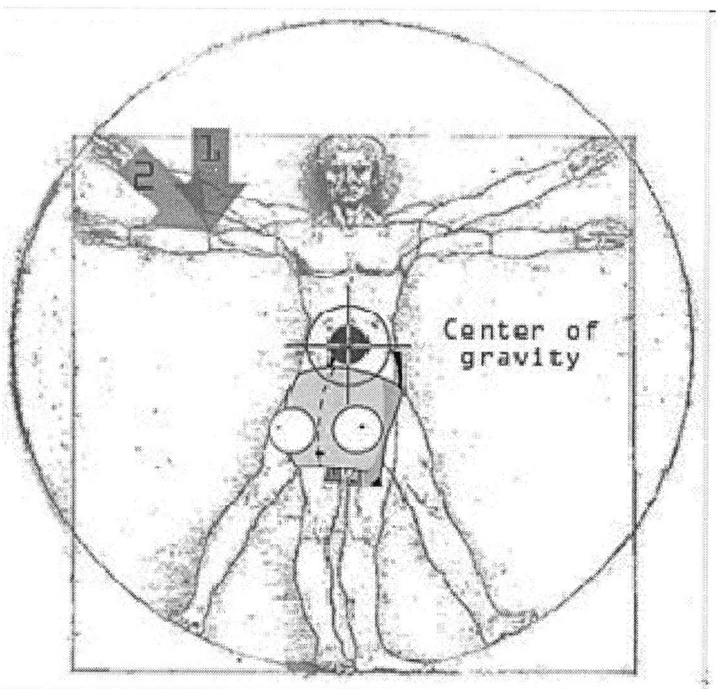

Purpose

Kinesiology claims to be a healing system that detects and corrects imbalances in the body before they develop into a disease, and which restores overall system balance and harmony. It is used to alleviate muscle, bone, and joint problems, treat all manner of aches and pains, and correct many areas of imbalance and discomfort.

Precautions

Since interpretation of the muscle tests is both complex and subjective, it should only be performed by a licensed health professional trained to look for "subclinical" symptoms (those which have not yet become a major problem). Kinesiology, itself, is more of a diagnostic technique and should not be thought of as a cure for any particular problem.

Description

Traditionally, the word "kinesiology" refers simply to the study of muscles and body movement. In 1964, however, American chiropractor George J. Goodheart founded what has become known as applied kinesiology when he linked oriental ideas about energy flow in the body with western techniques of muscle testing. First, Goodheart noted that all muscles are related to other muscles. He observed that for each movement a muscle makes, there is another muscle or group of muscles involved with that movement; one muscle contracts while another one relaxes. So when he was presented with a painful, overly-tight muscle, he would observe and treat the opposite, and necessarily weak, muscle to restore balance. This was then a very new technique.

Further, Goodheart argued that there is a definite and real connection between muscles, glands, and organs, and that by testing the strength of certain muscles he could learn about the health or condition of the gland or organ to which it was related.

Applied kinesiology is based on the idea that the body is an interacting unit made of different parts that interconnect and affect each other. Everything we do affects the body as a whole; therefore, a problem in one area can cause trouble in another area. According to kinesiology, the muscles eventually register and reflect anything that is wrong with any part of the body, whether physical or mental. Thus, a particular digestive problem might show up in the related and corresponding muscles of the legs. By testing the strength of certain muscles, the kinesiologist claims to be able to gain access to the body's communication system, and, thus, to read the health status of each of the body's major components.

The manual testing of muscles or muscle strength is not new, and was used in the late 1940s to evaluate muscle function and strength and to assess the extent of an injury. Applied kinesiology measures whether a muscle is stuck in the "on" position, acting like a tense muscle spasm, or is stuck "off," appearing weak or flaccid. It is called manual testing because it is done without instruments, using only the kinesiologist's fingertip pressure. During the first and longest appointment which lasts about an hour, the kinesiologist conducts a complete consultation, asking about the patient's history and background.

During the physical examination, patients sit or lie down, then the kinesiologist holds the patient's leg or arm to isolate a particular muscle. The practitioner then touches a point on the body which he believes is related to that muscle, and, with quick, gentle, and painless pressure, pushes down on the limb.

Patients are asked to resist this pressure, and, if they cannot, an imbalance is suspected in the related organ, gland, or body part. This diagnostic technique uses muscles to find the cause of a problem, and is based on traditional Chinese medicine and its idea that the body has common energy meridians, or channels, for both organs and muscles.

Kinesiologists also claim that they are able to locate muscle weaknesses that stem from a variety of causes such as allergies, mineral and vitamin deficiencies, as well as from problems with the lymph system.

Risks

There are no major risks associated with this gentle, noninvasive therapy. It is generally safe for people of all ages and has no side effects.

Normal results

If applied kinesiology does what it claims, patients should expect muscle testing to discover the cause of their physical complaint and to be told how to correct it.

Key Terms

(a) Acupressure - A form of acupuncture in which certain points of the body are pressed with the fingers and hands to release energy blocks.

(b) Alleviate - To make something easier to be endured.

(c) Complementary - Something that serves to fill out or complete something else.

(d) Deficiency - A shortage of something necessary for health.

(e) Diagnostic - The art or act of identifying a disease from its signs and symptoms.

(f) Flaccid - Flabby, limp, weak.

(g) Meridian - In traditional Chinese medicine, the channels which run beneath the skin through which the body's energy flows.

(h) Spasm - An involuntary, sudden, violent contraction of a muscle or a group of muscles.

Muscle Fiber Types

There are two types of muscle fibers, fast twitch (FT) and slow twitch (ST). Fast twitch fibers are used for explosive type movements and are easily fatigued. Slow twitch muscle fibers contain more mitochondria than Fast twitch. Mitochondria are cell structures that contain specific enzymes, which are required by the cell in order to use oxygen for energy production.

Fast twitch muscles fibers have less mitochondria and therefore less capacity for oxygen utilization in the production of energy within the muscle. This makes them better suited to anaerobic activities such as weight training, sprinting, jumping and other explosive type activities. FT fibers create energy anaerobically, that is, without oxygen. This system uses glucose as a prime energy source. The by-product of this anaerobic energy production is heat and lactic acid. Lactic acid accumulation in the muscle causes fatigue and

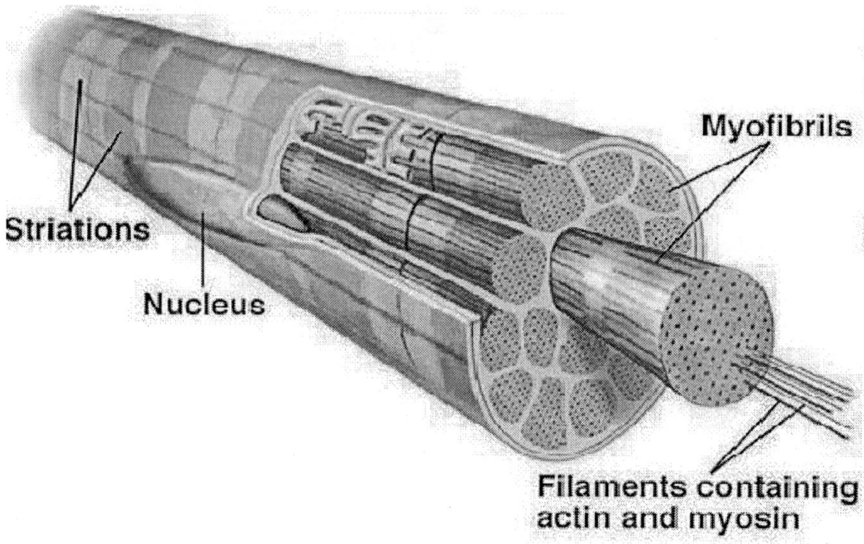

soreness. The anaerobic energy system is a limited system for energy production.

Slow twitch fibers are used for endurance type activities and are particularly suited to aerobic type activities. These type fibers contain an increased number of mitochondria and therefore are capable of utilizing oxygen for the production of energy within the muscle. This system uses glucose or fat in combination with oxygen to produce energy. The by-product of this system is carbon dioxide, water and heat.

Each person has a specific ratio of FT to ST fibers. A person with a high ratio of FT fibers may find it easier to train for specific activities that involve explosive movements. Conversely, a person with a higher ratio of ST fibers might find it easier to train and excel at endurance type activities.

There is a third type of muscle fiber that exists only

in humans. It is considered a FT fiber of type IIA. These fibers are less powerful than the type IIAB discussed above. What makes these type IIA FT fibers unique is that they can adapt somewhat to aerobic activities. These fibers provide the capability to alter our original genetic FT/ST ratio.

Energy Production

There are basically two types of energy systems that the body utilizes, Aerobic and Anaerobic. Each energy system produces Adenosine Triphosphate (ATP), which is used by the muscles to contract.

The Aerobic System can utilize carbohydrates, proteins or fat to supply an unlimited amount of ATP as long as oxygen is present. The Aerobic system provides medium to very long duration energy production with low to moderate power (less than 85% of maximum output). The by-product of this system is heat, water and carbon dioxide.

The Anaerobic System can only utilize carbohydrates for ATP production. This system does not use oxygen in the metabolization of it's fuel source. The Anaerobic System provides short duration (45 - 70 seconds) and high power. The by-product of the metabolization of glucose (glycolysis) in this system is heat and lactic acid, the cause of muscle soreness immediately after exercise. Muscle soreness 24 to 48 hours after exercise is due to torn muscle fibers and connective tissue. This type of soreness can be reduced by adequate warm-up and cool-down stretching exercises.

Aerobic capacity is the ability of the body to collect

and transfer oxygen from the air through the lungs and blood to the working muscles. This is related to cardio-respiratory endurance and is referred to as Maximal Oxygen Consumption or VO2 max. Aerobic Capacity reduces at about 10% per decade after 30 years of age.

The Anaerobic Threshold is defined as that point where the body can no longer meet the oxygen demand and it's anaerobic metabolism is accelerated. This point varies on an individual basis and is dependent on fitness level. For healthy individuals, this occurs between 50% and 66% of their maximal working capacity. This would be equivalent to running faster than half speed.

Cardiovascular and Respiratory System

Air is inhaled into the lungs where oxygen is exchanged through tiny gas permeable sacs within the lungs for carbon dioxide from the blood. The heart pumps the oxygen rich blood from the left atrium through the arteries then through tiny vessels called capillaries to the tissues of the body. At the cell level, oxygen is given up for metabolism and the carbon dioxide produced by this action is picked up by the blood. The oxygen depleted and carbon dioxide rich blood is then pumped back to the heart, through the veins to the right atrium to the lungs where the process is repeated.

Aerobic activity increases the strength of the heart muscle. The result is a greater volume of blood per stroke. This is referred to as Stroke Volume or the amount of blood ejected from each ventricle of the heart during one stroke. Cardiac Output is a measure of the amount of blood pumped through each ventricle in one minute. Vital Capacity is the volume of air that can forcibly ejected from the lungs in a single expiration. Aerobic activity provides a Training Effect on Vital Capacity, Stroke Volume and Cardiac Output.

An artery carries blood away from the heart while a vein carries blood towards the heart.

Bone Density Tests

Many consider osteopenia (a symptomless measurement of low bone density) to be an early sign of osteoporosis, but an article by New York Times science reporter Gina Kolata questions the significance of this diagnosis. In 1992, the World Health Organization (WHO)

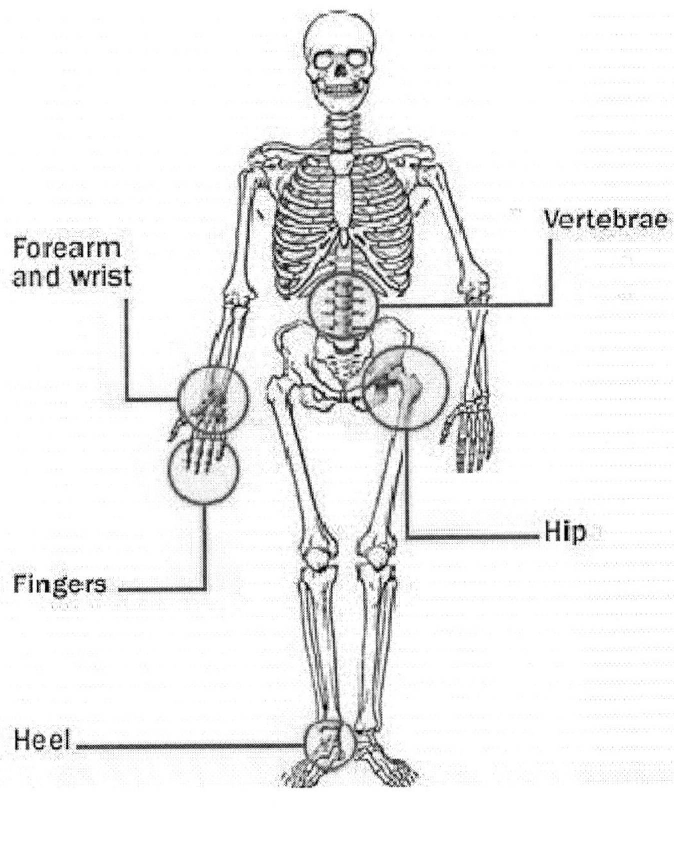

arbitrarily defined osteopenia as "bone density that [is] one standard deviation below that of a normal young adult"--i.e., a healthy 30-year-old white woman or man. Osteoporosis is defined as 2.5 or more standard deviations below normal. Low bone density is only one factor that predicts fracture risk, however. While half of all middle-aged men have osteopenia, according to the above definition, they have only 35% the risk of hip fractures, compared to women. Age, family history, and, perhaps most important, bone quality also contribute to osteoporosis. In addition, variation in bone density measurements further shadows the significance of a diagnosis of osteopenia. The incidence of osteopenia varies 28 to 45%, depending upon the machine used for diagnosis, according to a Merck study.

Your Body Doesn't Lie

One of the simplest ways to gain information about the body's needs and condition is behavioral kinesiology (BK) as described by John Diamond, MD in his book Your Body Doesn't Lie. Dr. Diamond's system for checking the body at an energy level is based upon the work of Dr. George Goodheart. Dr. Goodheart discovered that "each large muscle relates to a body organ. A weakness in a muscle usually means that there is a problem at the energy level in the associated organ." Dr. Goodheart found that strengthening the muscle led to improvement in the corresponding organ. Full kinesiology testing involves most muscles in the body and over 100 test-touching points for full diagnosis and treatment. The technique in Your Body Doesn't Lie, however, uses one muscle (the deltoid) and the point over the thymus gland to determine how environment, diet choices, and emotional attitudes affect the body at an energy level. In addition to its immunological function, the thymus monitors and regulates the body's energy system, according to Dr. Diamond.

The BK basic test requires two people. The test subject stands erect with one arm relaxed at the side and the other arm held out parallel to the floor, elbow straight. The tester faces the subject and places one hand on the subject's extended arm just above the wrist and the other hand on the subject's shoulder. After instructing the subject to resist, the tester pushes down on the extended arm. "The idea is to push just hard enough to test the spring and bounce in the arm," writes Dr. Diamond, "not so hard that the muscle becomes fatigued." Testing the strength of the deltoid muscle in this way indicates the body's energy supply. If the muscle gives way, that supply is weak. If it remains strong, the energy supply is strong. Dr. Diamond recommends repeating the process while the subject touches the skin over the thymus area (the point where the second rib joins the breastbone) with the fingertips of the free hand. If the deltoid muscle in the extended arm weakens when challenged, either the thymus gland is underactive at that time or its energy supply is low.

The effect of food, supplements, and environmental factors on the energy system can be tested using this system. Test edible substances by holding a small sample in the mouth while doing the testing. If the substance is harmful to the body, the deltoid will weaken. Sometimes the deltoid may be unaffected until the subject touches the thymus area. A weak response while touching the thymus point indicates that the substance is detrimental to thymus function. Sometimes, a substance may cause the deltoid to test stronger than it had moments earlier when no stimulus was used, indicating that it is beneficial. Dr. Diamond also recommends that supplements be tested, noting that one brand may strengthen the indicator muscle while another brand may weaken it, possibly because of the colorings, fillers, and binders used. He has also noticed that "lower-potency, more natural substances are more likely to correct a specific muscle weakness than those of higher potency. The more refined supplements and vitamins may even weaken the patient generally."

Sounds and music, social environments, types of cloth, and personal hygiene products--anything to which we expose ourselves--can be tested as well.

Through his own investigation, Dr. Diamond has found that wearing sunglasses, wristwatches, hats, synthetic clothing, disposable diapers, or metal, weakens many people. Exposure to fluorescent light, cooking gas, smoking, household chemicals, auto exhaust, some sound waves (including the whistle given off by television sets), ionization, magnetic fields, X-rays, microwaves, some rock music, and digital sound (achieved through Pulse Code Modulation), also tend to stress and weaken the body's energy system.

When under stress, many people develop a state of cerebral hemisphere imbalance that Dr. Goodheart called 'switching'. If switching becomes the normal mode of operation, the results from BK testing flip. Substances that weaken the deltoid in most people appear to strengthen those with cerebral hemisphere imbalance, and beneficial substances weaken them.

It is as if his body no longer can distinguish what is beneficial and what is harmful. In fact, his body now actually chooses that which is destructive over that which is therapeutic.

The body "should be the final arbiter of treatment, not the textbook or even clinical experience. If the body's Life Energy (as measured by test-touching the thymus gland) is strengthened, then the substance may be given; if it is weakened, then it should not.

Through BK testing, Dr. Diamond has found that many patients test weak when asked to say "I want to be healthy." Since attitudes affect the energy system, a self-defeatist attitude can affect outcome.

Biomechanics

Biomechanics is the science concerned with the internal and external forces acting on the human body and the effects produced by these forces.

At the highest levels of sports in which techniques play a major role, improvement comes so often from careful attention to detail that no coach can afford to leave these details to chance or guesswork. For such coaches knowledge of biomechanics might be regarded as essential.

Linear Kinematics

Kinematics is the branch of biomechanics concerned with the study of movement with reference to the amount of time taken to carry out the activity.

Distance and Displacement

Distance and displacement are quantities used to

describe the extent of a bodies motion.

Distance is the length of the path a body follows and displacement is the length of a straight line joining the start and finish points e.g. in a 400m race on a track the length of the path the athlete follows (distance) is 400m but their displacement will be zero metres (they finish where they start).

Speed and Velocity

Speed and velocity describe the rate at which a body moves from one location to another. These two terms are often thought, incorrectly, to be the same. Average speed of a body is obtained by dividing the distance by the time taken where as the average Velocity is obtained by dividing the displacement by the time take e.g. consider a swimmer in a 50m race in a 25m length pool who completes the race in 60 seconds - distance is 50m and displacement is 0m so speed is 50/60= 0.83m/s and velocity is 0/60=0 m/s

Speed and Velocity = distance travelled ÷ time taken

Acceleration

Acceleration is defined as the rate at which velocity changes with respect to time.

average acceleration = (final velocity - initial velocity) ÷ elapsed time

From Newton's 2nd law:

Force = Mass x Acceleration

Acceleration = Force ÷ Mass

If the mass of a sprinter is 70kg and the force exerted

on the starting blocks is 700N then acceleration = 700 ÷ 70 = 10 msec²

Acceleration due to gravity

Whilst a body is in the air it is subject to a downward accleration, due to gravity, of approximately $9.81 m/s^2$

Vectors and scalars

Distance and speed can be described in terms of magnitude and are known as scalars. Displacement, velocity and acceleration which require magnitude and direction are known as vectors.

Components of a vector

Let us consider the horizontal and vertical components of velocity of the shot in Figure 1.

Figure 2 indicates the angle of release of the shot at 35° and the velocity at release as 12 m/sec.

Vertical component Vv = 12 x sin 35° = 6.88 m/sec

Horizontal component Vh = 12 x cos 35° = 9.82 m/sec

Let us now consider the distance the shot will travel horizontally (its displacement).

Range (R) = $((v^2 \times \sin Ø \times \cos Ø) + (v \times \cos Ø \times \text{sqrt}((v \times \sin Ø)^2 + 2gh))) \div g$

Where v = 12, Ø = 35, h = 2m (height of the shot above the ground at release) and g = 9.81

$R = ((12^2 \times \sin 35 \times \cos 35) + (12 \times \cos 35 \times \text{sqrt}((12 \times \sin 35)^2 + 2x9.81x2))) \div 9.81$

R = 16.22m

The time of flight of the shot can be determined from the equation (2 × v × sinØ) ÷ g

" Time of flight = (2 x 12 x sin 35) ÷ 9.81 = 1.4 seconds

Uniformly accelerated motion

When a body experiences the same acceleration throughout some interval of time its acceleration is said to be constant or uniform.

In these circumstances the following equations apply:

Final velocity = initial velocity + (acceleration x time)

Distance = (initial velocity x time) + (½ x acceleration x time^2)

Moment of Force (torque)

The moment of force or torque is defined as the application of a force at a perpendicular distance to a joint or point of rotation.

12

KINEMATICS

Kinematics is the science of motion. In human movement, it is the study of the positions, angles, velocities, and accelerations of body segments and joints during motion.

It's important to define these terms precisely.

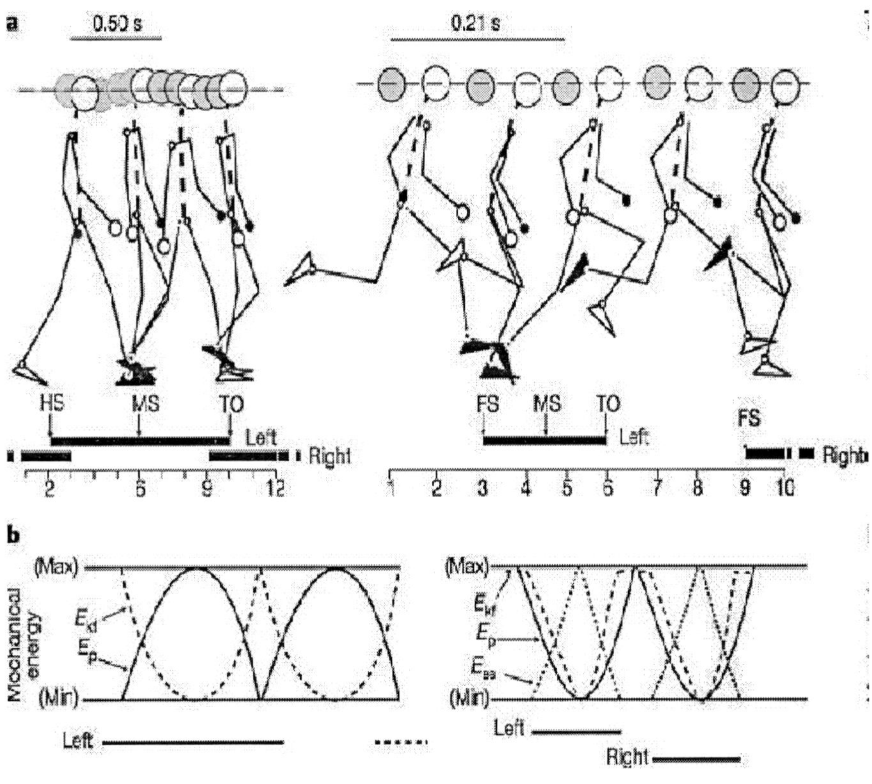

Body segments are considered to be rigid bodies for the purposes of describing the motion of the body. They include the foot, shank (leg), thigh, pelvis, thorax, hand, forearm, upper-arm and head.

Joints between adjacent segments include the ankle (talocrural plus subtalar joints), knee, hip, wrist, elbow and shoulder.

Position describes the location of a body segment or joint in space, measured in metres. A related measure called displacement refers to the position with respect to a starting position.

In two dimensions, the position is given in Cartesian co-ordinates, with horizontal followed by vertical position.

e.g.

In three dimensions all three directions must be defined:

e.g. (1.5, 6.2, 3.2), (2.8, 9.6, 7.8) etc.

Joint angle (also called inter-segmental angle) is the simply the angle between the two segments on either side of the joint, usually measured in degrees and often converted to clinical notation. Since joint angles are relative to the segment angles, they don't change with the body orientation.

Segment angle is quite different. It is the angle of the segment with respect to the right-hand horizontal. Note that it is an absolute measure, meaning that it changes according to the orientation of the body.

Velocity is another word for speed. Velocity may be

linear (change in position) measured in metres per second (m/s or ms-1), or angular (change in angle), measured in degrees per second (deg./s or deg.s-1). Normally, velocity is derived from position or angle data by the process of differentiation.

Velocity = distance moved / time taken

Thus if the knee moves from a horizontal position of 1.5 m to a position of 1.6 m in 1/50 of a second, it has a velocity of

Velocity = (1.6 - 1.5) / (1/50)

= 0.1 × 50 = 5 ms-1.

Acceleration is change in velocity. Again, it may be linear (change in linear velcocity) measured in metres per second per second (m/s2 or ms-2), or angular (change in angular velocity), measured in degrees per second per second (deg./s2 or deg.s-2). Acceleration, too, is usually calculated from the position data by differentiating twice. It can also be measured directly by an instrument called an accelerometer.

Use of Kinematic Measurements

Kinematic measurements are limited in what they can tell us about the causes of motion is - for this we need to look at the kinetics. However, they do provide a description of the motion which can be valuable for certain purposes.

Stance-Phase Kinematics

One important observation we can make from looking at the kinematics is the amount of up-down and sideways motion. In actions such as walking and

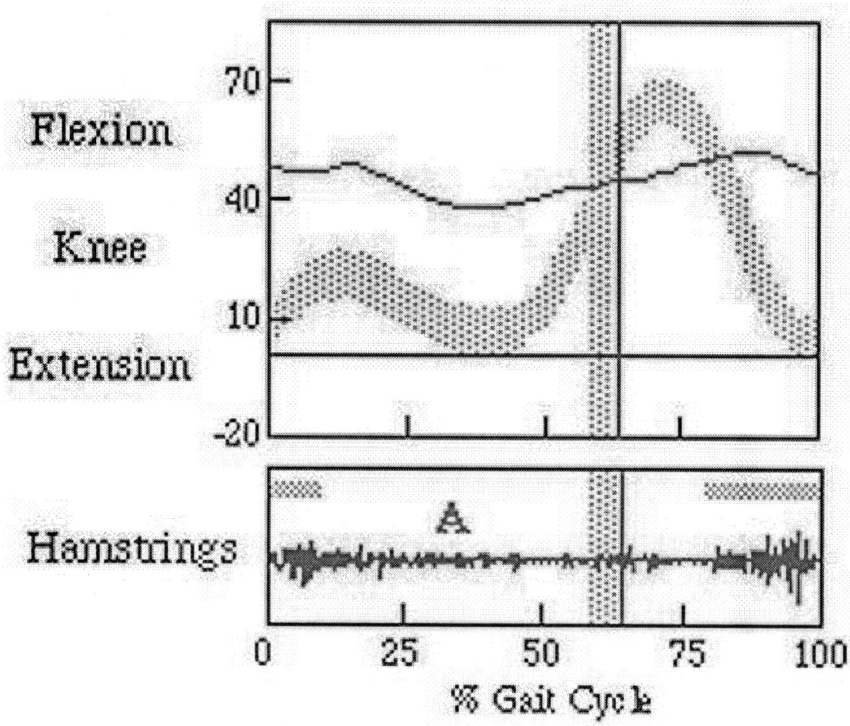

running, the body is attempting to move horizontally across the ground - any other motion, especially vertical, does not help this objective, and uses up precious energy.

If the body had wheels it could avoid vertical motion all together, but since we have legs, there must be some vertical motion. The reason for this is that at heel-strike and toe-off the two legs make up the sides of a triangle, while during mid-stance the stance leg is vertical.

This has the effect of lowering the upper-body (often called the HAT segment for Head-Arms-Trunk) at heel-strike and toe-off (which together make up the phase known as double stance, when both feet are in contact with the ground), and raising it during mid-stance:

By the way, the funny cross-like sign means the body centre of mass (CoM), which is located in the HAT segment (in the pelvis). In order for the CoM to rise up between heel-strike and mid-stance, energy must be expended, which is not gotten back when it drops back down again at toe-off. This up-down motion of the CoM is therefore inefficient, and we will see the locomotor system has several methods to try to reduce its amplitude.

Heel-strike ----------> Mid-stance ----------> Toe-off

The Determinants of Gait

After the second-world war, there were a large number of limbless ex-servicemen in the United States. The Government realised that a major effort was needed to develop improved prostheses, particularly lower-limb prostheses, to get these people walking again. As part of this large research project, the University of Calfornia at Berkely was requested to perform comprehensive studies on normal and disordered locomotion.

Out of this research came much of our present understanding of the biomechanical mechanisms used in walking and running.

Several of these key mechanisms relate to the methods used by the body to reduce the up-down and side-to-side motion of the body CoM, and because of their fundamental importance to walking biomechanics, they have been called the Determinants of Gait.

The determinants have two main goals: to reduce

the maximum height of the body CoM during mid-stance, and to increase the minimum height of the body CoM at heel-strike and toe-off.

a) Pelvic rotation

The pelvis rotates anteriorly at heel-strie, and posteriorly at toe-off to increase the effective leg-length at these times:

b) Pelvic list

The pelvis lists downward (obliquity) to increase the effective leg length at toe-off and heel-strike:

c) Stance Phase knee flexion

A slight flexion of the knee lowers the CoM during stance:

d) Ankle rockers

The ankle is dorsiflexed at heel-strike and plantar-flexed at toe-off. Both these actions increase the length of the leg.

e) Transverse rotation of leg segments

The lower-limb is lengthened by external rotation, and shorted by internal rotation.

In the foot, these rotations are facilitated by the torque-converter effect, whereby pronation at heel-strike is converted to internal tibial (and subsequently femoral) rotation, and external rotation of the femur at toe-off is converted into supination of the foot. These actions are a consequence of the axes of the talo-crural and talo-calcaneal (subtalar) joints:

f) Genu valgum The anatomical valgus at the knee

permits a narrower walking base, and thus a smaller lateral shift, than would otherwise be necessary:

All these actions in themselves contribute very small reductions in the amplitude of the CoM (pelvis) motion, but added together, they reduce it considerably, to around 50 mm (up-down and side-to-side) in normal gait.

Swing-phase kinematics

An essential pre-requisiste for gait is to be able to shorten the swing leg before propelling it foward. The main way this is achieved is by flexion of the knee.

This amount of swing-phase knee-flexion is proportional to the stride length, and thus the gait velocity:

Many gait pathologies (e.g hemiplegia, diplegia, knee osteoarthrosis) impair swing-phase knee flexion, causing compensatory mechanisms to be used, such as hip-hiking, lateral-tilting and circumduction.

Summary of sagittal-plane joint angles

So, basically, you can think of the actions of the knee and ankle joints as compensating for the flexion-extension motion of the hip. At extreme flexion of the hip (at heel-strike and toe-off) the knee is extended, while during stance knee flexion and ankle dorsiflexion help to reduce the effective height of the body.

Other useful kinematic measures

Other useful kinematic measures relate to the risk of falling. In general, there are two types of fall: the trip, and the skid. The former is a result of the low foot clearance during mid-swing, typically about 1.5 cm, while the latter is caused by a high forward velocity at heel-strike.

Moreover, it is possible that the vestibular organ may be disorientated by high accelerations from the lower-limbs if they are not (as is usually the case) attenuated by the spine. Thus, the head to hip forward acceleration ratio has been used to gauge the efficiency of this spinal damping mechanism.

13

LEVERS

A lever is a rigid structure, hinged at one point and to which forces are applied at two other points. The hinge or pivot point is known as the fulcrum. One of the forces that act on the lever is known as the weight that opposes movement and the other is the force that causes movement. For more details see the page on Levers.

For your arm, leg or any body part to move the appropriate muscles and bones must work together as a series of levers. A lever comprises of three components -

Fulcrum or pivot - the point about which the lever rotates

Load - the force applied by the lever system

Effort - the force applied by the user of the lever system

The way in which a lever will operate is dependent on the type of lever.

Classification of Levers

Class 1 - The fulcrum lies between the effort and the load

Class 2 - The fulcrum is at one end, the effort at the other end and the load lies between the effort and the fulcrum

Class 3 - The fulcrum is at one end, the load at the

other end and the effort lies between the load and the fulcrum

Class 1 Lever

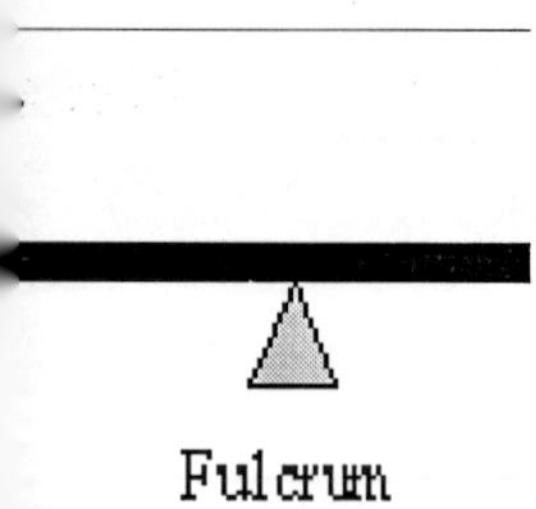

Class 2 Lever

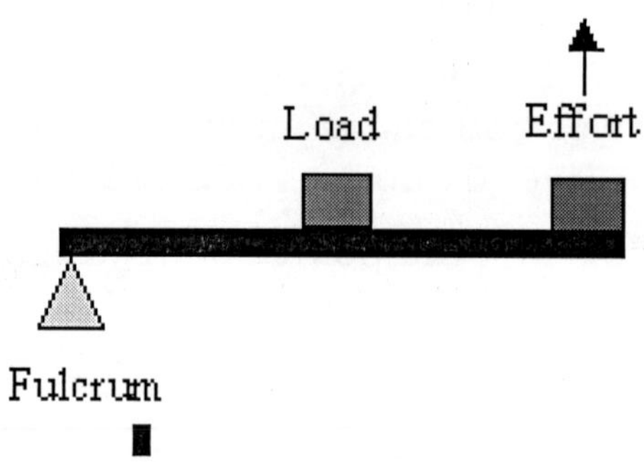

Class 3 Lever

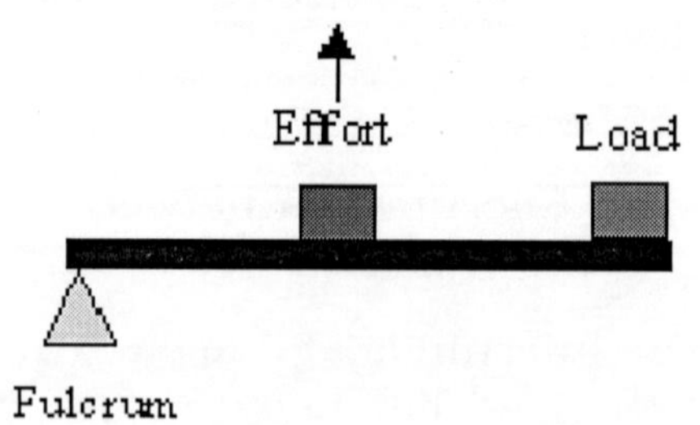

Examples in strength training

Class 1 - Seated dumbbell triceps extension

Class 2 - Standing heel lift

Class 3 - Seated biceps curl

Class 1 Lever in the Body

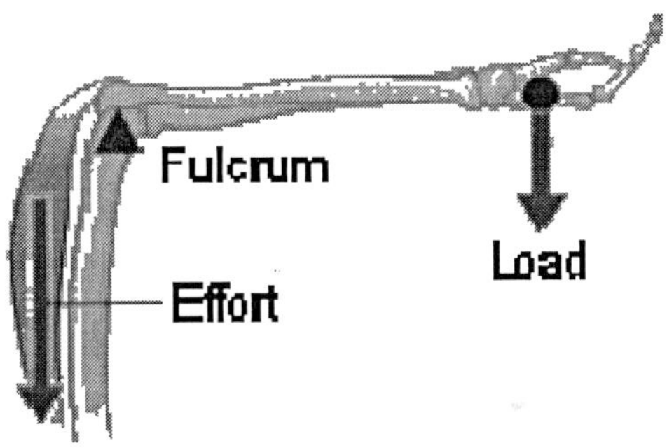

Class 2 Lever in the Body

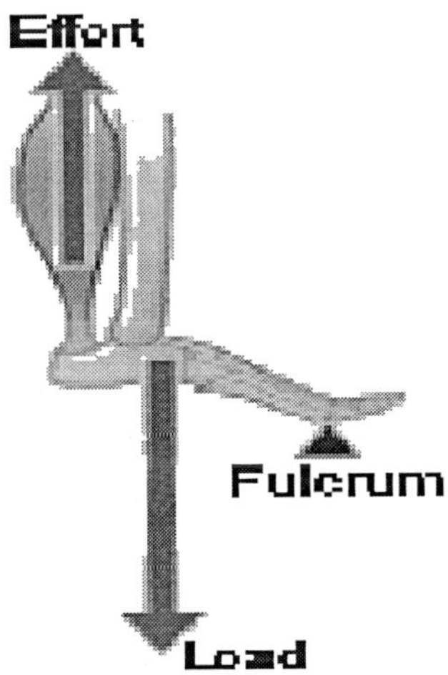

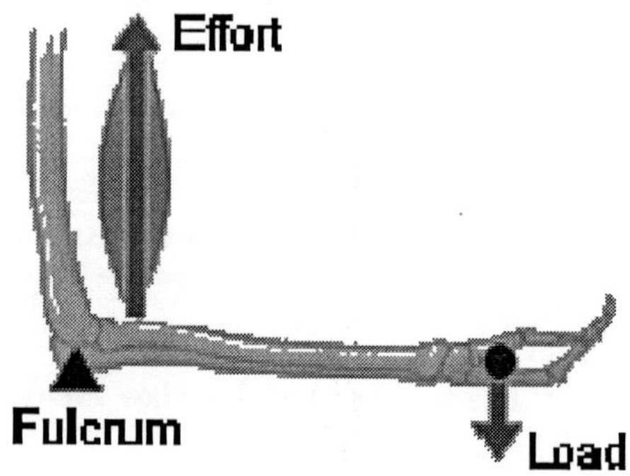

Class 3 Lever in the Body

TYPES OF LEVER

Lever of First Class

Classification of lever depend upon the position of fulcrum on which rigid bar is suspended or rests. If the fulcrum is exact in the middle P and W means and is equal than that kind of lever will called as first type of lever. Thus we can conclude that when fulcrum is situated exactly in between P and W it will a lever of first class. The example of lever of First class or class I lever are.

Hence if length of power arm is greater than weight arm, less power will be required to lift weight. Mechanical advantage will be greater than one for lever of first Class, if power arm's length is less than the weight arm than greater power will be required to lift the weight and Mechanical advantage will be less than one. Finally if the power arm's length is equal to the weight arm than equal power has to be applied to lift the weight because in this condition p=w.

Crowbar, see saw handle of water pump, spade, Cydebrake, plies and the pair of scissors are the example of Class one levers.

To understand the instance one which has been given in above explanation than if power arm is greater than the weight arm than mechanical advantage will be greater than one, we can take the example of crowbar in which fulcrum is in between weight and power applied. But whenever fulcrum is kept nearer to the weight and power arm is long we can lift a heavy load by small effort application.

As we usually see, when two boys playing up and down game on the see saw; first those boys adjust their position on the plank. Fatty boy sits near the fulcrum while thin bodied boy sits away from Fulcrum. Adjustment of the position is for obtaining equilibrium. When the bulky boy sits near the fulcrum and a thin boy sits away from over the fulcrum thin boy can lift the heavier boy.

When both the boy obtained equilibrium and they want to have continuous swinging the boy who goes up inclined/bends his body toward the fulcrum, the other boy who got down inclined his body the away from the fulcrum, by doing so the boy who goes up and inclined towards the fulcrum decreases the length of A and the boy who goes down increase the length of B. Thus when one boy wants to go up he moves his body away from the fulcrum. By doing alternatively this boys can swing continuously.

Lever of Second Class

In this type of lever W (weight/load) is situated in

the middle of fulcrum of efforts applied.

Lever of third Class

In this type of lever P is situated in between fulcrum and weight load.

FA=A Effort Arm.

BF= B Weight Arm.

Advantages of Levers

1. Levers are useful in developing movement and velocity in various sports activities.

2. Levers are used in producing force.

3. Levers are the basic Fundamental techniques for various sport skills.

4. Functions of various body joints are based on principles of lever.

Bony levers in Body

Usually muscles of body joined with the bones at the joints. And due it length of efforts arm become less. All kinds of levers present in human body effort arms are usually shorter that weight arm. It has it won technical advantages.

Constriction of muscles produce required force for functioning of joints. Though the produce force is low but it gives greater mechanical advantage. Due to such specific structure of muscles and bone attachment; quantum of produces force power is less but muscles can contract very swiftly.

The reaction in which much distance is not covered that required more power. Hence, the less which is suffered due to less power/forced could be recovered by achieving distance.

When any lever move around any fixed point, all the organs of the lever also move along with it in a circular path.

Any point of the lever move in the specific path and as much distance it cover's that distance is in fixed ration with axis and the point.

Many points of the lever move for different distance at the same, at that time the furthest point achieve more distance than the point which are nearer to the axis. At this situation lever get advantage of distance and motion.

Muscles of the body levers are usually attached with the bones longitudinally hence they are quiet nearer to the bone joints, due to the constrictions of muscles movements of hands and legs become very earlier. A cricket bat or tennis racket or hockey stick increase the length of weight are due to which force/ power of muscles and movement of weight arm also increase. But when we pushes any cart or any such instrument, its reduces the length of weight arm and length of power arm increases which also increase the mechanical advantage. In this specific condition, much work can be done by generating little power by the muscles of the lever but movement cannot be obtained.

Uses of Lcvcr In Sports

1. Uses of first class lever

In performing any sport skill in which basic principle of first class lever is applicable, we must have to keep in our mind that the point of force application is ncarer to the axis than the weight point length of power arm will be more beneficial in generating motion. Contrary to it if fulcrum is nearer to the point of weight than the point of application of force than length of weight arm will be less than the power arm. In such a situation lever will produce more technical advantage for producing force.

2. Use of Second Class Levers In sport

In it weight arm is always shorter than power arm, hence it is always used to produce more force.

3. Use of Third Class levers In sport

As we know that in third class lever power arm is always shorter than weight arm, hence these type of levers are mostly used in producing motions.

1. Basic technique used in various sport skills are for obtaining maximum leverage.

2. All kind of lever found in human body are velocity producing levers because power arm is shorter then weight in human body lever.

3. In human body third class levers are more in number than first and second class levers.

4. Technical advantage of various joints and lever is different at different place and different kind of motion.

14

REVIEWING SPORTS PERFORMANCE

It is an astonishing fact that performance of Indian players in the Asian Games and Commonwealth Games has remained better than in the Olympic Games. Now the question arises that what are the responsible factors for such occurrence.

Why Performance of Indian Players is Declining

Indian is being ranked on second position in terms of population, but it is a surprising fact that the country having such a huge population can only bring single or two medals in any international competition. Various small countries have emerged in the international competitions who perform well and get more medals than Indian players. It is a matter of shame for us and to improve the reputation of the country on international level, it is necessary to find out the reasons for this occurrence and to put a check on them.

Before discussing the responsible causes for this fact, it is necessary to throw some light on the views of some experts on performance of Indian players in some international level competitions.

Views of Experts on Sports Performance of Indian Players

In the words of Kamaljit Sandhu (First Indian Woman Athlete winning a gold medal in Asian Games) :—

– sports system has decayed. In the other words, its condition has deteriorated.

– She further blaims the members of International Olympic Association, who do nothing for the betterment of sports and games, but rather fight for their personal motives.

According to Mrs. Nirmal Milkha Singh (Former International Volleyball Player)

– performance of our players in the Olympics held at Sydney was not satisfactory. Although, there are some players and even hockey team who played well than previously, but still their performance cannot be called encouraging in any way.

– Our players can win medals only by becoming mentally and physically more tough.

– She also blaims International Olympic Association is responsible for such performance of players to a lot of extent.

Pargat Singh (outstanding player leading the country in two consecutive Olympic Games) feels very shocked at the performance of Indian players. According to him:—

– All national federations are corrupted by politics, which has influenced the performance of players negatively.

– There are various national sports federation which are being run by non-professional people, who do not have any knowledge to run these organisations.

– Indian players do not receive training throughout the year, but it is before six months or so from the international competitions that training programmes are being started.

Rupa Saini (who led Indian women's hockey team in

Olympic Games) has blaimed the Indian players for not trying to achieve the excellence. She said that:—

– There are various players belonging to small and weaker countries who performed well in competitions. Thus only the players should be blaimed as they do not try to achieve higher goals.

Gurdishpal Singh (Former Hockey player) feels very disappointed on the poor performance of Indian hockey team in Olympic Games. He says :—

– Inspite of the fact that India has improved in terms of infrastructure and other facilities, but still performance of players is low.

– In our country, participation base is shrinking and various facilities are remained un-utilised.

– To improve our condition, it is necessary to widen the participation base and to include dedicated people in the sports administration.

In the words of Uday Chand (Olympic Grappler)

– wrestling federation is corrupt and he also took a step further when he said that while selecting the women wrestlers, wrestling federation exploits them in different ways.

The facts of corruption found in the field of sports and games can be prove by the fact that in order to represent India in the world women wrestling championship, Manju, the Indian Wrestler was asked to pay Rs. 13,000 to the wrestling officials.

– He said that it is because of the wrong sports policy used by Indians that its players cannot perform well in the competitions of international level.

Thus, from the views of experts, following can be considered the responsible reasons for deteriorating state of performance of Indian players in international competitions :—

Some Influential Persons hold the Control on various National Sports Organisations

Generally it is found that various national sports organisations are controlled by not any sports-persons, but by politicians and wealthy businessmen. These persons do not possess any kind of knowledge of games and sports because of which they do not keep needs and requirements of players in mind. They only concentrate on the benefits which will accrue in terms of money or other forms to them. These persons are not held accountable for the bad performance of players as they are very powerful in the society.

For instance, around 200 officials were gone in the Sydney with the 60 players, but out of them most of them were absent from the competition as they were busy in doing their personal works. Thus, management of national sports organisations by non-professional personnel is a very important reason which contribute to the deteriorating performance of Indian players.

Poor Management of Sports Authority of India

Sports Authority of India was organised with the objective of constructing more and more stadiums in the country. In this way, the main function of sports authority of India was to promote sports and games in the country, however, nothing has been done by this authority in this direction. Instead of promoting sports, sports budgets have increased considerably but without any benefits.

Here again we found that people managing this authority are not sports-persons, but they are some influential persons of the society. They do not have any knowledge of managing such a highly reputed organisation. No doubt that a large amount of money is being allocated for promotion of games and sports, but these officials do not know how to make proper use of the available money, because of which it cannot be used for the desired purpose. Thus, because of this a large amount of money is being wasted and cannot be put on the work for which it was allocated.

Wrong Information to the Government

Before sending any player in competitions of international levels, national sports federation provides the information to the government that all the players are competent to take part in such high levelled competitions. Because of these fake claims, government clear the players for such competitions, while in reality, they are not competent for the same. Its result can be seen clearly in the competition when these players are defeated by other players very easily.

This fact can be prove by the fact that Ms. Beena Mole, who was a 400 metre runner, was selected in the team sent in the Olympic competition, inspite of the fact that earlier she was disqualified even in the trails. Nobody knew the reason except Federation officials. Neither the government nor the International Olympic Association tried to find out the reasons for her selection. As the federation officials know that they will not be asked by any person or authority for their task, they do the things keeping in them personal motives. This is also an important reason which can be held responsible for the poor performance of Indian players.

Inefficiency of Physical Educators

The responsibility of making a player to meet the challenges of various competitions rest with the physical educators or the coaches, but our Indian coaches remain inefficient in performing their function upto the satisfactory level. It is the duty of the professional players to make the game popular in the country, but they have failed in doing this task. Even today, some people do not consider games and sports important in the life.

At the school and college levels, parents feel hesitated in allowing their children to participate in games and sports as they think that it will affect their studies adversely, which is nothing but a myth. Physical educators have remained fail to convince the parents as well as the children that by participating in games and sports, they will gain in all the respects. Because of this, the talented students do not get the opportunity to make use of their talents and in this way, standard of games and sports remain low.

Improper Importance given to the Physical Education

Players who are send to participate in the international competitions are those who get training right from their school days. It is believed that outstanding players cannot be made as they are born, but these kind of players can be prepared to face the challenges of participating in international competition by continuous training. In our nation, although, all the universities are permitted to organise or include physical education in the curriculum, but it is found that this subject is considered to be unimportant by some authorities, because of which they prefer other subjects in place of it. Because of this, very few students get the opportunity to make full use of their talents, while some talented students remain un-utilised. Thus, a narrow based pyramid for selection of the players is one of an important reason which affects the performance of Indian players considerably.

Fundamental Objectives of Physical Education are being Ignored

At the school and college level, the fundamental objective of physical education is to provide students with an opportunity to participate in sports and games at the maximum possible extent. It is through the participation in sports and games that students can be made physically and mentally healthy and alert in all the respects. With this, they can be prepared to face different kinds of challenges in the life. But from the various studies it has been found that coaches or physical educators do not provide opportunities to all the students, but they prefer only some students because of different reasons. These students will represent the country in the future in international competitions. This is a kind of hindrance which is proved to be an important reason of low performance of players in competitions.

Commercialisation of Sports Activities

These days, the motto of participation in the competition has changed from outstanding performance to win at every cost. All the competitions have been commercialised in the sense that every player wants to win the prize or the trophy. This kind of thinking has led to emergence of use of improper means by the players. Players use different means for victory. For the sake of winning, various kinds of negative tactics or means are being employed by the players.

This kind of change in the motto cannot be seen only in national championships, but even at the Olympic, this tendency can be found. With this kind of tendency, players even at the school and junior levels have turned out to bc professionals. Everybody wants something in return of their good performance. It is not possible that every player become a champion, but for getting the victory, they adopt various foul means. It is because of this zest for prize or trophies that players make use of unprohibited drugs in the championships.

Ineffective Functioning of U.G.C.

Physical education has not provided with the place it should be provided in the universities. Nobody take pain to stimulate this area in our country, and even University Grants Commission, does not bother to give proper attention to this field. In order to monitor physical education in schools and colleges, there should be a qualified physical educationist in this commission, but no such arrangement have been made in this respect. For teaching physical education, competent or qualified teachers are not appointed, but the teachers teaching other subjects are provided with this task, who fail to promote games and sports in the school with the result that very few students get aspired to take part in sports activities.

Indian Government has a Biased Attitude

It is generally seen that government of India provide various facilities to the players who do not deserve it, while ignores some outstanding players who have performed very well in international competitions for the country. This kind of treatment by the government discourage the players from performing well in the competitions, even they are capable of it.

Media is not Fair towards All the Sports Events

The role of media has become very important in imparting information to the general public. For its projection, sports activities depends to a lot of extent on print and electronic media. But it is unfortunate that media in our country do not provide same kind of treatment to all the sports. They concentrate on the cricket and some other specific games. This fact can be prove by the fact that there is hardly any person or citizen of India who knows all the hockey players of the Indian team, but everybody knows the name of cricket players, whether they are included in the team or not. There are some sports activities which suit our country because of the non-availability of equipments, e.g., kabaddi, kho-kho etc., but these are neglected by media, because of which students are not aspire to participate in them.

Government of also found very much biased towards players of some specific game. For instance, for good performance, generally it is found that government provide some kind of assistance or gift to cricketer, but no such gift or assistance is being provided by them to the players of other games, because of which other players do not get any kind of motivation and their performance remain low in the international competitions.

Measures for Improving the Performance of Players

The responsibility of improving the deteriorating performance of Indian players rest with the authorities, and for this purpose, it is necessary to take some important steps, some of which are as follows :—

i. Till now it is obligatory for the universities to include physical education as a separate subject in the curriculum, but now the authorities should wake up and take the steps of making it compulsory for all the schools and colleges to include this subject in the curriculum.

ii. In educational institutions, physical educators should be guided that their main objective is to provide opportunity to participate in games and sports to maximum number of students. They should not concentrate on some specific students, but the opportunity should be provided to all the students, however, it is their right to exclude the incapable students. To choose the talented students present in the school, they should organise intramural competitions in the school from time to time, as it is the most convenient and effective method for this purpose.

iii. For imparting physical education teaching, one should appoint only technically qualified teachers, who can do this function properly and effectively. Person with such knowledge knows the needs and requirements of students and have thorough knowledge relating to games and sports. Thus, while appointing the physical educator, due consideration should be provided to his or her technical qualification.

iv. Physical educators should perform the function of selecting the players for the competitions in a fair manner. No kind of treachery should be done on the part of teachers while doing this function.

v. The task of managing institutions where training of sports and games is imparted should be provided to the professionally qualified personnel. If possible, these persons should be experienced players. Such kind of persons know each and every aspect of the game and they also know the needs and requirements of the players, because of which they can perform the function of managing such institutions efficiently.

vi. Good performance of all the players should be appreciated by the government as well as general people, irrespective of the fact that to which sport the player belongs. The biased manner on the part of media as well as general public should be stopped, otherwise, it will affect the performance of players belonging to other activities considerably.

vii. For imparting professional qualification to the physical educators, more and more institutions should be established where one can get proper training to become a coach. These coaches will do the function of imparting training to the players, which will improve their standard of performance in the international competitions.

viii. The responsibility of ensuring that money allocated to the development of sports activities is being used fairly should be provided to the government. Government agencies should be held responsible for controlling or keeping a check on the use of money granted for this purpose.